GROWING UP
AN AMERICAN
MUSLIM ARMY
BRAT

A Memoir

Authored By: Julde Halima Ball

Copyright Page

Book Editing By: Alfa Ramadan

Cover Photo (Front) By: Asaleh Mahdi

Author Bio Photo (Back) By: Fatima Janneh

About the Author Photo (Page CCCLI): Stanley Steril

Book Cover & Interior Design By: Julde Halima Ball

Paperback ISBN: 978-1-7339758-1-0

Hardback ISBN: 978-1-7339758-4-1

E-Book ISBN: 978-1-7339758-7-2

Contents

Foreword

In recent times, American Muslims are contributing to a more realistic narrative of what it's like growing up Muslim in America. Too often, our stories are written and controlled by those who are not Muslim, which tends to convey a very narrow and sometimes inaccurate portrayal of our collective experience as Muslims in America.

As a new convert to Islam, I left the United States in 2001 in search of a deeper understanding of my religion. In 2007 I graduated from the University of Madinah, in Saudi Arabia, with a concentration in classical Arabic and Sciences of Prophetic Traditions (Hadeeth). Currently, I am a public speaker, Islamic Studies teacher and author of *He Came to Perfect Moral Character: The Persona of Prophet Muhammad Through My Eyes* and other publications.

I have spoken at many colleges and universities discussing a plethora of contemporary subject matters from socio-spiritual paradigm. Recently, the Muslim Student Association of Hunter College in New York invited me to speak on the topic of *'Racism and Colorism: The Muslim Pride In Prejudice'*, where I met Julde, who purchased my book and spoke briefly about how excited she was for an Imam to speak so candidly to the exact experience she has had as an African American Muslim woman.

After reading *He Came to Perfect Moral Character*, Julde reached out to me about some of the highlights that my book mentioned regarding the character of Prophet Muhammad and that she learned a lot about him by reading my book.

Julde also made mention that she was currently working on her own memoir titled *Growing Up an American Muslim Army Brat*. This memoir will highlight Julde's childhood as a Muslim born to parents working for the United States Military living near other Muslim families all having the same experiences. The purpose of this memoir is for Muslims, who grew up a part of the cultural fabric of America post-9/11 while media propaganda was pushing the all Muslims are terrorists narrative, to begin piecing together their Islamic identity.

Julde Halima Ball

In her memoir, Julde also explains her family's extensive travelling ventures due to her father's military career. She speaks about the Muslim families who also lived on base and how they eventually became family to one another under the same circumstances.

In addition, Julde discusses the peer pressure she experienced as an American Muslim teen and how she managed to overcome the challenges and obstacles associated with it to finally become a more traditional Muslim woman. I recommend reading this memoir, which showcases authentic American Muslim literature that connects the reader with what it means to be a Muslim growing up in America in today's time.

Shadeed Muhammad

Acknowledgments

After telling my community that I was planning on publishing a memoir of my life, everyone was excited. Many people I knew at the time didn't have a clue about my military brat childhood. The people I knew while I was an Army Brat happened to be living in other parts of the world and weren't a part of my present community. So, people who I had recently built relationships with exclaimed, "Wow! I didn't know that you grew up as a United States military brat?" That's partly because it's not my first instinct to run up to every person I meet and say, "Hey! I grew up as a U.S. military brat!" That's just ridiculous. I'd expect that regardless of how I look, people would treat me with dignity and that certainly doesn't require me telling everyone about my military childhood.

Once I had committed to writing the memoir and my community witnessed me go through the countless steps to get my book published, they began taking me seriously and assisted me in every way they could to get my memoir published. My community members were now counting on me to release my memoir, *Growing Up an American Muslim Army Brat*.

They would constantly ask, "When are you going to announce the release date for your memoir?" while others would say, "I'm ready to read your memoir, let me know when it's ready."

I realized that I had also made a commitment to my community that I was going to release my memoir. I could no longer take back what was spoken into existence.

This book is not only for the reader, who hopefully learns the lesson of not judging every individual who crosses their path, but also for me, in that writing this book taught me a valuable lesson. While writing this book, I learned that regardless of Americans sharing different values, beliefs, or ideas, they'd come together and listen when a person is trying to advocate for change. People of every background, nationality, race, religion, sexual orientation, or political view joined in to make my memoir a reality. In current times when social issues seem to be so polarizing, there are portions of Americans on every side that truly care about one another. My memoir is not a political book and I would appreciate if people recognize my memoir as a call for social change. Democrats, Independents, and Republicans donated money towards the production of my book. People of every political party shared word about my book and let people know about the release date. Some people helped develop different parts of it, so I'd dislike for people to see the book as political when individuals from across the spectrum of all political parties helped with its development.

I spoke to several college professors which work in the City University of New York (CUNY), which I attended, and they provided input to assist in the layout of the manuscript. The professors never actually looked at the manuscript but through talking to me they could get an idea of where I was at in my manuscript and sometimes the short conversations which I had with my college professors presented better ideas for my memoir. I enjoyed the dedication that the CUNY professors had in providing me ideas, even when our discussions weren't directly related to the course at the time.

I was researching literacy agencies which could help me publish my book and after reaching out to a few literary agents, my submissions were rejected. Some people mentioned that they don't see the purpose of my story or that my story wasn't their subject of interest. I didn't let query rejections discourage me from publishing my book, so I decided to self-publish my manuscript. To me, my story is important, and I personally see the point in my story because it speaks to my daily struggle.

I began telling people in my community that I wanted to publish my book, but I was at a disadvantage because I didn't have a literary agent to represent my manuscript. I asked members in my community if they could donate money towards the production of my book so that I could begin building my author platform. Members of my community came together and donated money to complete my book. This enabled me to buy the necessary things to release my memoir.

Writing a memoir can be a lonely process, especially when you aren't working with an agency or publishing company. My community aided in making my writing process less lonely by inviting me over to workshops and events where I could speak to other people about my book.

I want to give a special thanks to City College Muslim Students Organization & Women in Islam-CUNY (MSO & WII) for inviting me over to their college to be a public speaker at their event *Our Responsibility to the Black Struggle in the Contemporary World.* Speaking at their event was an honor and it was unexpected because I was unaware of how far my story was reaching in the community. The Board Members at the City College MSO & WII welcomed me to speak for Black History Month and they were pleased with the presentation that I provided for their event. I'm truly honored to have met the Board Members at City College and they were pleasant people to speak with.

The Muslim Writers Collective (New York Chapter) was holding a storytelling workshop in partnership with the Moth. Only a few people were to be selected to partake in the workshop, and participation of the workshop determined through applying online. After applying online, I waited a couple of days before I was contacted by the Muslim Writers Collective NY to inform me that I was invited to attend their exclusive workshop with the Moth. I was excited to accept the opportunity, and working with the Moth helped me boost my public speaking skills. The Moth recorded a 3 to 5 minute podcast of me telling a story at the end of our two-day meeting. That workshop boosted my confidence in speaking in front of a crowd of people.

I'd like to thank the Lehman College Muslim Students Association and Muslim Women in Leadership (MSA & MWL) for the continued support while writing my memoir. The Lehman College MSA & MWL Board Members let me speak at their event about my upcoming memoir. During the Spring 2019 semester, the MWL club was looking to fill new board member positions and I chose not to run for board member. Despite not putting my name on the list, the MWL asked that I run as Secretary for our school club. The Sisters nominated me to be Secretary of the MWL club on their own and I was honored. I took the position and remained committed to helping the Sisters with all the MWL club events.

A special thanks for Asaleh Mahdi, because she stayed committed to helping me with photography and videography that I needed in the assistance of releasing my book. Asaleh would stay for hours helping me take photographs and video content that I could use for the release of my book. I rarely had money so Asaleh would take the money I could pay her and then afterwards we'd eat together before taking the train home. In fact, Asaleh took the picture used on the front of this book. She did an awesome job because this picture is a perfect touch to my memoir.

My older brother Alfa Ramadan has been helpful in editing my memoir. I wasn't planning on having anyone edit my memoir because people were giving me ridiculous prices. I was scraping change together and thought I'd try to read over my work as closely as possible, because I couldn't afford an editor. Then my older brother came to visit me and asked to edit my book. I asked my brother if he wanted me to pay him and he said he'd gladly edit my book for free. I was excited when my brother offered to edit my book because I was literally drained of finances and my brother is a bookworm. He always loved reading more than any of my siblings and he's excellent at grammar, so I was honored to have him look over my manuscript.

Finally, I'd like to thank my mom and husband for being by my side during the production of my memoir. My Mom was there to encourage me whenever I felt that releasing my memoir would be difficult. I normally don't share my story, but I had to gain the courage to do so over the months. It's been a difficult journey and I figured that I'd be myself and transparent, regardless of the outcome. I don't want other Muslim girls to continue facing what I face daily. My husband ran around the city with me trying to get everything done for my book. He was by my side when I had to speak with different companies, organizations, and he accompanied me to my events. My husband was always on the sidelines cheering me on while I was preparing to release my memoir.

My community and I did everything we could to get this memoir to what it is now. Just know that together we tried everything we could to put the best version of my book out. With the lack of professional assistance, the most important thing that I want the reader to understand is that I hope that you can read this memoir and learn from it. You cannot judge an entire group because of their race, gender, sexual orientation, national origin, religion, or political views. Prejudice is destructive to the rapid growth of diversity in the United States. Thank you for taking the time to read this memoir and I hope that you'll appreciate the work of my community, being that we aren't professional but still put this project together.

Preface

I'd sit in my bedroom after a long day and turn to the news networks to catch up on news occurring around me. Sometimes while watching the news, I'd dread the stories of American Muslims being attacked or killed because of our religious faith, or Muslims being attacked while worshipping in the mosque. Those stories spoke to the realities that I am currently facing as an American Muslim woman. While leaving my house, I'd recognize the likelihood of me facing similar attacks because my hijab makes me identifiably Muslim. To me, the hijab isn't an option because I truly believe this to be a portion of my Islamic faith. I cannot stand when people tell me to take off my hijab so that my life won't be in danger for wearing it. Why should I be uncomfortable wearing my emblem of Islamic faith, a commandment I believe to be given by Allah, to make another individual comfortable? My life shouldn't be at risk because of someone else's refusal to understand that Islam is a religion of peace. I feel comfortable dressing this way, and I should be granted the freedom to dress this way, just as a non-Muslim woman has the right to not wear this attire. The problem is Muslim women's lives are more subject to hate crimes because of the growing stereotype that all Muslims are terrorists.

On Saturday, August 13th, 2016, two Imams were fatally shot in Queens, New York after leaving the mosque for afternoon prayers. The New York police department refused to call the shooting a hate crime and concluded that their death wasn't the result of their faith. After appallingly watching this coverage on the news, I believed that this crime was meant to target the only two primary religious leaders of Mosque Al-Furqan Jame. Later that Saturday, Maulama Akonjee (Imam) and Tharam Uddin (Assistant Imam) were pronounced dead. The Muslims from the Ozone Park Queens community stood in solidarity for the two Imams that lost their lives.

On June 17th, 2017, an American Muslim girl named Nabra Hassanen was killed in Virginia while walking towards All Dulles Area Muslim Society (ADAMS) Center mosque with her 15 friends for Ramadan Taraweeh prayer. The man who killed Hassanen first nearly ran her group of friends over before beating her to death with a baseball bat, later placing her body in a nearby man-made pond. Hassanen's murder wasn't identified as a hate crime. Instead this crime was identified as road rage —— despite the driver coming out of his car and purposely using a baseball bat to murder Hassanen. "How could this horrendous murder be considered road rage?" I thought to myself, especially being that the man intentionally came out his car with the motive of hitting Nabra Hassanen. After watching the news coverage and witnessing law enforcement plainly attesting that Hassanen's murder wasn't the result of a hate crime, I began worrying about my personal safety as a Muslim woman.

There are countless instances when Muslim people are attacked or killed in the United States for our religious beliefs and their stories are a representation of other struggles that I face as an American Muslim woman. After a while, I worried about going outside alone, especially late at night. Not knowing if I could be the next victim resulting from the growing stereotype of Muslims.

Before reaching the decision to publish my memoir *Growing Up an American Muslim Army Brat*, I ran into my personal struggles. Nearly every day, someone was treating me harshly because of my religious faith. People would curse me out, shove me, or make smart remarks about my religion. Sometimes I'd say something back to the person or sometimes I'd just leave the entire situation alone.

After a while, I was shifting into my post-Army Brat life as an adult who was trying to figure out how I can live in America independently from my parents. This transition is faced with its own challenges, especially since people treat me like I don't belong in the United States. My opportunities in the United States are far worse and more limited than my other military brat counterparts.

Besides being mistreated by other members of my community, I've been having a harder time attaining my desired career path, although I can easily find minimum wage or temporary work. For a long time, I settled for less by accepting minimum wage paying jobs or temporary work while trying to earn a living for my family. Most of the time, minimum wage paying jobs led me to depending on welfare benefit programs such as food stamps,

Medicaid, and Supplemental Nutrition Program for Women, Infants, and Children (WIC). I sat in welfare offices for hours trying to receive government benefit programs and being mistreated by welfare workers who treat me like I'm another "lazy" individual trying to extract resources from the government. I am not "lazy," I am a hardworking individual who has committed to community service and volunteer work around my neighborhood. I love everything about being there for my neighborhood, but after a while it becomes tough working a full time job where you aren't earning a sufficient income to take care of your family. So, I continued to fall into the loop of committing to community service, relying on welfare, and then being called "lazy" by those who don't understand my circumstances.

I continue going to job interviews to secure employment with benefits so that I can get off welfare, hoping that the interviewer contacts me for the job, but I get denied positions. I work temporary assignments with more than one staffing agency and whenever the employer doesn't need me anymore, they tell me to stop coming in for the assignment without any given notice. Most Americans receive benefit packages with their employment such as medical coverage, paid time off, corporate perks, a 401K, etc. I am a portion of Americans who aren't fortunate to receive employment with a benefits package.

I got tired of being mistreated while trying to go about my day and having my opportunities limited by people who thought I wasn't "the right fit" for their employment opportunities. I knew that I was facing these shortcomings and challenges because I am a Muslim woman who wears the hijab. There are many stereotypes revolving the hijab and I cannot prevent an employer from holding onto prejudice that they had already developed through repetitive propaganda on the news media.

I got to a point where I wanted to revisit the time in my life when I lived on United States military bases. The best way for me to revisit my past was by purchasing a journal from a local Rite Aid store and using the journal to document the memories I developed as a child. In the beginning, documenting my childhood was an emotional process because I was still trying to cope with the things I was experiencing as an adult Muslim woman. While documenting my story in a journal, I didn't know how far I'd go with writing my memoir, but after reaching 200 pages, I knew that I was serious about getting my story out. I am normally a person who enjoys a private life, but despite the challenges, I am willing to use my story to make a difference. I know that by telling my story I am about to enter a tough journey, but this journey is worthwhile. I do not want any other Muslim girl growing up to experience what I am currently experiencing. I hope that my story brings awareness about the American Muslims who are committed to protecting the United States of America and how our religion in no way contradicts our loyalty to the United States. I want the American people to know that I, Julde Halima Ball, am a Muslim, but I am also an American, and I love everything about the two.

Army Brat: Not a spoiled or obnoxious child; rather it's the opposite. A child born and raised to military family whose whole life revolves around protecting their country. This term commonly represents the lifestyle of a military child living on military bases, changing public schools, and traveling around the world (states and countries). Sometimes being overlooked, people seem to forget a soldier's family also plays a role in protecting their country and military children are also affected by circumstances revolving a war.

Part One: My Life as a U.S. Army Brat

Chapter One: Introduction

"Where are you from?"

"I'm from the United States," I respond.

"No, where are you *really* from, like which country?"

"I just *said*, I'm from the United States."

The man stares at me in disbelief and proceeds to ask me, "Okay, which state are you from?"

As an Army Brat, the most challenging question that a person can ask is, "Which state are you from?"

I pause for a moment to genuinely think which state I am from because every three years my family and I had to move to a new location. While I'm staring at the man, I try to quickly think of a response because if I take too long to respond, he may assume that I'm lying.

I've always struggled with the question of where I'm from, but now I am living the post-Army Brat nightmare. Since my renewed commitment to wearing the hijab[1] in May 2014, people automatically assume that I'm an immigrant. New York happens to be the state that I've lived in the longest, but most people who live in New York are immigrants from foreign countries. New Yorkers rarely claim they are from New York unless they travel to any of the forty-nine other states. If I tell any person that I'm talking to, "I'm from New York," would they really believe that I'm actually from New York? Umm nope, people hardly believe that I'm a United States citizen.

In an effort to explain where I'm from, I tell the man, "I don't know which state I'm from because I grew up as a United States Army Brat and I moved around due to my dad's military career."

"When did you convert to Islam?" the man proceeds to ask me.

---

1 Hijab: a term used to mean cover or conceal. In most cases, hijab is used to describe a Muslim woman's head scarf or veil.

"I was born and raised as a Muslim Army Brat," I tell the man. At this point, the man looks at me like he had seen a ghost. He gives me a blank stare as if he's in disbelief that I could be a woman who grew up as a United States Muslim Army Brat, while also upholding the commitment of wearing a hijab.

"Okay, where are your parents from?" the man asks.

"My dad is from Hague, Virginia; and, my mom is from Kono, Sierra Leone," I respond.

"Oh! So, you're a Sierra Leonean!" the man responds to me with excitement.

Wow, that is amazing. Did he just ignore the fact that I just *said* my dad is from Virginia? The first time I've ever been to Sierra Leone, I was eighteen years old. For goodness sake, I was only there for two weeks and that's not long enough for me to claim Sierra Leonean as my nationality.

It's common for people to see me wearing my hijab and automatically assume that I'm an immigrant, when I am in fact an American. I wear the hijab for religious reasons, but ever since I began wearing it, it has also become a test of faith. I have faced many challenges and confrontations with people unaware of the reality that Muslims can be American. My hijab has made it harder for me to be accepted within the realm of the American society. After all, Muslims are the lazy, immigrant terrorists who enter countries to spread their evil influence of Islam.

I made the ultimate decision of wearing the hijab during the Spring of 2014, and ever since I began wearing the hijab, I have felt a difference in my everyday social interactions. Whenever I walk outside while wearing my hijab, most people treat me like a foreigner, but I am not; I grew up on various United States military bases.

My dad, who is a Muslim, has been serving to protect the United States of America since 1992. I grew up around other Muslim soldiers who were also fighting to protect the United States of America. While I continually dispute I'm an American, there are Americans who have no clue that there are numerous Muslims living on United States military bases. Islam is not a culture or country, Islam is a religious faith. Just like any other religious faiths, Muslims can coexist with being an American.

My oldest sibling is Mariam Ramadan, my second oldest sibling is Alfa Ramadan, and I'm my parents' third child. My oldest sibling, Mariam, used to watch Alfa and me while my mother, Khadijah Barrie, was at work. My mom didn't have to work, but she preferred working to financially support her family living in Guinea, West Africa. My dad paid one-hundred percent of all of our household bills while everything my mom earned was her own money.

My mom is from Sierra Leone, West Africa and she often speaks about the horrors her family faced trying to escape the civil war in Sierra Leone. It just so happens that the choices my family made to remain safe from the war required them to seek refuge in Guinea, West Africa. My grandmother often told my family stories of the things she experienced during her escape. While trying to find places to hide, my grandmother witnessed some of the horrific actions of the rebels. At many points through my grandmother's journey to Guinea, she was an onlooker who was unable to help many of the other victims.

"Do you think it is a boy or a girl?" one of the rebels asked the other.

My grandmother sat in a bush, hiding her presence from the rebels. The rebels entertained themselves by asking each other whether they thought the pregnant lady was carrying a boy or girl in her womb.

"I think it's a boy," one of the rebels joked.

"I think it's a girl," the other rebel laughed out.

"Let's settle this with a bet!" the other rebel exclaimed.

Both rebels put their money together to begin betting the gender of the unborn baby. One of the rebels used a knife to cut open the abdomen of the pregnant woman. while the pregnant woman was fully awake and conscious, they searched through her abdomen to pull out the baby. The woman screamed in pain. My grandmother was still watching from the bush, but she was terrified that one of the rebels would catch her watching them.

When the rebels finished pulling the baby out the woman's abdomen, one of the men cheered as he had successfully discovered the correct gender of her baby. The woman was still in pain while lying down on the ground, but her pain didn't concern either of the men. My grandmother remained hidden in the bushes as one of the rebels laughed out loud with joy. Afterwards the rebels exchanged cash with each other; the winner of the bet had received his money. This is one of the many haunting narratives that my mom's family used to continually tell me as a child. It took a couple of life-threatening weeks before my mom's family managed to escape Sierra Leone, but they finally found refuge in Guinea, West Africa and have stayed there till present day.

Fortunately, my mom, Khadijah Barrie, wasn't living with her family at the time. While Sierra Leone was experiencing a horrific civil war, my mom was living in Germany.

My dad, Bilal Bani Ball, is in the United States military. He was born and raised as a Southern Baptist Christian in Hague, Virginia. My dad was brought up in a household where Christianity was observed. Nearly every Sunday morning, my dad's family got ready to attend church. My dad told me that when he was a child, he questioned some of his Christian practices. In 1992, he joined the United States Army. The first location my dad was sent for military assignment was in Germany. My dad spent his first year in the Army as a Christian. During this time, he was still learning about Islam and multiple other religions. Then in 1993, he made the ultimate decision to convert to Islam. Before taking his shahadah[2], my dad wanted to make sure that he properly understood the principles of Islam.

My dad took his shahadah at a local American mosque in Kaiserslautern, Germany, where the Islamic lectures were provided in English. My dad was still single, but he planned on getting married. Marriage in Islam holds high importance because it completes half of a person's deen[3]. My dad decided

---

2 Shahadah: A Muslim's declaration that they only believe in one God, Allah, and Prophet Muhammad is the seal of the Abrahamic prophethood.

3 Deen: an Arabic term which means religion or faith.

that the best place to find a Muslim wife was at the mosque he regularly attended.

My mom and dad attended the same mosque for Jummah[4] services. Men and women entered the mosque through different entrances, so my parents didn't know each other through socializing outside of the mosque. A lot of the people in the community who were looking for a spouse would tell the Imam[5]. The Imam would act as an intermediary between the men and women, to see if the people were a good match. The Imam related news to my dad that there were a few women looking for husbands. The Imam explained that some of the women had never married or didn't have children; however, there was one woman who had lost her husband a couple years ago and she has two children. My mom's previous husband passed away a few years back while having a medical procedure done in a German hospital. Immediately, my dad was ready to meet my mom. He thought that since Khadijah Barrie could take care of two children on her own, it showed that she was responsible and mature.

With the Imam's blessing, my parents went on a few dates. They wanted to make sure that everything was done Islamically, so the Imam attended the courtings as a third person. After going out a few times, my parents decided that they wanted to get married. In 1993, my parents held a Nikah[6] ceremony in the same mosque in which they were introduced to each other.

By 1998, my family and I were living in El Paso, Texas because my dad got stationed at Fort Bliss, the local Army post. The benefits of being in the military is that you don't have to worry about looking for a house for your family to stay in. The military provides housing for military families on their bases. I loved living on Fort Bliss and as a four-year old child, I spent most of my days playing outside with the neighbors' children. All the children living

---

4 Jummah: a weekly Friday service which Muslims attend in a mosque around noontime, ending with a gathered prayer. (This religious service is an obligation for Muslim men; however, this religious service is optional for Muslim women.)

5 Imam: A Muslim leader who gives lectures and leads congregational prayers in a mosque.

6 Nikah: A Muslim wedding ceremony.

on Fort Bliss had one thing in common: either one or both of our parents served in the United States military.

In the morning, all the children in my neighborhood would go out under the hot sun to play hopscotch, tag, jump rope, and get to know one another. Children would sit out on the lawn, sidewalk, or street, socializing together. On my street, you'd find a group of children dribbling their basketballs, riding on their skateboards, or handling a deck of Pokémon cards on the sidewalk.

There were set guidelines which I had to follow if I wanted to play outside. First, I had to be in the presence of either my mom, dad, older brother or older sister. Second, I could play outside on my street all day, but once the sun began setting or the street lights turned on, I had to return home. Third, if I wanted to visit anyone's house, my parents had to meet their family first. As long as I followed those guidelines, I could continue playing outside whichever way I wanted.

The children in my neighborhood ran around freely while giggling and laughing, exhibiting the liveliest looks on their faces. Whenever a car drove down our block, all the children habitually got on the sidewalks and waited for the car to drive by. Some of the parents had their sprinklers connected to a water hose so that they could water their grass, but sometimes they allowed the children to run through the sprinklers with their swimsuits on. For hours, we'd continuously run through the sprinklers so that we could cool our bodies off from the dry summer heat. Regardless of the sun's intensity, the children remained outside to constantly run in and out of the sprinklers until we were exhausted. Other parents would hook up a pistol grip nozzle and allow the children to shoot water at each other with the water hose. Other children would bring out their water guns, buckets and water balloons to soak each other in water. Children would try to avoid being hit by the water, so they ran around the lawn restlessly while gasping for breath. Sometimes, a rainbow would form near the sprinklers and the children would call out, "I see red, yellow, purple, blue, orange!" Everyone was competing to call out the colors they saw in the rainbow, shouting above each other.

A rainbow is amazing because you can see its light, but you can never tell where exactly the rainbow is originating from. The children always tried their best to touch the light of the rainbow; however, touching a rainbow is scientifically impossible. All the children playing near the sprinklers were fascinated by the formation of the rainbow.

During the mid-afternoon, faint music could be heard coming from a distance. As the faint music slowly approaches our street, the children immediately recognize it. Most of the children playing in the neighborhood prepare to run back to their homes so that they can ask their parents for money. Other children begin looking for their parents socializing outside. The street that was once filled with children playing is now nearly empty, with every game and toy left behind on the lawns and sidewalks. Only a few of the children stay behind to continue playing.

I run into my house asking, "Mom, Dad, can I get a dollar?"

As the sound approaches our street, the song playing from a distance becomes louder and clearer. The tune being played in the distance is called, "Turkey in the Straw". Some of the children begin humming along to the tune while holding money in their hands. Most of the other children manage to get their parents out of the house with cash in their hands. A big white truck slowly approaches our street. On the outside of the truck, there is a display showing the selection of ice creams people can choose from. The ice cream truck finally comes to a full stop, the window opens, and people form a line in front of the ice cream truck. After playing all day under the hot sun, I am longing for a popsicle and I feel too impatient to stand in line. The children wait their turn until it finally becomes my turn.

My favorite ice cream was the Tweety Bird popsicle. I not only loved its flavor, I also loved that there were two blue gumballs placed on the popsicle as Tweety Bird's eyes. My older siblings ask me to choose the ice cream that I wanted from the ice cream truck. I stand on my tippy toes and point towards the picture on the truck while saying, "Tweety Bird!" My siblings tell the person working in the ice cream truck that I wanted the Tweety bird popsicle and then they hand money over to purchase my popsicle. When my siblings finish purchasing my popsicle, Mariam helps me open the package.

I stand a couple of feet shorter than Mariam as I wait for her to open my popsicle. Mariam has a mahogany skin tone, she's very tall for her age, with an hourglass figure (despite wearing modest clothing), and she's wearing a hijab.

Immediately after helping me open the popsicle, it already begins dripping down my hand. I try to quickly lick every part of the popsicle before it continues melting, but I'm unsuccessful. Each lick of the popsicle is a tart flavor of orange and lemon. Some licks of the popsicle were both the combination of lemon and orange flavors. My hands become sticky, but I continue to eat the popsicle anyway. When I finish eating my popsicle, I go to a nearby water hose to wash my hands, then I continue playing outside with the other children in my neighborhood.

I get in my electric Barbie Jeep, which is my favorite toy, to begin riding around the neighborhood, and I normally do so with my friends. My Barbie Jeep is a two-seater vehicle, colored pink, purple, and white, and reads "Barbie" on the front. Sometimes more than two of my friends attempt to jump on the top of my vehicle, but they're never able to hang on.

While driving around the neighborhood, me and my friends use the above power lines as our imaginary street lights. While driving up to the power lines, one of the children shouts out, "You must stop, it's a red light!" Immediately, I press my foot down and stop at the power line, until the light "turned green".

I resume driving past imaginary traffic lights in my neighborhood, then my friends and I switch seats. We take turns looking up towards the power lines and stopping the vehicle at a "red light." After a few seconds of waiting under the power line, we continue driving. Sometimes we intentionally run past the power lines and everyone bursts out laughing, "You were supposed to stop!"

My friends and I drive my electric Barbie vehicle until the afternoon skies become hued with yellow, orange, purple, and blue. The evening sky replaces the afternoon day and soon after, the street lights turn on. My siblings and I know that whenever the street lights turn on, we must return home. The street light rule similarly applies to many other children living on

Fort Bliss. The streets previously filled with children playing, giggling, and having so much fun, are once again empty and serene.

Sometimes, my parents wanted me to come home earlier than when the street lights turning on, so they'd call out from the front door of our home while shouting, "Julde! [Jul-DAY], it's time for you to come back home!"

"I have to go back home," I tell my friends. "I'll come back outside tomorrow." Without hesitation, my friends jump out of my Barbie Jeep, wave goodbye, and then I drive my Barbie Jeep home.

During the week, my parents scheduled activities for me on Fort Bliss. My older brother, Alfa Ramadan, loved reading books, so my family made numerous trips to the Fort Bliss library. My older sister, Mariam Ramadan, also loved reading books, but my older brother was seriously addicted to reading. Alfa taught himself how to read books before he even learned the alphabet. My family always jokes around with Alfa because we thought it was bizarre that any person can learn to read before knowing the alphabet. You can read a whole sentence in a book, but you can't identify each letter in the sentence? It's truly weird and it also displays Alfa's childhood intellect.

My family and I spent most of our days at the Fort Bliss library because I enjoyed their scheduled story times. I can still remember waiting in the library for the storyteller to come out and read books to us. The library always had several bean bag chairs set in place for children to sit on while listening to the storytellers read us a book. I typically chose the bean bag chair closest to the storyteller, so that I wouldn't have a hard time seeing the illustrations. I was much smaller than the bean bag chair, so sometimes after sitting on the bean bag, I would sink into the chair. If the children had enough time, we would plunge into each of the bean bags and pretend that we couldn't get out of the chair. "Help, help! Can you help pull me out the chair?" we'd joke out.

There were many books which I enjoyed listening to during story time. The storyteller sometimes wore a costume or put on makeup which resembled the theme of the book. For example, while reading a book called, *The Very Hungry Caterpillar*, the storyteller would wear a costume or props which made them resemble a caterpillar. There would be props set up around the storytelling area for children to use while the story was being read aloud. For instance, a huge green play tunnel would be placed near the story area and while the storyteller told a part of the story when the caterpillar was eating so much, all the children would enter the play tunnel, one by one, and army-crawl through the tube, pretending that we were eating through the food like the caterpillar did. When we got out of the tube, we'd laugh and giggle. The children constantly interacted with the storyteller, while also listening to the story.

When the storyteller was finished reading us a book, the storyteller would give the children an opportunity to walk around the library and choose a book we'd like to take home and read. I'd walk around the bookshelves in the library to slowly look through the selection of books I found interesting. There were different genres of children's books, but most often I loved reading fictional children's books with lots of illustrations. The illustrations in a children's book helped me imagine the characters and scenes as the book was being read to me. One of my favorite authors during my childhood was Dr. Seuss. Sometimes I'd picked up a children's book written by another author, if the book looked interesting.

Whenever I found an interesting book to borrow, I'd walk over to the librarian and check out the book. My parents would hand the librarian our card, the librarian would turn to the due-by-date page and stamp the date I must return the book to the library.

I enjoyed receiving gifts from the Fort Bliss library. After checking out a certain number of books, I was eligible to receive a gift from the librarian. Sometimes the librarian would place a book, toy, or bookmark inside of a plastic bag with my checked-out library books. Every gift that the librarian gave me was important to me, even if it was only worth 50 cents. I especially enjoyed the perks of those gifts for being a frequent visitor of the library.

Every Friday, my family and I attended Jummah prayer on Fort Bliss. Fort Bliss had an ordinary-looking military building which was used as a mosque for Muslim service members to observe their Islamic religious services. Although the building's appearance didn't resemble a genuine mosque, the service members still referred to the building as a mosque. Whenever my family and I entered, we'd sign our names into a logbook and record the date that we'd visited. My family and I always tried to attend mosque services early, especially when it was Jummah. Inside the mosque, the floor was carpeted with a huge curtain cutting across the middle of the room, used to divide the men and women attending religious services. Behind the prayer area was a kitchen, dining room area, a children's playroom, and far to the left of the prayer area were the restrooms.

On the walls of the mosque were signs displaying many of the 99 Names of Allah, beautifully calligraphed in Arabic, and books containing information about the lives of Islamic prophets. The building wasn't big, but it was big enough for us to attend religious services without leaving base.

Sometimes the children who followed their family to Jummah services played in the playroom behind the prayer area. The children's playroom was the best way for us to play around without jumping around the adults who came for mosque services. In the playroom, there were toy cars, balls, dolls, rocking horses, play telephones and numerous other toys for children to play with. Not only did the playroom have toys, there were also multiple Qurans and scrolls placed on the shelves around our play area. Sometimes, the older children would pick up the scrolls from the shelves and begin reciting the Arabic text aloud. Whenever there were too many children in the playroom, we made so much noise that it disturbed the adults trying to listen to the Jummah Khutbah[7]. It's not that we intentionally made a lot of noise, but the more children added to the mix, the louder we got.

One of the parents would leave the prayer area and walk back towards the playroom and say, "Children, can you please quiet down? We can hear all of you from the prayer room and your noise is interfering with the Jummah Khutbah."

All of the children would calm down for a brief five minutes. Then about six minutes later, we'd all begin hollering again. There was always some

---

7 Khutbah: an Islamic preaching or sermons which presents the teachings of Islam.

reason why we got loud again. Whether it was one child pushing another child, another child taking someone else's toy, or we just wanted to continue playing the game we were previously playing before the adult came in to quiet us down. It's nothing intentional, but we felt like we were having the time of our lives.

Some days I decided I didn't want to play in the playroom. I'd sit in the prayer area near the other adults and listen to the Jummah Khutbah. Normally, I sat near my mom in the women's section of the mosque. In the mosque[8], men typically sat in the front near the Imam and women sat in a sectioned off area behind the men. Muslim men and women typically do not sit within mixed gatherings for any mosque services.

When I did sit in the prayer area, I was quiet for the Islamic lectures. I remained quiet because I enjoyed hearing the Imam's lectures. The lectures soothed me, and, in most cases, I felt in touch with lectures given by the Imam. The Imam spoke about being a good neighbor, the consequences of gossiping, and how we should live our lives to be better people. The Islamic lectures were comforting because it provided me with good morals and guidelines to follow. These teachings would help me reach my main goal, going to Jannah.[9] After the religious services were done, everyone cleaned the mosque, collected any garbage left behind, and went home.

Sometimes the Muslim families living on base would go to the mosque to have family gatherings or eat dinner together. These gatherings were especially important since all of us had at least one family member in the military who was, more often than not, deployed. In the meantime, we were our support system and the families were there whenever we needed their help. I absolutely didn't have any blood related family in El Paso, Texas except for my nuclear family. So, the Muslim military families became my extended family. We may not have known each other for a long time, but we made it worthwhile for the time being. Frequently, family members who attended the mosque arranged meals to bring to the social gatherings, so

---

8 Mosque: a place of worship for Muslims.

9 Jannah: literally meaning heaven in the Quran. The highest level of heaven is Firdaus.

that we could eat together for dinner. We rarely left someone solely responsible for meal preparations.

"Assalamu Alaikum everyone!" one of the parents pronounces. "Sister Sarah said that she was going to bring baked chicken and baked ziti, and Sister Rabbiya mentioned bringing Baklava, dates, and shish kebabs. What is everyone else bringing for the gathering?"

"I'll bring the beverages and cups," another parent calls out.

"Can someone else bring the eating utensils? We'll need spoons, forks and butter knives."

"Brother Kareem said that he would bring potato salad, macaroni salad, and coleslaw."

"Sister Monica is making fried chicken, lasagna, and mashed potatoes."

"Sister Hafsa is bringing chicken curry and tikka masala. Sister Fatima will bring Banku and Waakye (Wa-Chi)."

Everyone would call out the items they were bringing for family dinner night at the mosque. All the Muslim military families stayed connected with each other, hung out with each other, and organized family trips together. It even got to the point where the children were told to refer to the other parents as their aunts or uncles, even though we weren't blood related.

Fall of 1999 was drawing nearer and my parents were speaking about enrolling me to attend Bliss Elementary School. After hearing my family's discussions of enrolling me into school, I couldn't wait for school to begin. My dad was supposed to be coming home from deployment and it was only a couple of months until I'd begin my first year of school at Bliss Elementary School.

After hearing news my dad was coming home the next day, I was thrilled. I was so excited that I couldn't sleep. I tossed and turned the entire night until the sun began to rise, signaling the arrival of a new day. It had been a while since I'd seen my dad and it was hard only having my mom around.

The sun rays extend between the cut of my bedroom curtains and the birds begin tweeting outside my bedroom window. Gradually, the bedroom transitions from an orange tint until my room glows a bright yellow. I wake up somewhat sweaty because Summer's heat is beating my skin. My mom is in the kitchen fixing a huge breakfast so that everyone can eat well before preparing for my dad's late arrival. The living room smells like freshly fried turkey bacon, pancakes, and scrambled eggs. I follow the sweet breakfast scent towards the living room and into the kitchen. There, I find that my mom has already finished preparing breakfast and I wait for my mom to fix my plate.

I enjoy having hot chocolate in my sippy cup while eating breakfast.

After giving me my hot chocolate, my mom drizzles syrup over my pancakes, and then she takes a fork and butter knife to begin cutting my pancakes into pieces. I like to eat my breakfast with a little bit of everything on my fork. I put a little bit of the pancake, egg, and bacon on my fork, then, I take a bite out of all three of them at the same time. I finish eating all my breakfast until I only see syrup remaining on my plate.

Everyone in my family finally finishes their breakfast, and then my mom specifies all the chores that my siblings must complete before my dad's return home. My family begins with cleaning up the dining room area first, before continuing to complete other chores. I'm too young to help my family get the house ready, so I sit in the living room watching *Mister Rogers' Neighborhood,* one of my favorite shows.

For whatever reason, the introduction to *Mister Rogers' Neighborhood* interested me; Mister Rogers would sing along to the introduction of the show while switching his clothing from formal business attire to casual business attire. It sounds funny, but the introduction to Mister Rogers' show made me feel like putting on formal business attire, just so that I can change into casual business attire myself. Don't ask me why, but I watched the show too many times. When the introduction to the show was over, Mr. Rogers would talk to people in his neighborhood. Some of his interactions were educational and the messages were important.

At some point during the show, Mister Rogers directs a red trolley to the Neighborhood of Make Believe. In this neighborhood, there are puppets which live in a castle and occasionally, the puppets interact with humans. Despite the puppets being pretend, they too have feelings and express their concerns or wishes during the show. Together, the puppets and humans in the Land of Make Believe help solve the problems that the puppets are facing.

While I am watching the show, the fresh aroma of lemon slowly whiffs past my nose. The lemon scent fills the air as my older siblings mop the living room floor. While the lemon scent is evident, there are other parts of the house which now smells like bleach. My family is nearly done cleaning the house and everyone begins putting away the cleaning supplies before my dad arrives home.

My mom burns an incense stick to mask the smell of the cleaning products. My mom commonly burned incense sticks on a wooden incense stick holder near our kitchen sink. She preferred having the incense stick's droppings fall into the kitchen sink.

The smoke from the incense stick slowly floats up in the air and forms a wavy trail. Sometimes I watch the smoke travel up and escape in its various directions. Within a few minutes, the whole house smells of the incense.

My family and I try to keep the house clean until my dad's arrival.

In the meantime, my mom makes her way to our kitchen to begin preparing dinner. Most of the time, my mom cooks African dishes for my dad's return from deployment. She also learned how to cook several American dishes which my dad loves to eat, and sometimes she'd make both ethnic dishes for him.

My mom commonly makes jollof rice for special occasions. For my dad's arrival, she makes jollof rice, fried chicken, and salad.

While Mom is cooking dinner, I watch her put all the seasonings which makes her jollof rice have a distinct taste from other jollof rice. A lot of Africans cook jollof rice, but everybody has their own methods and ingredients of making it.

My mom is short, heavy-set, and has a light-skinned complexion. A lot of people don't automatically assume that my mom is African, despite her African accent. Some people assume that my mom is from a Caribbean Island because of her light-skinned complexion. As for stereotypes, many people think that Africans are the darkest shade of brown, but my mom proves that stereotype to be wrong. There are many light-skinned Africans and it has nothing to do with them being biracial.

When my mom finishes cooking dinner, she places all the food in decorative serving dishes. She sets up the dinner table with plates and eating utensils. No one is allowed to eat the food until my dad comes back home.

I remain steady in the living room for most of the afternoon until my dad comes back. If I moved out of my spot, I'd most likely mess up the house and get in trouble. It was better for me to listen to my family and stay in my spot until my dad got back.

"Julde [Jul-DAY], your dad is here!"

My dad is a tall, muscular African-American man with broad shoulders and a medium-brown complexion. Every time my dad came back home, he was wearing a green, beige, brown, and black camouflage patterned uniform. On the right side of my dad's uniform jacket it reads, "Bani Ball", and on the left side of my dad's uniform jacket it reads, "U.S. Army". My dad walks into the house while wearing his uniform and reaches out to hug everyone. Everyone in my family is excited that my dad finally came back home from deployment. After my dad settles down, he opens his camouflaged backpack and gives each of my family members items which he received from his deployment.

My favorite thing that my dad gave out were his MRE food packages. The MRE food packages came in brown, suctioned, plastic packaging, and inside the packages were meals which military personnel ate while they were deployed in the field. MRE stands for "Meal Ready-to-Eat".

As usual, I sit near my dad to spend time with him. Later into the evening, my dad lets me taste one of the MRE meals he brought home. The meals are not that tasty, but it allows me to see what my dad ate while he was deployed.

My family and I spend the rest of our evening listening to Quran together on the stereo or listening to lectures of well-known Imams. Most of the Islamic lectures we listen to are pre-recorded on cassette tapes. While the family listens to Islamic lectures, my mom calls the family to eat dinner. Finally, my family could eat the food that my mom prepared for my dad's arrival. We sit around the round, wooden dining room table, and begin preparing our meals, and eating together. My family starts up a few conversations, but I just munch my food while sitting at the dining room table quietly watching everyone talk. As a young girl, I was quiet because I loved absorbing everything that was going on around me. When my family finishes eating dinner, we all help to clean the dining room table.

As soon as the sun begins setting, everyone in my family gets ready to pray the evening prayer called Maghrib[10]. Muslims pray five times a day and Maghrib is the fourth daily prayer that Muslims perform. To get ready to pray, everyone in my family goes to the bathroom to make Wudhu[11]. When everyone finishes making wudhu, my family members take prayer rugs out of the cabinet and we spread the prayer rugs neatly in the living room.

Either my dad or older brother makes the call for prayer, which is called the Adhan[12]. It is not traditional for Muslim women to call out the adhan, especially when there are Muslim men in the room who could call out the adhan. I only witnessed women say the Adhan for prayer if there were no men present to lead them in prayer, but when women said the Adhan, they normally said it in a quiet, soft tone. After deciding who would state the Adhan, that person would go to the prayer rug spread out in the front and stand in position. The person calling out the Adhan would place their hands over their ears and recite in Arabic:

Allah is the Greatest, Allah is the Greatest
Allah is the Greatest, Allah is the Greatest
I bear witness that there is none worthy of worship except Allah
I bear witness that there is none worthy of worship except Allah
I bear witness that Muhammad is the Messenger of Allah
I bear witness that Muhammad is the Messenger of Allah
Come to Prayer
Come to Prayer

---

10 Maghrib: the fourth daily prayer Muslims pray after sunset.

11 Wudhu: a method which is used by Muslims to cleanse themselves before praying. This cleansing must be done, otherwise a Muslim's prayer is invalid.

12 Adhan: an Islamic call for prayer. When Muslims hear this call, they know it's time for prayer.

> *Come to Success*
> *Come to Success*
> *Allah is the Greatest*
> *Allah is the Greatest*
> *There is none worthy of worship except Allah*

While my dad or older brother calls out the Adhan, everyone else in my family respectfully listens to the Adhan in silence. A true and believing Muslim knows that they're not supposed to interrupt the Adhan while it's being called. Muslims normally stay quiet throughout its duration and say their blessings under a soft, whispering tone. Immediately after the Adhan is done being called, everyone in my family lines up for prayer, women behind men, so that we can begin praying.

My mom, my older sister, and I stand in the back and followed behind in prayer.

I knew every part of the movement and it felt good to pray alongside my family members. My favorite part of prayer was when the leading person of the prayer would recite a chapter in the Quran called Surah[13] Al- Fatihah. Surah Al-Fatihah is the first chapter of the Quran and it means, "the Opening". The translation for Surah Al-Fatihah reads:

> *In the Name of Allah, the Most Beneficent, the Most Merciful.*
> *All praises and thanks be to Allah, the Lord of the World.*
> *The Most Beneficent, the Most Merciful.*
> *The Only Owner of the Day of Recompense.*
> *You Alone we worship, and you Alone we ask for help.*
> *Guide us to the Straight way.*
> *The way of those on whom You have bestowed Your Grace, not the way*
> *of those who earned your Anger, nor of those who went Astray.*

Then everybody says, "Ameen."

As a child, I shouted out, "AMEEN!" with a lot of force. I would almost be competing my shout for Ameen with the person leading the Islamic congregational prayer. I even did that during the Jummah prayers at the mosque. That was the only part of the prayer which everyone in the

---

13 Surah: an Arabic word which means chapter. Any time this word is used it literally refers to the chapters in the Quran.

congregation could say anything; every other part of the prayer, everyone had to remain silent.

When my family finishes praying Salat, everyone remains seated on the prayer rugs. Shortly after praying, it's good for Muslims to remain seated so that they can either make dua[14] or dhikr[15]. When everyone finishes making their dua or dhikr, we put our prayer rugs away to have family night.

Family nights in the 90s were the best nights I experienced as a child. Everyone would gather around the dining room table to play board games or card games. My family and I kept all our board games in a specific spot in the living room. When we're ready to play games, someone would go to a designated spot and grab the game the family wanted to play. The games that my family and I had stockpiled were Parcheesi, Monopoly, Uno, The Game of Life, Scrabble, Dominos, and so much other games.

I never played the games; I mainly observed my family playing them instead. Some of it had to do with the fact that I didn't understand the rules to the games, but it was fun just to watch my family. My family agreed on which games they wanted to play. If everyone agreed that they wanted to play Uno, my family members would sit around the dining room table and get ready to play Uno. One person in my family would shuffle the deck of Uno cards and evenly distribute them to each player. Meanwhile, I'm sitting on the side of the dining room table watching everyone in my family receive their share of Uno cards. After everyone's hands have been dealt, the first card pulled from the top of the deck begins the game.

The night is steadily approaching. Everyone sitting around the dining room table is yelling out, "Draw four!", "You just got skipped!", or "Reverse!".

---

14 Dua: an informal act of worship in which a Muslim calls out or supplicates to our creator. This prayer form is like "saying grace".

15 Dhikr: a continuous praise of Allah, the God of Abraham. In Dhikr, a Muslim continuously says Allahu Akbar (God is Great), Subhan Allah (Glory to God), Alhamdullilah (Praises be to God), or Astaghfirullah (I seek forgiveness from Allah).

"Did you draw your card from the deck? I didn't see you draw your cards! You're trying to cheat! Come on now, that's not how we're supposed to play the game. Draw your card from the deck!" my family members yell out.

I look over everyone's shoulder to see which cards they're holding, but I never expose my family member's cards. The game carries on until Alfa yells out, "Uno!" Collectively, everyone around the table chuckled. At this point, everyone's palms are sweating as they clutch onto the Uno cards in their hands. The cards are getting all bent up and crushed as the game approaches peak intensity. I'm on the edge of my seat, curious as to who will prove to be the victor. Some of my family members chuckle as they are forced to grab another Uno card from the deck.

Finally, Alfa plays his last card. We've finally reached a winner! Everyone around the table is in disbelief that they had just lost in the game of Uno. "I cannot believe that I just lost!" my family members exclaim.

I watch as my older brother Alfa celebrates his win in the game of Uno. Alfa wears glasses, he's tall, slender, a tawny-beige skin color, and when he smiles, his cheekbones bunch up.

These games were one of the many ways in which my family came together, especially after my dad returning home from deployment. I couldn't participate in game night because I didn't understand the concept of the games, but I loved the feeling of togetherness which they brought to my household. During the daytime, everyone was busy doing various activities. In the evening, I knew that my family would be home together reading the Quran, praying, watching television or playing board games.

Now that the game ended, everyone in my family begins preparing for our final prayer of the night, Isha'a. Isha'a is the fifth and final prayer of the day. Isha'a prayer is the night prayer, performed after darkness has completely approached. Everyone in my household takes turns entering the restroom to make wudhu. Without proper cleansing, a Muslim's prayer is considered invalid. When they finish cleansing themselves, everyone grabs a prayer rug and places it in the living room to get ready for Isha'a prayer.

My dad stands in position to begin calling out the Adhan for Isha'a prayer. Everyone in my family remains quiet until my dad finishes calling out the

Adhan. After he's finished, my family stands up in position for Isha'a prayer.

It felt good whenever I prayed alongside my family; it is what kept my family close together.

When we finish praying Isha'a, we remain seated on the floor so that someone can make Dua for all of us. Everyone cuffs their hands together, looks into the palms of their hands and listens to the one person making dua. As we listen to the dua, we say, "Ameen," for every part of the dua that we wish Allah would grant us.

"I pray that Allah grants everyone in the family good health."

"Ameen."

"May Allah reduce any burden which someone may be experiencing in their daily lives right now."

"Ameen."

"May Allah guide our family to the straight path and keep us from sinful temptations."

"Ameen."

When the duas are done, my siblings and I got ready to go to sleep. During this time, I wasn't attending public school, but I was enrolled at a daycare center on Fort Bliss. My family had glow in the dark stars placed above my bed on the ceiling. I normally looked up toward the glow in the dark stars until I slowly began dozing off to sleep. Next thing I knew, I'd be completely asleep. The next day, my parents got my siblings and me ready for school and daycare.

Chapter Two: Eaglets First Day of School

By September 1999, I was preparing for my first day of school at Bliss Elementary School. My family and I headed towards the school to register me for kindergarten. My parents completed all my school documentation and spoke with the school administrators about other paperwork they needed to bring before I could begin school. My parents were provided my school's supplies list, uniform requirements, and a list of vaccinations I needed to get. After getting all the information they needed, my parents scheduled me a doctor's appointment for my vaccinations. In the meantime, my family and I went school shopping.

My family went school-shopping at the Fort Bliss Post Exchange, so we entered our green van and drove towards the Fort Bliss PX[16]. After parking our van in the parking lot, my family and I made our way into the PX and immediately walked towards the school uniform section.

Mariam and Alfa repeatedly told my parents that they wanted the Dickies branded school uniforms. My parents headed directly to the area containing Dickies clothing brand and begin picking out our school uniforms.

For my uniform, I was required to wear a collared-shirt in the colors red, white, or blue. My bottoms, whether they were skirts or slacks, were supposed to be the colors blue or black. After picking out our uniforms, we went to grab school supplies. We made sure to grab everything listed on my school supplies list. I got my backpack, jumbo pencils, jumbo crayons, glue, markers, watercolors paint, erasers, a ruler, and notebooks.

My mom purchased bobos[17] and a relaxer for my hair. She told me that I needed to get my hair done for the first day of school.

The night before school, my older sister, Mariam, relaxed my hair using the Just for Me hair relaxing brand my mom purchased.

---

16 PX: a short abbreviation for Post Exchange, a retail store that is found on military bases.

17 Bobo: a hair accessory that is used as a ponytail holder. Bobos [Plural] are wrapped around hair that is braided or twisted.

Mariam places gloves on her hands before relaxing my hair. Afterwards, she places a sufficient amount of Vaseline at my hairline. Mariam then carefully sections and parts my hair so that she can place the relaxer in each section of my hair. Mariam begins placing the relaxing cream at the roots of my hair, while slowly working her way out to the ends.

"Let me know when the relaxer begins burning, Julde," Mariam tells me.

"Okay, I'll let you know," I tell Mariam.

Within twenty minutes of Mariam placing the relaxer in my hair, I holler "Mariam, it's burning!" The relaxer is stinging my skin and I can barely stand the burning I am feeling from the relaxer.

"Okay, let me massage the relaxer in a little bit longer," Mariam replies.

After five minutes, Mariam and I rush back into the bathroom to begin rinsing the relaxer out of my hair.

"Julde, keep your eyes shut! Try not to open your eyes! Don't let the relaxer enter your eyes!" Mariam repeatedly shouts.

I firmly close my eyes shut while Mariam rinses the relaxer from my hair. When Mariam finishes rinsing all the relaxer out of my hair, she uses shampoo and conditioner to make sure my hair was thoroughly rinsed from all the hair relaxing chemicals.

After getting my hair relaxed, my mom picks out my pajamas, and prepares me for bed.

On school nights, it was customary for me to be in bed by 9:00 p.m. I shared my bedroom with my older sister Mariam. Mariam's bed was on the right side of the bedroom and my bed was on the left side of the bedroom with my glow-in-the-dark stars placed above it, I'd stare at those stars until I finally dozed off to sleep.

This school night would be different from all the other nights which I ever slept. I was finally beginning my first day of school the next day. For so long, I had been waiting for the day I'd finally sit in a classroom. I tossed and turned that entire night, finding it difficult to sleep because of the excitement. There was nothing better than finally attending school.

"I'll go to school, learn, and make friends," I think to myself as I fight to sleep.

"I'll finally be able to use the school supplies my family bought for my first day of class," I think some more.

With all the excitement, I continue tossing and turning because to me, there's nothing better than beginning my first day of kindergarten.

"The sneakers which light up with every step I take, those are the sneakers I want to wear. My mom's going to style my hair with the bobos in the morning."

I toss and turn some more, then the next thing I know, my parents are coming into my room saying, "JULDE! Get up, today is your first day of school!" I'm astonished at how fast morning approached. I really didn't sleep at all.

I instantly get up from my bed smiling with excitement.

My dad comes into my bedroom with a big, black, camcorder placed on his shoulder. He wants to record the very moment I woke up for my first day of school. My parents wanted to preserve this memory forever, so they begin recording the video from the hallway leading to my bedroom. Dad bursts out laughing because it didn't take them much to wake me up for school. While my Dad is laughing, it also looks like his eyes are also smiling. I have my Dad's eyes, they're round, big and they'd glow whenever we smiled.

I'm instantly and fully awake.

I'm ready to put on my school uniform, get my hair done with the bobos, eat breakfast, and attend my first day of kindergarten at Bliss Elementary School. After getting ready for school, I'm handed my lunch bag. I then wait for my dad to get ready so that he can take me to my first day of school.

My dad and I drive towards Bliss Elementary School in his red Nissan. Bliss Elementary was walking distance from our home; however, my dad had to go to work after dropping me off for school. While driving towards my school, my dad says, "Julde, look! That's your school playground." My dad uses his forefinger to point towards a huge playground behind the school building. I look out the car window staring at the playground. It contains monkey bars, swings, tetherball poles, a jungle gym and a basketball court. The playground is full of green grass, but in certain areas of the playground there are patches of dust where the grass eroded, likely from children playing roughly on the grass. After absorbing the view of my new playground, I'm eager to finally play there during recess. Recess was one of the things I looked forward to the most while attending elementary school.

After driving past the playground, my dad turns into the school parking lot and parks his car. When my dad was finished parking, we head towards the entrance of my school, where I await my kindergarten teacher.

The sun is nearly out, and the morning sky is light-blue. A slight breeze kisses my face as I walk alongside my dad to my school entrance. There are other students standing near their parents while waiting outside the school's entrance. The area is crowded and students are wearing their brand new red, white, and blue collared uniform shirts. Everyone was told that the teachers would come out to walk us into our school classrooms on the first day. My dad converses with the other parents standing near the school building. I'm too shy to talk, but I stand near my dad, listening to his conversation.

Finally, the huge double doors of Bliss Elementary School burst open and a group of teachers walk out of the double doors, smiling. Their smiles give me the impression that they couldn't wait to finally begin the new school year. All the kindergarten teachers welcome the students to a new school year and begin telling the parents to walk their children to their assigned teachers. I eagerly search with the rest of the students for who our new kindergarten teachers will be before heading into our classrooms. I'm even more excited when I find out which classroom I belonged to.

It is only *after* finding my kindergarten teacher, when my dad says he has to leave for work, that it suddenly hits me: I'd have to be in class the entire day without any of my family members.

I grow empty on the inside, thinking how awkward it would be to sit next to other students I didn't know. I had only just met the teacher five minutes ago but would have to be under her supervision until I returned home later in the day. My dad starts to leave for work, but with every step he takes away from the school, my feelings of emptiness grow deeper. Earlier in the morning, I was excited to attend school, but I never took into consideration that I'd be in school without my family members. I was unfamiliar with everyone in my class and this frightened me.

"I have to go to work, Julde," my dad tells me as he looks back towards me. I feel a rush of tears welling up in my eyes. I wipe my eyes to get a clear vision of where my dad is. My dad is already taking small steps away from the school hallway but looks back at me every now and then to tell me, "Julde, I have to go to work." At this point, my dad stops looking back towards me, and he heads directly toward the school parking lot. I get one last glimpse of my dad while he walks away from my school. One of my classroom teachers comes to get me from the school hallway and escorts me into the classroom.

I look back outside the double doors to see if I could find my dad in plain sight, but he's no longer there. That left me with no other option but to follow my kindergarten teacher into her class. This was the beginning of my public school experience.

When class began, my classmates and I were given assigned seats. Once all the students settled down, we were told to place all our school supplies under our classroom desks. The teachers used their rosters to call out the attendance of each student sitting in my classroom. My name was normally one of the first names to be called because my last name begins with the letter "B".

The teacher slowly goes down the list and finally gets to my name. "Juldy Ball? Or Ball?"

"No, my name is pronounced Jul-DAY," I correct my teacher.

"Oh, Judy. I'll make a note of that in my roster."

I had a hard time with my name while I was younger. Sometimes I'd wonder why my parents didn't opt to give me a more common name. A name which didn't require me explaining how to pronounce it every time I met someone new.

My teacher finishes calling the attendance of everyone in class, then she hands us some papers to know if some students could spell out their names. When I began kindergarten in 1999, I knew how to write out my name, but it was funny because I wrote out my name with some letters backwards. So, whenever the teachers asked me to write down my name, I'd often wrote my name out as Julbe because I couldn't make out the difference between the lowercase letters "b" and "d".

It took a couple months of practice for me to get used to writing some of the letters properly. The teachers understood that I struggled with some of my letters, so they worked together to teach me the difference between the letters "b" and "d".

After getting settled in the class, the school administrators made a morning announcement over the loudspeakers. The school administrators greeted the Bliss Elementary School students with a good morning and expressed their excitement for a new school year. While speaking over the loudspeaker, the school administrators told all the students to stand up, face towards the American flag and place our right hands over our hearts. The morning announcement was going to be concluded with the "Pledge of Allegiance", "Star-spangled Banner", and "America the Beautiful". The two kindergarten teachers in class quickly went over to each student, helping us get into proper positioning towards the American flag. The class was full of a bunch of four and five-year old children acting like they had ants in their pants. The teachers tried their best keeping the students in position, then the school administrators began saying the "Pledge of Allegiance" over the loudspeaker. The students followed along, declaring:

> *I pledge allegiance to the flag of the United States of America, and to the Republic for which it stands—one Nation, under God, indivisible—with liberty and justice for all.*

After a few minutes, the school administrators put on "Star Spangled Banner" over the loudspeaker and it played:

> *O say can you see by the dawn's early light*
> *What so proudly we hailed at the twilight's last gleaming?*
> *Whose broad stripes and bright stars through the perilous fight*
> *O'er the ramparts we watched, were so gallantly streaming?*

> *And the rockets red glare, the bombs bursting in air*
> *Gave proof through the night that our flag was still there*
> *O say does that star-spangled banner yet wave*
> *O'er the land of the free and the home of the brave?*

The students who knew the song, sang along to the "Star Spangled Banner". Many of the students were four or five-years-old, so some students were still attempting to learn the lyrics. Some of the students mumbled the lyrics they didn't know. The students remained facing towards the American flag even after the "Star Spangled Banner." Both Kindergarten teachers made sure that they helped us stay in proper positioning towards the American flag so that we can listen to "America the Beautiful". The staff at Bliss Elementary didn't play "America the Beautiful" except for special occasions. Being that this was the first day of school, it was necessary for us to remain standing for "America the Beautiful". The lyrics played over the loudspeaker:

> *Oh, beautiful for spacious skies,*
> *For amber waves of grain,*
> *For purple mountain majesties*
> *Above the fruited plain!*
> *America! America!*
> *God shed his grace on thee,*
> *And crown thy good with brotherhood*
> *From sea to shining sea.*
> *Oh, beautiful for pilgrim feet,*
> *Whose stern, impassioned stress*
> *A thoroughfare of freedom beat*
> *Across the wilderness!*
> *America! America!*
> *God mend thine every flaw,*
> *Confirm thy soul in self-control,*
> *Thy liberty in law.*
> *Oh, beautiful for heroes proved*
> *In liberating strife,*
> *Who more than self their country loved,*
> *And mercy more than life!*
> *America, America!*

May God thy gold refine,
Till all success be nobleness,
And every gain divine,
Oh, beautiful for patriot dream
That sees beyond the years
Thine alabaster cities gleam,
Undimmed by human tears!
America! America!
God shed his grace on thee,
And crown thy good with brotherhood
From sea to shining sea

When "America the Beautiful" ended, so did the school announcement. The two kindergarten teachers began the first day of Kindergarten by asking all the students to introduce themselves. Each of the Kindergarten students introduced themselves to everyone in the class, then afterwards, the teachers had us begin our kindergarten curriculum.

Later in the afternoon, it was lunchtime and my teachers got ready to escort all the students to the school cafeteria. I had my own lunch bag, so I went over to my classroom's lunch table and began eating the lunch my parents prepared for me that morning.

A peaches fruit cup, a turkey and American cheese sandwich, a pack of chips, and a Capri-Sun; those were the common lunch items my parents packed me for lunch. After lunch, it was time for recess. I went outside with the rest of my kindergarten class to play.

Recess! I finally get the chance to play on the monkey-bars, swings, and slides my dad pointed out to me earlier in the morning. I was ready to go out and play with some of my classmates who I was shy to meet earlier in the morning. As soon as my classmates and I went outside, we began getting to know each other. Although in the morning I was terrified with the idea of my dad leaving me behind at school for work, at that very moment I was comfortable playing with the other students from my classroom.

That initial hollow feeling I had in the morning was soon gone, and I found myself feeling relieved that I was finally comfortable at school. My classmates and I ran around under the hot beaming sun, laughing and having a significant amount of fun. It didn't make a difference how hot it was, I continued running around. Some students were playing soccer, other students were playing tag. Students who came to school with brand new, neat uniforms began getting creases and wrinkles in their uniform. Some students said, "My parents are going to be *mad* at me when I get home."

I'm sweating because of the sun's heat and I feel out of breath. I'm running around so much that I begin gasping for air. I barely gave myself any break from running around. At this point, I'm completely out of breath and fully dehydrated.

I am thirsty.

I notice other children running back towards the school building to this thing that looks like a huge white sink. I run behind the other students to this huge white sink. After getting there, I see the students twisting the knob to get water out and drink. The students stand over to sip water. I impatiently wait my turn because some of the students appear like they're not willing to move. I watch them take mouthfuls of water and walk away. When the students in front of me finish drinking, at last I get my turn to drink water. I don't know how to turn the knob, so I ask one of the students to help me. He walks over to my side and turns the knob as I drink water. Another student watches us while laughing out loud, asking me, "You don't know how to turn the knob for the water fountain?"

Then a girl shows me how to work the water fountain. The knob on the water fountain is sturdy and I have a hard time getting the water out of the fountain. Eventually, I learned how to work the fountains. Water fountains became my lifesaver while attending elementary school, especially during recess.

By the time recess ends, I've sweated out my relaxer a little bit. Typically, when someone gets a hair relaxer, you try your best not to sweat out, dampen, or wet your hair. Any moisture which your relaxed hair absorbs can cause the relaxed parts of your hair to become frizzy and return to its natural curly state. That's the shortcomings of being an African-American girl who always relaxes her hair. I could barely do any activity which required me wetting my hair. When school ended, I didn't look the same way I looked when my parents sent me off for school. Compared to how I looked in the morning, I looked a wild mess! That's the perks of being a child. Your parents send you off to daycare or school looking nice and neat, but after playing and having lots of fun, you come home looking untidy. Most of the time I got in trouble for looking a mess, but I only had one chance at being a child. I was going to live my childhood to the fullest.

For the next three months, I followed the same routine of getting ready for school. I wore my Bliss Elementary School uniform with pride. My favorite shoes to wear with my school uniform were the light-up shoes; they lit up with every step that I took. Sometimes the students who had flashing shoes would jump on purpose to show off the many colors their shoes made whenever they lit up. Those shoes gave me every reason to get out of my classroom seat and walk over to my cubby. Sometimes while walking over to my cubby, I hit a pose and got back towards my classroom seat as my shoes flashed.

The first thing that my school routinely did every morning was face the American flag to sing along to the "Pledge of Allegiance", "Star-spangled Banner", or "America the Beautiful". Whenever I arrived to school late and missed the "Pledge of Allegiance", I already felt out of my normal school routine. With being late to class, not only did I miss the morning announcement, but I also fell behind in my classwork. I disliked falling behind in my learning material because I sat confused for the remainder of my teacher's curriculum. Not to mention, students who didn't have perfect attendance weren't invited to the school pizza party and I wanted to be invited to the school pizza party. On the days that the school did have pizza parties for students with perfect attendance, you'd watch all the staff bringing in boxes of pizza you wouldn't eat because you were late to school a few times. There's nothing worse than smelling pizza from the hallways of the school building, knowing that you don't get to be a part of it.

On some weekends, my family and I drove off Fort Bliss to go out and eat at restaurants in the city of El Paso, Texas. Other times, we ate at other families' homes. After having a long day out in the city, my family and I would drive back to our housing unit on Fort Bliss. If we happened to pass by the Franklin Mountains, I'd see the huge bright star placed on the mountain. The star on the mountain is made from huge light bulbs, shaped and designed to form a five-point star. It can be seen from a distance and its presence is right above the city of El Paso. I never understood why there was a huge glowing star located on the mountain, but it seemed to be El Paso's landmark.

On other weekends, my family and I went to the Halaqas[18] being offered by the Islamic Cultural Center of El Paso. At the time, the Islamic Cultural Center of El Paso was a two-story house, but the house was being used for religious services. Some of the Muslim families who attended religious services on Fort Bliss also attended the Halaqas held by the Islamic Cultural Center of El Paso. Some people brought food along with them if they wanted and waited for the Imam to come and discuss various topics in Islam. Some of the topics the Imam covered were the lives of the prophets and some chapters in the Quran. In the meantime, the children attended Quranic study classes on the second floor of the house. My parents enrolled me in some of the classes, so that I could become familiar with Islamic doctrine. Religious services at the Islamic Cultural Center of El Paso normally ended at noon during Dhuhr[19] prayer, which is the second prayer Muslims perform in a day. When it was time for Dhuhr prayer, I'd run downstairs with my hijab and get ready to pray. Some of the students went into the bathroom to make their wudhu, but at the time, I wasn't taught how to make proper wudhu. I'd run to my mom, who was sitting in the sister's section of the mosque, and get in position for prayer. One of the Imams would call out the Adhan, which was familiar to me, and slowly the prayer room would steadily become packed. Everyone stood in prayer, toe-to-toe and shoulder-to-shoulder while the Imam recited the verses of the Quran. When we were done praying, my parents would get ready to leave the mosque and we'd return home.

It was nearing the year 2000, and my dad was told he'd be stationed in Germany again due to military orders. This meant that my entire family would have to relocate alongside my dad to his next duty station. I was

---

18 Halaqa: [Plural-Halaqas] an Islamic gathering purposely for Muslims to study Islam and the Quran.

19 Dhuhr: the second daily prayer Muslims pray during the midday.

disappointed after hearing the news that my family had to move. I was never going to see the friends that I made again. I was going to leave behind my neighborhood on Fort Bliss, and I'd have to start all over when my family moved to New Argonner Kaserne in Germany. I had made so many memories while living on Fort Bliss. At least, I could take all those memories with me, but I'd have to leave behind the many people I created those memories with. I thought back on the times that I got to know many of the children on a personal level, especially now that I had to leave those neighbors behind and start a new life in Germany. I was dreading this reality. As a military brat, my memories became a very important part of me.

During my family's last months in our house, we began packing up all our belongings into boxes. We wanted the moving company to begin sending our furniture and other items to Germany ahead of our departure. The sooner my family sent off our belongings to Germany, the faster we'd be able to retrieve those items.

Before my parents turned our housing unit over to the Fort Bliss housing office, my parents did excessive cleaning in our housing unit. You would've thought that my parents were renovating the entire interior of our housing unit, especially if you saw the type of work my family was doing in that house. My parents always said, "The military gave us this housing unit clean, so we'll return this housing unit back to them clean." So, we stayed in that housing unit to scrub every and any part of the house until my parents thought it looked clean enough. It was a serious back breaker; I kid you not.

"Mom, Dad, isn't the housing office going to send people to clean our housing unit anyway?"

Like for real, we weren't allowed to go outside for nearly a week, until the unit looked "tip-top clean," as my parents would say. My parents didn't want the military to go through a lot of trouble cleaning our housing unit; especially before turning it over to another incoming military family.

All the blame was on me while my family was cleaning the house, for I was the child that thought the wall, carpet, and tiles were a "sheet of paper." If any part of my house had an open surface, I most likely drew on it. My parents opted to throwing our carpet away because it was tough scrubbing the marker stains out. They also had to buy Brillo pads to scrub out all the stains I made. In a continuous pattern, my family sprayed the stains and scrubbed. I tried my best to remain silent for the duration of my family's cleaning process because anytime I spoke, one of my family members would get upset. My family and I were scrubbing the walls and floors for days. I tried to help my family scrub some parts of the walls in the house, but it was so hard for me to scrub the stains that I had to stop helping them. The house smelled of bleach, Lysol, Pine-Sol, and any other cleaning agent you could think of. My family members were wearing gloves to protect their hands from the cleaning agents. Occasionally, someone's glove would break from scrubbing the stains so aggressively.

Then in the most innocent and lovable tone I turned to my family and said, "I am sorry that I drew in the house." My family just turned and gave me a serious look. On children's television shows the puppy dog look works, but I realized that I couldn't expect an old television trick to work on my family members. While trying to pucker up my face, everyone looked back down to the part of the house they were scrubbing and continued trying to get all the stains out. My family was UPSET!

Geesh! Sorry about that.

Chapter Three: A New Year in New Argonner

Before leaving El Paso, my family and I drove to the nearest airport for our departure towards Frankfurt, Germany. It was common for my parents to leave home hours before our plane departure. Sometimes that meant that my family would be in the airport five hours prior to our flight's departure. When my family and I got to the airport, we waited there until it was time for our flight to depart.

The flight to Germany was the first flight that I could remember during my childhood. I had been on a couple of flights as an infant; however, I didn't have a vivid memory of any of those flight experiences. This time, I was going to know and remember what it felt like to be on an airplane flight. My family and I were scheduled to land at the Frankfurt Airport, the closest airport to Hanau, Germany; which was my dad's new military duty location. New Argonner Kaserne[20] was going to be my family's new neighborhood.

When it was time for the passengers to board the flight, the airlines called the passengers according to the section of the airplane they were sitting in. My family always flew economy, so we were one of the last people to board. My family stood in line and waited to board the airplane. Once we had boarded, we all sat in our assigned airplane seats, as written on our boarding passes, and waited for the airplane to take off.

The flight attendants began the flight takeoff by demonstrating the mandatory instructions for flight safety. It was always good to be informed on what actions you should take in case you're on a flight which experiences technical difficulties. My family watched the flight attendants demonstrate the exit routes, oxygen masks, and help some passengers buckle themselves into their seats as the flight prepared for takeoff.

---

20 Kaserne: translates to meaning "barracks" in German.

My family and I flew numerous airplanes before finally landing in Frankfurt, Germany. Along the way, my family had to transfer onto different connecting flights. It almost felt like we were travelling on airplanes for two days. There were no direct flights from El Paso, Texas to Frankfurt, Germany. Every time my family and I had to switch to a connecting flight, I felt nauseated.

The thing that I disliked the most about flying on airplanes was my ears popping. Whenever the flights took off or landed, the change in atmospheric pressure would make my ears pop uncontrollably. Not only did I have to bear the pain of my ears popping once, but I had to bear the pain of my ears popping every time we took a connecting flight. My family finally landed at one of our many stops, but we had to rush to our next connecting flight.

Right after the airplane is done taxiing and comes to a full stop, my family reaches to grab our carry-on items in the overhead compartment. The aisles on the airplane are narrow so we wait to exit the airplane. Everyone else on our plane gradually walks off the flight as we're waiting near our seats. My parents, who are holding the boarding passes for our next flight, read the ticket, so that we can know which gate we'll need to catch our connecting flight at. My family and I only have minutes to get to the subsequent gate and I had barely slept. We run through the airport so that we can make it to the next gate on time.

"I'm tired!" I cry out.

"Julde, we're all tired. If we don't hurry up, we'll miss our next flight."

Everyone in my family is carrying a carry-on item while running through the airport terminal. As soon as we see the high-speed moving walkways, we get on them to speed up our travel towards the next gate. The airport has large windows which face outside towards the terminals and runways. While I'm running alongside my family, I look outside the window and observe workers placing luggage under the airplane and people performing ground control. I'm amazed at the sight of the airplane workers outside, so I start slowing down.

"Julde, hurry up, we're almost at our gate!"

I pick up speed again, running behind my family members on the moving walkways. A whiff of food from the nearby restaurants brushes past my nose and it smells very good. The savory scents of garlic, onions, bay leaves, and other seasonings, permeate the air. I just want to stop and eat! The food being served on the airplanes haven't tasted good, but my parents won't stop to buy any food since we're running late.

Finally, we make it to the gate and begin boarding our next flight. At this point, I'm both tired and hungry.

"Passengers please remain seated and keep your seat belts buckled as the plane prepares for takeoff," the flight attendant announces over the loudspeaker. The flight attendants begin their routine demonstration of flight safety, as they did on the other flights.

Sometimes I'm extremely tired while boarding a flight, then immediately after the flight takes off, I'm wide awake. The pain I get of my ears popping while the plane is taking off wakes me up, no matter how tired I feel. The higher the plane flies up into the sky, the more my ears pop. Now I'm wide awake and cranky because I haven't slept well for the last few hours that I've been riding on airplanes. Travelling makes me feel nauseous, which is especially unpleasant while you're running on an empty stomach. Airplanes barely have space to make free movement. It becomes worse when the passenger sitting directly in front of you decides to recline their chair. Not to mention, you cannot lie down flat while flying on airplanes, unless you're riding in First Class. I always felt that whenever I didn't lie down flat while sleeping on airplanes, I wasn't well rested.

"Mom, my ears are popping!" I say while sobbing in pain. I begin holding both of my ears tightly with my hands. It didn't matter how tightly I held my ears, my ears were still popping. I looked towards my mom who didn't appear to be experiencing any sort of pain.

"There's nothing that we can do, Julde. Do you want to chew on a piece of gum?" my mom asks me.

"Yes, please! I want to chew on a piece of gum," I respond without hesitation. My mom gives me a piece of gum and I instantly notice that chewing on gum is easing the pain of my ears popping. I start chewing the gum extremely fast to keep the pain from returning.

When my family and I finally arrive in Frankfurt, Germany, we temporarily stay in a hotel until we get assigned to our new housing unit on New Argonner. After a couple of days, my family gets news that we've been assigned a housing unit, but this time we're going to be placed in an apartment building.

Getting my siblings and I enrolled in school was one of the first priorities that my parents had after moving to Germany. My siblings and I left El Paso, Texas during the middle of a school year and it was nearly the year 2000. My parents felt that the sooner we got registered for school, the faster my siblings and I could catch up with our school's curriculum. My parents were going to enroll my siblings and me into the schools located on military bases. The United States' military bases in Germany had their own American public schools for military dependent children to attend. On the military bases, the students were taught primarily in English, but one class period was reserved to students learning how to speak conversational German. Learning some of the German vocabulary was especially necessary whenever our families decided to travel off base to shop or enjoy various parts of the country. The majority of the students attending the schools on base were dependents of military members; only a few of the other students attending our American schools were native Germans.

The school that my parents tried to enroll me in for kindergarten was called Argonner Elementary School, located on the Old Argonner Kaserne. New Argonner, which I lived on, was connected to Old Argonner via a bridge. When I began school at Argonner Elementary School, I'd walk across from New Argonner Kaserne to Old Argonner Kaserne using this bridge. New Argonner and Old Argonner were directly across from each other with a local road outside the confines of either base dividing the two bases.

The school administrators at Argonner Elementary School told my parents that I couldn't begin kindergarten at their school until I turned five years old. At the time, I was still four years old, but I was going to turn five years old in nearly a month. My parents tried explaining to the school administrators that I was going to be turning five years old a few weeks from then, but the school administrators insisted that I was too young to be registered for their kindergarten class.

"Even though Julde is going to turn five years old soon?" my parents tried reasoning with the school administrators at Argonner Elementary School.

"Yes, your daughter must wait for the upcoming school year, beginning Fall 2000. Come to register your daughter next fall so that she'll begin kindergarten."

"Julde already began kindergarten at Bliss Elementary School. She began her kindergarten classes September 1999. How come she has to wait an entire school year to begin kindergarten here?"

"We do our kindergarten registration differently from Bliss Elementary School. When Julde turns five years old, she'll begin kindergarten at our school."

Despite my birthday being December 20, 1994, I'd have to start my school year after turning five. I quietly watched my parents dispute with the school administrators about how Argonner Elementary School should let me continue kindergarten for the remainder of the 1999-2000 school year. My parents persisted; however, the school administrators stood firm that I'd have to begin kindergarten in September of 2000. The Argonner Elementary School administrators said that the school age requirements in Texas are totally different from the age requirements of the students attending their school in Germany.

My parents enrolled me at a daycare center located on Old Argonner in the meantime. This was especially necessary now that my parents needed to get back to work. On the days that I didn't attend daycare, I played with other children who lived on New Argonner. My parents developed relationships with some of our new neighbors, who also offered to babysit me whenever my parents needed them to watch me. This would help my parents reduce the costs of daycare. Military families don't know each other from a hole in the ground, but we end up resembling a family. It only takes a few conversations for my parents to bond with neighbors in our neighborhood.

I used to enjoy going to the playground located across the street from my apartment building. Even when I didn't know the names of the children I was playing with, I'd play with them anyway. It was important that I introduced myself to the other children playing on base so that we can begin developing a relationship with each other. Sometimes we'd play tag, hide-and-go-seek, or jump rope together. After getting familiar with some of the children living on base, not only did we hang around together outside in the neighborhood, but we also went over each other's houses to play. All I had to do in my day was get up in the morning, get ready, and go outside to play. It was always safe for me to go out on my own, I just had to make sure I asked my parents' permission before leaving the apartment.

All the apartment buildings on New Argonner had large basements where children liked to play various games. When the children wanted to play hide-and-go-seek, we'd go downstairs to the basement of the buildings. The basement was nice and dark, and there were many spots where the children could hide from the seekers. The children would play a round of rock, paper, scissors to begin choosing the first person who would seek all the hiders.

"Rock, Paper, Scissors!" then everyone would see who won that round, and the loser would become the seeker of the game during hide-and-go-seek. Other times, the children would play a round of "Eeny Meeny Miny Moe", to find out who'd be the next seeker. Everyone would stand in a circle while one person chants:

> *Eeny, meeny, miny, moe*
> *Catch a tiger by the toe*
> *If he hollers let him go,*
> *Eeny, meeny, miny, moe*
> *My mother told me*
> *To pick the very best one*
> *And you are not it!*

Now that we finally found a seeker, we'd begin our game of hide-and-go-seek. The first seeker would count to 20 while all the other children scattered in the basement to find a good hiding spot.

"One, two, three…"

Promptly, everyone begins running to find a room they can hide in.

Inside the basement of our apartment buildings were storage rooms for military families to store their belongings. Some areas of the basement had dimmed light bulbs and other parts of the basement had bright light bulbs. Just like many other basements, there were barely any windows, which made the basement look dark. At certain parts of the basement, there were ceiling windows so high up, that none of the children could reach them.

I continue running through the hallways of the basement, trying to find a good hiding spot. When I find a room that looks good enough to hide in, I try my best to hide from the seeker. Sometimes the best places to hide were inside the furniture or empty boxes in the basement. Other storage rooms were impossible to hide in because the families locked those rooms.

"Ready or not, here I come!" the seeker hollers out. Everyone who's hiding gets prepared to potentially be found by the seeker. I really didn't like hiding around other children who giggled, snickered, or screamed, because immediately after the seeker entered our storage room, we'd be found. The whole point of the game is to not get caught, and if the other children were going to mess that up, then I didn't want them hiding next to me. On occasion, it was nice to get caught by the seeker because now you'd have the chance to find the other children, but I didn't want to be the seeker all the time.

New Argonner didn't have a mosque that we could pray in but with the help of the chaplains the Muslim military were able to secure a small prayer room on Pioneer Kaserne where they could hold Jummah prayers.

On the weekends, the mosque would have Islamic and Quranic Studies classes for the children. My parents got my siblings and me enrolled for the Islamic weekend classes. The children would go to their Islamic Studies teachers to begin learning whatever was required of them that week. Sometimes, the parents stayed in the mosque to talk with the Imam about various topics which they questioned in Islam. At the age of five, I still wasn't learning how to read in the Arabic text, but I did learn about the lives of the prophets. It's important to know that Muslims believe in all the prophets from the Abrahamic prophethood. In Arabic, the name Abraham translates into Ibrahim.

As in the previous Abrahamic religions, the Muslim children were taught that the human creation began with Adam, who was the first man, and Eve, who was the first woman created after Adam. Adam and Eve were told to not eat from the forbidden tree. They weren't given an explanation as to why, but they were commanded to respect God's instruction and not eat from the tree. Then came along Iblees[21], who was jealous of the human creation, and lured Adam and Eve into eating from the forbidden tree because he despised the human creation. Iblees was a good Jinn[22] who offered his prayer to God so often that his behavior resembled that of an angel. At certain points, God reminded Iblees that he wasn't an angel; rather, he was a Jinn. Iblees successfully lured Adam and Eve into eating the forbidden tree out of envy. Muslims learn that because of Adam and Eve's disobedience, humans were made to struggle on Earth until the day of resurrection.

The many prophets that I learned about while attending Islamic studies class were Noah, Enoch, Abraham, Ishmael, Isaac, Ezekiel, Lot, David, John, Joseph, Solomon, Aaron, Jesus, and so much more. After mentioning the prophets' names, you must give them their respect by stating, "peace be upon him." When the Islamic studies class ended it was time for all the students to pray Dhuhr prayer. Everyone would pray Dhuhr prayer together and leave to go back home.

When the winter season began drawing near in Germany, I went outside less. It was now getting too cold for me to go play outside. Although I enjoyed hanging out with the other children in my neighborhood, I'd rather stay home to avoid going out to the cold weather. I began occupying myself

---

21 Iblees: the chief of Jinn which is believed to have rebelled against Allah. (He is also known as the Devil)

22 Jinn: a classification of spirit made from smokeless flames, different from an Angel because they can choose to be good or bad.

with other things at home like watching television, playing with my toys or playing games on my computer. Even though my family and I were living on a United States military base, the television stations on base barely had any English channels. Some days I watched Cartoon Network and other days I watched British channels. While watching the British channels, I often did an impression of British English. There are many variations of the English dialect being used around the world, such as Australian, Jamaican, American, and Nigerian, but they're all speaking a form of English. However, I really loved the British dialect when I was younger. Some of the shows which aired on the British channels were fascinating and I loved their usage of vocabulary.

December 31, 1999 was the first time that I celebrated New Year's Eve in Germany. While I was living in El Paso, I never celebrated New Year's the way that I celebrated in Hanau, Germany. Celebrating New Years in El Paso was rarely fun because fireworks were illegal. Being that El Paso is a desert, fireworks were banned from being used due to the high temperatures they reach. On the other hand, in Hanau, Germany, my family bought many firecrackers and fireworks.

My family and I went outside to join our neighbors close to sundown, to begin preparing for the new year. People who drove through the neighborhood were careful not to hit the children who were playing outside on New Year's Eve. The trees outside were missing leaves from their branches and whatever remained of the leaves was blowing around on the sidewalks or streets, looking dry and brittle. All the children in my neighborhood were running around outside while wearing their big winter coats, gloves, and hats. Despite all the winter clothing the children were wearing, some of their faces were slightly pink in color.

The winter air was remarkably crisp and cold. The wind continually blew the dry brittle leaves across the pavement and the leaves made a ruffling sound as they dispersed their different ways. Every breath of winter air felt refreshing. Some of the children playing outside breathed out the winter air so hard, you could see the gas escaping from their mouths. A few of the children playing outside deliberately began breathing out hard, so that they could pretend they were smoking cigarettes. Children were placing two fingers around their lips, pretending to draw in smoke and then, they breathed out hard, while pulling their fingers away from their mouths. My parents caught me pretending to smoke and they became infuriated.

"Julde, cut that out!" they hollered after watching me pretend to pull a smoke.

All the children played outside until the sun began setting and the sky looked the streaked colors of yellow, orange, purple, and baby blue. We ran tirelessly around the neighborhood street while playing tag, until the clouds began spacing out and the navy-blue sky steadily appeared. The night sky finally arrived, so some of the children began running back home to bring their firecrackers and fireworks outside.

It was too cold to stay outside for long especially after the cool night air arrived, so I occasionally went upstairs to my family's apartment to sit in the company of my parents. My parents themselves didn't want to be outside all night because of the frosty weather. My parents decided to watch the New Year's Eve celebration on television. The news channels were showing New Year's Eve being celebrated in Times Square. Crowds of people were standing in Times Square preparing to watch the ball drop for the year 2000. There were concerts, people dancing, and news reporters bringing up New Year's resolutions for the year 2000.

My apartment had a balcony, just like many of the other apartments on base, so I stood out on our balcony and watched the other children play outside for a little while. Some of the children had already begun setting some of their fireworks off because they wanted to see how they burst into the night sky. Other children brought out snacks and desserts they could eat with their friends. I just stood out on the balcony briefly before returning inside to my apartment to join my parents, who were still watching television.

Inside my home, my family had sparkling juice to celebrate New Year's. For religious reasons there were no alcoholic beverages present in my home. Muslims don't consume alcoholic beverages, so my parents normally bought sparkling juices for our New Year's celebration. My parents opened a couple of sparkling juice bottles and we began drinking some of the juices while eating the food my parents prepared earlier in the day. As I drank the sparkling juice, I could feel it fizzling down my throat with each swallow.

I was using the sparkling juice to rinse down the food I was eating, but it didn't do a good job in that regard. The food that my parents cooked for the New Year's celebration was scrumptious. Both of my parents were marvelous cooks. Whenever one of my parents couldn't cook for whatever reason, my other parent could accomplish the task. My mom was known for cooking her African dishes and my dad was known for his American dishes. Sometimes, they both cooked food for a celebration or event. This night, my parents teamed up to make all the food for our New Year's celebration.

When midnight drew near, I ran downstairs from my apartment to go outside and watch the children throw their fireworks or play with their sparklers. My older siblings gathered with the other children in the neighborhood, collectively lighting up their fireworks. Children tried their best to jointly throw up their fireworks. We felt that the more fireworks that burst into the night sky, the more fascinating the fireworks looked altogether. Red, Blue, Green, Yellow, Purple, Pink, each firework flashed their own styles and colors.

"Wow, look at that firework! That one's so nice," I tell my older siblings.

"Oh yeah! Well, I like that firework too, Julde," my older sister replies to me.

When the New Year's celebration ended, it was finally the year 2000. Now that it was the year 2000, I was going to attend school again, but this time I'd be attending Argonner Elementary School. That year, my mom was pregnant with my younger sibling. Not only did my family and I have to adjust to our new surroundings in Germany, but we were also getting ready to introduce a new family member.

I was glad that the school year was approaching, and I'd be able to continue attending kindergarten, just as I did at Bliss Elementary School.

One of my favorite things about living in Hanau, Germany was learning a little bit about the German culture. My family went off the military base frequently to visit various cities in Germany. I cannot recall exactly which cities we visited, but I do remember loving the places we visited. My family commonly made these trips around Germany in our green van. Germany didn't have a speed limit, so my family drove at the speed they felt comfortable with, towards any city they wanted to visit.

My family would shop for groceries in the German supermarkets and exchange the goods with the Euro currency. One of the things my family learned about Germany is that they're an Earth-friendly country. After shopping for German food items, the cashier would ask us if we preferred purchasing a shopping bag or if we already had our own tote bag.

"We have to purchase a shopping bag?" Dad asks.

"Yes, remember?" Mom replies. This was nothing out of the ordinary for her; she'd lived on the German economy for years before she'd met my father. "The Germans encourage the usage of reusable shopping bags."

"Oh yeah, I forgot. Next time we decide to go shopping off base, we'll have to bring our own bags."

Afterwards, my family and I resume shopping at clothing stores.

We'd have to learn our clothing sizes in Germany because they don't size their clothing the same way Americans dog. While my family and I are shopping, we ask German store associates to help us find our clothing sizes according to the European clothing metrics.

Sometimes while my family and I were out in the city, we'd go out to eat at German bakeries. The pastries at the German bakeries were so yummy. Some of the German bakers spoke English, but if the German bakers couldn't speak English, my mom could translate the orders for me. My mom, Khadijah Barrie, could speak German fluently. She lived in Germany for years prior to her marriage with my dad, Bilal Bani Ball. She had borne and raised both of my older siblings there before my dad took my mom to the states in the 90s. In fact, I was born in Germany while my dad was stationed in Kaiserslautern, commonly known as K-town.

My favorite cake from the German bakeries was the German cheesecake. It tasted delicious ——*mmm-mhmm*. I can assume that cheesecakes prepared in Germany were baked because the top layer of the cheesecake was always a golden-brown color. The cheesecakes were also warm, as if they were recently taken out of the oven. Another food I often ate whenever my family and I went out were their French fries with curry ketchup. I got the chance to do even more sight-seeing in Germany when I began school, attending multiple school field trips.

In September 2000, I began my first day of school at Argonner Elementary School. I already knew what to expect of school since I previously attended Bliss Elementary School.

First, my family made plans to prepare me for my first day of school. Argonner Elementary School had a no-school-uniform policy. Students could wear whatever they wanted, and this meant that my parents had to purchase numerous outfits I could wear during the school year.

I got up for my first day of school, got dressed, and my parents took me to my new school. My parents decided to walk along with a bunch of other families who were heading in the same direction.

All the parents begin introducing themselves to each other. As we walk over the bridge, I can hear the cars driving under us in both directions. We finally get off the bridge and there are lots of tall trees and pine cones which fell onto the sidewalk from pine trees. I hop from side to side and I step down on the pine cones.

Crunch, crackle, snap!

On my right-hand side, there's a huge field of green grass and on my left-hand side, there are other apartment buildings. Parents are asking their children, "Are you ready for your first day of school?" Some of the children enthusiastically voice their excitement to attend their first day of school. As for the other children, well, they seem decidedly less ready than the rest of us.

The autumn air feels cool and a slight breeze makes the trees dance. Leaves slowly fall off the tree branches in their marvelous colors of gold, orange and brown. Swaying back and forth, the leaves eventually hit the green grass, which smells freshly cut. I look out to the grassy field and I notice a small, furry animal bouncing across the field. Then a few more of the same animals trail behind the other until they hop into a hole. They're extremely cute, but too fast for me to recognize which animals they were.

"Did you guys see the bunnies?" one of the parents asks the children.

"Yes, I saw them, I saw the bunnies!" I say with excitement.

"Yes," she replies back, "and the bunnies live inside those holes, dug into the ground.".

Now I understood why there were holes dug into the ground; the rabbits were going into their homes. Five minutes later, I see Argonner Elementary School from a distance and I know that I'm about to begin kindergarten again.

"Julde, that's your school," Dad says.

"I remember!" I respond.

I remembered exactly how Argonner Elementary School looked like from the time of school registration. This time I was seeing my school from a different angle because last time my family came here, we drove directly through the front of the school.

After making it to Argonner Elementary School, everyone waited outside to the side of our school building to wait for our teachers to come outside and get us for our first day of kindergarten. After several minutes, teachers finally come outside and get the students who belonged in their classes. Students quickly said goodbye to their parents, grandparents, aunts, or uncles. After saying our goodbyes, we were on our way into our new kindergarten classrooms. The teachers gave all the students their assigned seats and then assigned the students a cubby outside of our classroom door. Before beginning our lesson, we were told to put all of our personal belongings into our cubbies.

In my kindergarten class, we were not only taught math, reading, and spelling, we also had enough time to engage in creative activities. Most of the time, I played dress-up with my two best friends. We frequently used costumes and toys to explore our imaginations. During playtime, we tried to be whoever we wanted to be. Whenever we wanted to be doctors, firefighters, cashiers, or police officers, we'd put on our costumes and role play scenarios in our pretend careers.

One of the students would be cooking a meal in our play kitchen set when suddenly, their meal was set on fire.

"Oh, my goodness, my food is burning, let me call 911!" The student dials 911 on their toy phone.

"911, what is your emergency?"

"My house is burning, hurry up and get here quick!"

The children wearing the firefighter costumes rush over to the play kitchen set and use toys to spray out the growing fire. Students wearing the police officer uniforms all take a piece of paper and a crayon to report the fire incident. Children running from the kitchen play set rush to the "doctor" and say, "My arm caught on fire while I was cooking, please help me!"

The doctor dutifully starts to medically treat the child. Before long, our classroom teacher begins singing the cleanup song and then, collectively, my classmates and I join in:

> *Clean up Clean up*
> *Everybody everywhere*
> *Clean up Clean up*
> *Everybody do your share*

All the students gather around while singing the cleanup song, to clean our play area. We return to our desks and wait for the next activity our kindergarten teachers have planned for the day. My classmates and I commonly spent time together doing other activities, such as painting, making pottery, or playing with clay.

In the middle of our school day, everyone in our kindergarten class is instructed to line up at our classroom door, so that we can head to the cafeteria and eat lunch. My parents remained consistent in packing my school lunch; however, other days, my parents let me eat the school lunch in the cafeteria, I just had to pay the cafeteria staff to eat school lunch.

After finishing my lunch, I'd walk my lunch bag over to my cubby, and then go outside to play in our school yard. Argonner Elementary School's yard was spread-out. I ran out to the playground area everyday after lunchtime, just so that I could get to the playground faster. As a child, the best method for me to get anywhere was by running. I rarely walked unless I had to accompany an adult.

While running to the playground, the autumn breeze hits my face and, once again, the aroma of nearby pine trees and freshly cut grass whiffs past my nose. I finally make it to the playground and run around tirelessly playing different games with my classmates. We slide down the slides, swing on the swings, climb the monkey bars, and we play hand games such as ring-around-the-rosie.

Teachers at Argonner Elementary School often wore whistles around their necks to get the students' attention. Sometimes the whistles were blown differently if children were playing too rough. If the whistles were blown with two short quick blows, it meant that the two students were probably tackling each other, and they should stop playing rough.

"Children, we don't play like that on the playground! If you don't stop, I'll place you in time-out," one of the teachers says.

Teachers begin blowing their whistles, signaling all the children to come back to class. Over and over, they blow their whistles, shouting, "Children let's go, you have to return to your class!"

Gradually, we students gather near our school building, waiting in designated areas for our teachers to escort us back to class. Some of the teachers hold up huge signs with their classroom name or number on it to let us know which area to stand in. The sign is supported by a yard stick taped to the back of the poster. After the teacher calls attendance, we return to our classrooms.

There were many activities I enjoyed doing in my kindergarten class. Some of the activities included making food. One day, my classmates and I were told that we were going to make our own individual pizzas. First, the teachers instructed us to clean off our classroom desks. When we were done cleaning our desks, the teachers handed each of us a ball of dough. Both of my kindergarten teachers would sprinkle flour on parchment paper so that the students could start forming the pizza crust to their individual pizzas.

My classmates and I began competing on who could make the widest pizza crust. We thought that the wider our pizza crust was, the larger our pizza would look in comparison to our classmates'. Afterwards, both teachers helped the students place the marinara sauce and cheese on our crusts. After everyone was done making their pizza, we all placed our pizzas on baking pans. These activities were not only fun; they also brought me closer to my classmates.

Other days, my kindergarten teachers walked my classmates and me over to the art room, so that we could paint on paper held up by an easel. The art teacher taught our class that mixing red and blue makes purple, mixing red and yellow makes orange, mixing blue and yellow makes green and, you know, the average basics of children learning art in a classroom.

While wearing a red plastic smock over my outfit, I grab a tray full of paint and a paintbrush and I stand in front of my blank easel, thinking of what I'm going to paint. I dip my fingers straight into the paint and begin my artwork. The kindergarten teachers walk around the classroom complimenting everyone's artwork, even though it looked like a pure blob of nonsense.

"Wow, your artwork looks so good Julde, keep up the great work!"

"Thank you! That's my tree, there's my grass, the sun is in that corner, and those people are my family," I respond to my teacher.

When I'm done painting, my artwork looks like a massive splotch of "*what is going on here?*", but my teachers are right by my side to applaud my artwork.

"Julde, your artwork is brilliant! You did a great job," she says, and after she finishes praising my artwork, she goes around complimenting my classmates' artwork. It makes me feel good to hear that my teachers value my artwork.

The teachers set aside our artwork, to let it dry. My classmates and I walk over to the sinks individually to rinse off our hands and arms. By the end of the day, our paintings are dry, the teachers have placed our names on our artwork and are attaching our paintings to the classroom's ceiling. Our classroom served as a gallery for our artwork and whenever the students had a chance, we'd point out which artwork we painted.

In that same classroom we made pottery. One time, I failed at making a teacup. The teachers told us to make a dish for our parents. That day, for whatever reason, I decided to make my parents a teacup instead. My classmates and I got a dollop of pottery clay to begin forming items we wanted to make our parents. At first, I formed the cup for my teacup, then I made the handle for my teacup, which was very thin. When everyone was done making their items, we painted our pottery work, adding as much detail as we could, to impress our parents. When I finished painting my teacup, I gave it to my teacher to bake. The next day, I brought my teacup home from school and gave it to my parents as a gift. Shortly after handing it to my parents, the handle to my teacup broke and I was sad that it didn't exhibit the gift that I imagined giving to my parents.

Spring was fast approaching in Germany, so I happily returned to playing outside with my neighborhood friends. As the months pass by, many of my neighbors slowly began relocating to other duty stations. It wasn't common for people living in my neighborhood to move during the Winter season, but when it was required, those families left. Even though I remained in the same neighborhood, I had to make new friends. Constantly making new friends is part of social survival for an Army child. It's disheartening to build a strong bond with children in your neighborhood only to watch them move away because their parents were reassigned to a new duty station. So, there I was in the playground feeling lonely and wondering how I'd make friends with the new children who moved on base. I swung on the swings, slid down the slides, and played on the monkey bars, all by myself.

One particular day, a few other children join me at the playground and begin playing with me without having a clue what my name is.

"Hello, my name is Ashley. What's your name?"

"My name is Julde."

"Your name is *what*? Can you *repeat* that?"

"My name is Julde."

"Julde? *Hmm ——* I've never heard that name before."

We start playing around the playground as if we've known each other for centuries. Then Ashley asks me, "What type of games do you usually play?"

"I like to play games on my computer like checkers, solitaire, and Mine Sweep. Sometimes I go onto websites like barbie.com, myscene.com, and sometimes I draw pictures on Kids Pix. When I'm not on the computer, I play with my dolls."

"Yes! I play with dolls too! Maybe we can bring our dolls outside and play with them."

"Okay, no problem. I'd have to let my parents know that I'm bringing my dolls outside though," I tell Ashley.

We continue playing outside in the playground until more children join us. That's pretty much the genesis of most of our relationships. We would just begin playing with each other randomly before formally introducing ourselves.

Another day, I notice a group of kids sitting outside, role playing with their dolls. I want to join the children, but didn't bring a doll outside to join them, so I decide to run back upstairs to my apartment and grab my own doll to play with. After returning outside, I start playing with the other children, but when I try to engage them, I quickly realize that they're ignoring me. I didn't understand why they were ignoring me, so I ask them point blank, "Why are you ignoring me?"

All the children stop and look at me before one of the biracial children blurts out, "We don't want to play with you because you're black."

I turn to look at the other children, who are all white, for validation, but they all give me a serious look. Not one of them said that they wanted to play with me. Instantly, I feel a rush of sadness overtake me before deciding to run upstairs to my apartment, crying uncontrollably.

At five years old, I just can't believe that I'm being excluded from playing with the other children because I was black. My whole face is full of tears and I can't see where I was going while running up the staircase leading up to my apartment. The biracial boy who blurted out he didn't want to play with me happened to be mixed and of African-American descent. The boy lived in the apartment below me and my parents knew his parents well. For the purpose of this book, I'll call the boy Derrick, even though that's not his actual name.

When I get home, my whole family sees I'm in distress and crying miserably. They ask, "Julde, what happened?" And while I fight to say it——with snot and tears all over my face, I manage to whimper, "Derrick told me that he didn't want to play with me because I am black. The other children who were sitting next to him were all white and they didn't say anything. The just gave me a serious look." Everyone in my family knew his family, but my family members still try to confirm the boy I was talking about. My dad asks, "You mean the African-American and Asian boy living downstairs?"

"Yes," I answer, while crying my heart out.

Then one of my siblings reconfirms, "Isn't his dad an African-American?"

It never really occurred to me that the boy was in fact mixed with African-American descent. So, guess what I do? I run downstairs in gloom, bawling and knock on the boy's door. His dad, a tall African-American man, opens the door confused because he doesn't understand why I'm crying. My parents try their best to get a hold of me before I can tell his dad what happened, but I'm too quick. Now that his front door is open, I tell his dad flat out, "Derrick said he didn't want to play with me because I'm black." I watch him get instantly enraged at what he's heard. Immediately, he calls Derrick home for the rest of the night.

At the tender age of five-years-old, I'm forced to realize that sometimes other children may not play outside with me because I'm black. It never really occurred to me that my skin color can determine my acceptance into a social setting until that very day.

Chapter Four: Mi Casa es tu Casa

Sometimes I'd wake up at four in the morning, while finding my entire family in the living room, wide awake, and praying Fajr[23] . I only woke up early in the morning if I saw the living room's light glowing under my bedroom door. After watching blush shadows walking past my bedroom door, I'd realize that my family members were awake, so I'd open my bedroom door to find my whole family finishing their Fajr prayer.

My family would ask me, "Julde, why are you up so early? Go back to sleep."

"I saw the living room light on, so I decided to walk out and see why the light was on. Why is everyone up at this time?"

"We're up praying Fajr, Julde."

"How come no one woke me up to pray Fajr?" I ask my family. I get upset when my family doesn't include me in praying Fajr because I loved everything about worshipping with my family. For as long as I could remember, I always prayed near my family.

While rubbing my eyes from tiredness, I proceed to ask my family again, "Why didn't you wake me up to pray Fajr? I always wanted to pray Fajr with everyone, but no one ever wakes me up."

"It's too early in the morning for you to be up, Julde. That's the reason why we don't wake you up for Fajr."

After questioning my family, I remain awake to watch both of my parents get ready for work. My dad irons his brown T-shirt continuously, flipping his shirt over to iron out any creases which are present. It was oddly amazing for me to watch my dad iron his T-shirt because he ironed his clothing to perfection. After my dad was done ironing his brown T-shirt, he'd hang it up and begin polishing his black military boots.

---

23 Fajr: the first daily prayer Muslims pray early in the morning before the crack of dawn.

There was so much attention to detail in the way my dad polished his black boots. Nearly every morning, I'd watch my dad place the black KIWI shoe polish on his boots, and then he'd gently brush the black shoe polish on. Occasionally, my dad would hit a lighter to the tip of his boots so that the shoe polish could melt onto that part of the boot. My dad continued the same brushing motion and melting, until his boots were glossy in appearance. By the time he was done shining his boots, it was as if you could see your own reflection in the tip of them. After preparing his uniform, my dad would leave the house and go to work. My mom made sure that my siblings and I got ready for school. Afterwards my mom got herself ready and went to work at the PX, or post exchange, on a nearby military base.

My mom mainly worked as a cashier at the PX, but she sometimes bagged groceries at the commissary for extra cash. It was easy for my mom, Khadijah Barrie, to work part-time without worrying about losing her employment. Whenever my dad was deployed to a new military base my mom easily transferred her employment status to that new base. Many military spouses have a hard time maintaining stable employment because of their spouses' military career. My mom knew that getting a job on base would accommodate her employment with my dad's career. The benefits of my mom working at the Post Exchange and Commissary became the start of my mom's stable employment.

By the year 2000, my parents had four children. My youngest sibling was born July 2000, but despite having four kids, my parents continued to accomplish so much.

My mom brought my grandmother, Halimatu Bah, from Africa to help watch both me and my younger sister. My mom wanted to build a house for her family in Guinea, West Africa, so my grandmother came to Germany to help my mom watch us while the house was being built. The benefits of my grandmother coming wasn't only watching my siblings and me, but it was also allowing my grandmother to visit the nearby clinic for medical checkups, which helped her get prescription medications. There are pharmacies in Guinea, but their pharmacies aren't always reliable like American pharmacies. Some medications provided to patients in Guinea are made from fake or inactive powders, in the form of a pill. In Guinea, it's important to find a trusted pharmacist who provides valid medications to their patients.

My mother worked very hard to send her older brothers money so that they could begin building the house and improving their living situation in Guinea. Before my mom's family fled from Sierra Leone's civil war, her family owned several parcels of land inside Sierra Leone. After seeking refuge in Guinea, they left those parcels of lands behind, no longer having a place of their own while living in Guinea. My family was adjusting to living in Guinea, but they were renting homes. Whenever my mom's family couldn't afford basic living necessities, such as rent, my mom sent them money. My mom was often responsible for helping her family after seeking refuge in Guinea. My mom is the only child my grandparents have living in a developed country, so she took the initiative to buy her family's first piece of land in Guinea and help them build a house on that land. My grandmother was still horrified at the thought of returning to Sierra Leone after the war because memories of the war haunted her.

Meanwhile, my dad was working hard to continue helping his family in Virginia with whatever they needed. The main people that my dad focused on helping within his side of the family was his mother, Daisey Ball, and his grandmother, Mary Tolson Smith. My dad's side of the family was better off than my mom's side of the family; however, a generation of my dad's family were survivors of the Jim Crow segregation era in the United States. My dad's generation of siblings and cousins had better opportunities to succeed than the previous generations. Shortly after completing high school, there were no potentials for African-Americans to fully advance in their college education. My grandmother and grandfather attended community college, but the social pressures revolving African-Americans made it difficult for them to complete their college degrees.

Being that the outcome for African-Americans was much more challenging than their white counterparts, it was easier for African-Americans to remain on full-time employment rather than being fully committed to attending college. My dad knew that his grandmother, Mary, and mother, Daisey, did everything they could to take care of him, so he tried his best to do what he could for them. My dad made sure to continue his routine of getting up early in the morning for work, in preparation to defend the United States.

My dad normally began getting ready for work after my family finished praying Fajr, the first prayer of the day. Some mornings my dad got ready to perform physical training (PT) with his military colleagues. PT is an exercise routine which military service members do in the mornings. My dad would put on black shorts, sneakers, and a grey shirt for his PT training. Then out the door he would go, to meet up with his colleagues for their morning exercise routine.

My mom kept on working towards building the house in Guinea, West Africa for her family. My dad continued working for the United States Army to provide for our family. I was never clear what exactly my dad did in the United States Army because that information was always private. I understood to never question my dad's job or what he did. All I knew was my dad stepped out early every day for work, he wore a military uniform and he was in the Army.

There were multiple playgrounds on New Argonner. Sometimes whenever I didn't feel like going to the very big playground across the street from my apartment building, I went to the playground near the military clinic. That playground was slightly smaller, but I liked that playground because the equipment was made from wood.

While playing at the smaller playground near the military clinic, I met a few other girls also playing at the playground. We began randomly playing with each other simply because we saw each other at the playground. We swung on the swings, went down the slides, rode on the seesaws and were enjoying each other's company.

"Hello, how are you? My name is Adriana, what's your name?"

"Hello, I'm good. My name is Julde."

"What did you say your name was again?"

"My name is Julde," and then I break my name down into syllables, so that Adriana can learn how to pronounce my name.

"Say Jul..."

"Jul..."

"Okay, now say, "day."

"Day. Oh, your name is pronounced Jul-DAY? That's a very interesting name! I've never heard that name before."

Me and Adriana meet up with a few other girls playing in the playground and we decide to swing on the swing set. "Let's see who can swing the highest!" one of the girls says with excitement.

All the girls rush to sit on a swing and begin kicking their legs forcefully as they swing back and forth. The breeze hits my face fiercely with each swing. Some of us look towards each other while swinging on the swing set, to see how much higher we are than the other.

One of the girls asks everyone, "Do you guys know how to jump off the swings while you're still swinging?"

Not everyone knew how to jump off while they were still swinging. For the girls who do know how to jump off the swing set, they do. As for the others, they slowly stop their swings while using their feet as a brake and get off. Some of the other girls jump off the swing set and land into the sandbox surrounding the swing set. After jumping off the swing set, the force of the landing causes our feet to dig into the part of the sandbox we landed in. The girls and I stay in the spots we landed in to estimate who jumped the farthest distance away from the swing set.

After getting tired of swinging on the swing set, everyone walks together towards Adriana's house. Adriana didn't live in one of the apartment buildings located on New Argonner; instead, she lived in a duplex housing unit. At Adriana's house, there's a sign near her front door and she tells me, "Julde, read the sign."

I tell Adriana, "I barely know how to read."

"It's okay Julde, just try your best and read the sign, you can do it."

At five years old, I still struggled with phonics and letter pronunciations, but I still attempt to read the sign. With great effort, I slowly sound out, "My *Ca..sa es tu ca..sa?*" At this point, I'm ashamed of myself because I don't understand what I'm reading. Thoughts begin racing in my mind that these girls will probably make fun of me for not being able to read. I stopped reading the sign at Adriana's front door.

"Sorry Adriana, I don't know how to read, I told you I just started learning how to read." Adriana then giggles and tells me, "You almost got it, Julde! The sign says *mi casa es tu casa.*"

I ask her, "What does *mi casa es tu casa* mean?"

Adriana tells me to guess first, but I have a difficult time trying to figure out what it meant. After realizing that I couldn't guess what the sign read, Adriana tells me that it says, "My home is your home." That's how you say "my home is your home" in Spanish. "My family put this sign near our front door to let our visitors know that our home is their home. Julde, this is your home. We can go inside now."

We enter Adriana's house to play. One hour later, Adriana's dad comes back home from work and he's wearing the same uniform my dad always wears. I look outside their window and realize that the sun is setting, so I tell Adriana's family I must return home before dusk. I knew the rules; I knew that if I didn't return home before sundown, I'd get in trouble. Adriana's family wanted me to stay over their house for dinner; but, I didn't even have my parents' permission to be over her house in the first place. I leave Adrianna's house and head back toward my apartment building.

The longer my family and I stayed on New Argonner Kaserne, the more comfortable I felt going out and spending time with other children. The other children and I sometimes played in our apartment building's front yard, trying to find a "lucky" four-leafed clover. There were numerous three-leafed clovers, or shamrocks, but we wanted our "lucky" four-leafed clover. When we got tired of looking for clovers, we'd walk over to the rose bush adjacent to our apartment building and try to find a rose to pick. The rose bush grew yellow roses, but they were always hard to pick because of the thorns on their stems.

Two apartment buildings to the right of my apartment building lived a Korean and African-American girl who became my friend, named Monica. Monica lived in the last apartment building down my street, just before reaching the dead-end, and sometimes we played jump rope, hula hoops, or hopscotch together. I always stayed over her house and her mom would make various Korean dishes that I ate with them. Monica loved to eat the Korean noodles that her mom made. We would sit in her house, wait for her mom to finish preparing the noodles and then we'd eat together at her dining room table. Monica's dad, an African-American, also knew how to make some of the Korean dishes, so sometimes he'd prepare us meals. When Monica and I would finish eating, we'd go into her bedroom and play with her toys. We role played stories for our toys, as if they lived realistic lives. When we got tired of playing with toys, we'd go outside and play in front of her building.

Further down on the right-hand side of Monica's building was a fence separating our neighborhood to what looked like a forest. Her building was near the forest where our parents did their PT exercises every morning. Monica and I sometimes went near the fence which gated the forest to try and find tiny frogs. The tiny frogs, which were smaller than a dime, lived inside the mud and if you paid close attention, you could see them making small leaps. Only God knows why, but we tried catching these frogs with our bare hands. After successfully catching one of the tiny frogs, we'd let it go because our parents wouldn't allow us to bring those frogs back into their homes. After catching frogs, we'd go to a nearby water hose and wash our hands off.

I basically dwelled outside in New Argonner because I didn't like staying home if the weather was nice outside. I was always ready to begin an adventure with the children outside. I only stayed home if I was on punishment, but most of my days were spent hanging out with the other children living on base.

One day, one of the children randomly decides to ask, "Hey, would you guys like to have a potluck in the gazebo down the street?"

"Yes, that sounds like a fantastic idea!"

"Okay, great! Let's ask our parents to help us with getting the snacks and drinks for the potluck."

On the far left of my apartment building was a gazebo where military families commonly held birthday parties, barbecue parties, and other social gatherings. It was a great setting to have a social gathering, provided it had a roof and you can go under the shade of the gazebo, whenever you got tired of being out in the sun. I go home that day and tell my parents I need them to purchase a few items for the neighborhood potluck.

"Mom, Dad! Can you please purchase some items that I can bring for a potluck?"

My dad looks at me with a strange look on his face and asks, "What potluck?"

"Me and a few other kids on base decided that we wanted to have a potluck at the gazebo."

"Okay, which *parents* are supervising this potluck? And exactly, which *parents* are involved in organizing this potluck, if I may ask."

"Dad, the children on base decided that we wanted to organize a potluck at the gazebo down the street. There are no parents organizing this potluck," I say nonchalantly.

"Oh really? How can a bunch of kids with no money and without any of the parents' knowledge organize a potluck?"

"I'll give you more information about it by tomorrow, Dad."

The next day, I speak with some of the other children outside and explain that we would have to bring our parents together to organize the potluck. We find ways to get our parents to speak to each other and it comes easy to us, being that we were neighbors. After a few conversations, the parents voice their willingness to support the shenanigans of five and six-year-olds coming up with their own potluck party. The children and I set a date for the potluck and the parents purchase food items. Some of our parents walk us over to the gazebo to help us bring the food and set up for our potluck. The gazebo was on the far left of my street in the middle of a grassy field. Some of the children go to play in the field, periodically running back to the gazebo to grab a handful of snacks.

With my parents having enough money to take care of my siblings and me, all I really worried about was being a child. Which is why the other children and I spent days pretending to go on adventures and other silly things.

Whenever I went to the huge playground, the other children and I would go into the small wooden cabins and pretend we were sailing a ship. We really dug into the depths of our imagination, play-acting different situations.

" *Whoa guys*, we just hit a huge wave! Mayday, mayday, this is the captain of the ship, and we're calling for your help. We are experiencing heavy waves on the sea and we need you to save our ship!"

Children rush and pretend that they're trying to save our sinking ship. Out of nowhere, one of the children starts pretending to be a shark.

"I'm a shark and I'm going to eat all of you on this ship, run!"

Then the shark begins chasing all the other children, so that they could be "eaten." The other children and I run around laughing, trying to break free from being eaten by a shark. Next thing I know, the child who is pretending to be a shark taps me on my back and I'm eaten.

"Oh no, I am *drowning*!" I call out.

The other children and I find ways to occupy ourselves until dusk before parting ways to go home for the night.

Occasionally, my parents had money to take us on road trips to other European countries. We rarely took flights if we were visiting neighboring European countries.

We'd drive for hours passing the various scenes of the European countryside. There were no speed limits in Germany, so my parents drove as fast as they wanted so they could get to places quicker. I would look out the car window and see farms fenced with cows and sheep. Occasionally, we'd drive past little towns. Whenever my family got tired, we'd stop our van and take restroom breaks at the public toilets near the highway.

On one of these road trips, we drove to Belgium to visit one of my mom's family members.

The tribe that my mom, Khadijah Barrie, belongs to is the Fulani ethnic group. My mom sometimes doesn't get the chance to see her family for years. After reuniting, they'd get comfortable and begin speaking either Creole[24] or Fulani[25] together.

My dad took advantage of the opportunity to learn some of the dialects my mom speaks through listening to her conversations. Sometimes my dad surprised my mom's family members by saying something in their language. Abruptly, everyone would burst out laughing because they weren't expecting my dad to know how to speak Fulani.

When my family and I were finished with our mini vacation, we returned to Germany.

Now that my grandmother, Halimatu Bah, was temporarily staying with our family in Germany, I began learning a few words in my mom's native language, Fulani. I call my grandmother *nene biro* or *nembiro*, which literally means grandmother in Fulani. I only say *nembiro* when I'm quickly joining the words together; it's like using contractions, but for Fulani.

Sometimes, whenever I didn't go out to play, I'd sit alongside my *nembiro* in the living room and watch the WWE wrestling shows with her. She'd become fascinated at the way the wrestlers picked each other up and slammed each other down in the boxing ring. After watching the WWE match, my grandmother would say, *"Ehhh!"* in astonishment to the wrestling match she'd finished watching. For her, watching the WWE matches were addicting. She rarely liked when we changed the channels from the wrestling programs.

During the day, my *nene biro* would stay in the house with my younger sister and me while my mom was at work.

Nembiro has fair skin, a straight nose, loose curly gray hair (mainly covered with a hijab), medium-sized eyes, and even though she is an elder, her skin is unblemished.

---

24 Creole: two or more languages mixed together. In my mom's case English, French and local languages from Sierra Leone are mixed together, to create a unique Sierra Leonean English dialect.

25 Fulani: an African ethnic group which are nomads due to cattle herding in the Northern east and west regions of Africa. They normally travelled to countries they'd find food sources for their cattle so they can be found in many countries.

If my *nembiro* had money, she'd go downstairs and purchase candy from the candyman who drove down our street approximately around the afternoon time. The candyman had a trunk full of different candies to choose from and you'd pick the candy you want so that he could put it in a bag. *Nene biro* typically liked purchasing gummy candy because sometimes, she'd also eat the candy with us. My younger sister and I would sometimes fight over the candy and my *nembiro* would say, "*Achu!* Stop!"

We'd stop what we were doing and share the candy between ourselves evenly.

Nene biro grew home sick while she was living in Germany with us. She always spoke about Guinea's warm tropical weather and some of the foods she was used to eating back home. *Nembiro* loved living with us, but she couldn't help continually bringing up what life was like in Guinea. She felt like life in Germany was too fast-paced for her and there weren't other elders living on our base who spoke Fulani nor were there many African elders in general. The few Africans that lived on base were always working, so she looked forward to my younger sister and me being at home after school.

Chapter Five: When a Home Comes Crashing Down (September 11, 2001)

During September 2001, I started my first grade school year at Argonner Elementary School. I got ready for my first day of school and left my apartment building to begin walking towards Old Argonner. Many of the other children who attended Argonner Elementary School were also leaving their apartment buildings, to head to our school. After getting off the bridge, we walked towards our school building. Nothing had changed about Old Argonner, everything was still the same. You could still see the bunnies hopping from afar, pine cones were lying down on the sidewalks, and the school building was the same. The only difference was, I was now six-years old and beginning the first-grade.

I can still remember my first grade teacher, but for privacy reasons I will not mention her name in my memoir. She was a blonde, Caucasian woman, and the only Elementary School teacher whose name I can remember from the top of my head. I believe that my long-lasting memory of my first-grade teacher has much to do with me beginning her class a couple of weeks prior to 9/11.

In first grade, I was learning advanced reading and writing skills, such as nouns, pronouns, adjectives, verbs and adverbs. For math, I was learning how to count money and my multiplication.

A couple of weeks into the school year, there was a lot of commotion in my school hallways. It was almost nearing our school dismissal time when teachers were trying to relate urgent news to all the students, but I was confused about the stir taking place in my school hallways.

I watch in a hush as teachers run by, crying as they rush to other classrooms to speak with their peers. Some of the school staff look disoriented. Students in my classroom have no clue as to what is going on. We stop learning course material for the remainder of that day; instead, we stand by as the school staff weeps and shows signs of hopelessness.

"Children, we need you all to behave yourselves and sit down, criss cross applesauce. Don't get up! Something urgent just happened."

Everyone in my classroom remains seated in criss cross applesauce position, looking puzzled.

Eventually, the teachers relay news that there was a plane crash in New York, where thousands of people died. Two airplanes dived into the World Trade Centers located in the lower end of Manhattan. For a while, my classmates and I, who were all between the ages of six and seven years old, were trying to figure out what happened in New York. The question that instantly ran through my mind is, "How do two airplanes accidently dive into buildings?" As a naïve and gullible child, I couldn't understand airplanes accidentally being flown into buildings. I wasn't expecting to later find out that those plane crashes were intentional.

The students weren't receiving the entire information about the airplane crash from the teachers because they were mainly talking amongst each other. School staff were grieving the attack because some of their loved ones were also harmed during the process of the attack.

Later that day, I enter my apartment, seeing my parents and grandmother sitting in the living room, watching the 9/11 attacks on the news channel. I'm instantly horrified at the images I'm seeing on the television. It suddenly begins to make sense to me. I understand why my first-grade teacher and other school staff were grieving for the remainder of the school day. The news channels show short clips of people running away from a huge cloud of smoke in the lower end of Tribeca, New York. I watch countless people running for their lives, all while sitting in my living room.

The president at the time, George W. Bush, released a statement on the news network that the attacks against the World Trade Center and the Pentagon were acts of terrorism and it was an attack against our freedom. The news reporters and investigators were still searching for answers to this disturbing attack, which directly targeted the World Trade Center.

Many people who were trying to flee the attack unfortunately got caught in the smoldering debris and lost their lives. Relatives of the casualties were left grieving the loss of those who were caught in the attack. Other family members depended on first responders to find their loved ones. Every news channel was playing clips of people trying to escape the smoke on an endless loop. While watching them, I wanted to be able to talk to them through the television set and let them know that they were almost out of the smog.

That they shouldn't give up on running.

I knew that it was helpless talking to the television set because they couldn't hear me. Surviving victims of the 9/11 attacks spoke on the news channels, explaining what it took for them to survive. Some people talked to the American people, mourning the loss of their family members, co-workers, and friends. Firefighters were still searching for lost victims under the rubble and debris.

It was horrifying.

Shortly after, everyone learned about the man behind the 9/11 attack, Osama Bin Laden, the leader and founder of Al-Qaeda. Osama Bin Laden was motivated to attack the Americans because he had a distaste for America's alliance with Saudi Arabia, Egypt, Kuwait, and Jordan. Osama Bin Laden especially detested America's alliance with Israel.

Osama Bin Laden was a son of Saudi Arabian elites who are millionaires, but he felt that his government was being hypocritical for maintaining an alliance with the United States.

Al-Qaeda was originally developed by Osama Bin Laden in 1988 after the Soviet Union invaded Afghanistan. Bin Laden didn't want to completely cut ties with Saudi Arabia because that was his main source of income, but he wanted to join forces with the Afghanistan fighters to defeat the Soviet Union within their country. After successfully dismantling the Soviet powers in Afghanistan, Bin Laden began to visualize further attacks in westernized nations. Bin Laden thought that he'd successfully dismantle every other western power that he felt had undue influence in the Middle East, just as he'd defeated the Soviet Army. The next step was to eliminate the other superpower, the United States.

In his eyes, the Saudi Arabian leadership were acting as puppets to the westernized world. He thought that by forming a rebel organization within their own country, Saudi Arabia, they'd successfully dismantle this Saudi-

American relationship. Al-Qaeda believed that their plans were motivated by Jihad[26] and that through this, they'd also stop the American-Muslim alliances with Egypt, Kuwait, and Jordan. Osama Bin Laden favored his country's alliance with other Muslim majority countries in his region and he faulted the westernized countries for the humiliation of Muslim majority nations. [27] [28]

That night, after going to bed, I couldn't sleep. Images of a mass of people trying to escape debris in Tribeca haunted me.

The next day, I went to school feeling overwhelmed. I was only six years old and couldn't understand why anyone would intentionally harm so many people. For me personally, I thought good of people and gave them the benefit of the doubt. I was still naive and young, without being aware that there were malicious people in the world, especially willing to attack thousands of innocent civilians.

Although the group of men who committed the crime were Muslim or at least claimed to be Muslim, it didn't mean that every Muslim should be held accountable for this appalling act. There are Muslim countries in alliance with the United States, and this is a fact. Osama Bin Laden had hatred for Muslim countries which maintain their alliance with the United States, deeming them "puppets." The September 11th attack occurred due to hatred developing inside the mind of a millionaire Saudi Arabian son of elites.

I just couldn't understand how one man's crime could cause an entire religion to be held accountable.

---

26 Jihad: an Arabic word which means struggle or effort. Muslims sometimes use this word to reference their personal spiritual struggle toward Islam. It is often erroneously translated as "holy war."

27 McAuley, Denis. "The Ideology of Osama Bin Laden: Nation, Tribe and World Economy." Journal of Political Ideologies, vol. 10, no. 3, Oct. 2005, pp. 269–287. EBSCOhost, doi:10.1080/13569310500244305.

28 Post, Jerrold M. "Killing in the Name of God: Osama Bin Laden and Al Qaeda." 2002. PDF file.

Every morning, I watched my dad, a Muslim, get ready to protect our country. I knew that every Muslim couldn't be held accountable for this severe act.

Every Muslim military member I knew growing up were dedicated to fighting for the United States of America, putting their lives on the line every day. Yes, some of the Muslim military members were immigrants, and they also dedicated their efforts to protecting the United States, a country they now call their home. Other Muslim military members were Americans by blood, from families that had been in America since the country's founding, but later converted to Islam like my dad did. Immigrant or American national, they're Muslim and they're always willing to protect the United States' country borders.

My dad was born and raised as a practicing Southern Baptist Christian his entire youth; however, my dad later converted to Islam one year after joining the United States Army. My mom was raised as a Muslim her entire life. Although my parents, with different religious and cultural backgrounds, are both currently Muslim, they're the same Muslim parents who raised me, and they never taught me violence.

Whatever I watched on the news is not a representation of my Islamic faith. To deliberately hijack four airplanes and crash the first two into the twin towers, while sending the third to hit the Pentagon, and a fourth crashing into a field in Pennsylvania? No, that's not what Islam represents. Islam is a religious belief system and not a criminal organization. I was upset because our religion was being ambushed by the new term "Islamic Terrorism" because of the hateful actions of one group of people. This wasn't about Islam, this was about a group with political motives to mass murder an entire community. This was a terrorist organization called Al-Qaeda trying to develop their renewed Islamic caliphate and eliminate Jewish-Christian relationships established with Muslim majority countries.

My dad and many other Muslim military members were fighting for the United States' Army. Muslim firefighters were running into the noxious plume that engulfed Ground Zero, rescuing victims of the attack. Muslim medics worked tirelessly to revive numerous patients coming from the attack. Muslim police officers gave their all to protect New York City residents and escort them to safer areas. Muslim employees worked in the World Trade Center and they, too, lost their lives that day. Muslims who were among the victims of 9/11 attacks were rarely acknowledged, as if their lives weren't just as important, because this attack was supposedly committed by the entire Muslim population. The news very much neglected the true stories of American Muslims who similarly suffered from the 9/11 attacks. It was as if our sentiments, the American Muslims, didn't matter, like we also didn't share the experience of what the 9/11 attacks did to the American population.

Muslims grieved the loss of their loved ones following September 11th. Muslims grieved the loss of other individuals following that day. Muslims grieved and we too were hurt by the 9/11 attacks, but many people disbelieved our grief.

As Americans, the attack on the World Trade Center presented us with many challenges, but specifically, American Muslims faced a challenge that was uniquely our own at that time. American Muslims were still grieving the 9/11 attacks when our patriotism began being called into question.

The September 11 attacks impacted my family. Being that my mother and older sister wore the hijab, it brought attention to our household while living on base. Our family was now recognizably Muslim. It's obvious that since my dad is in the military, he was going to be deployed following the 9/11 attacks. This meant that my future family outings would no longer include my dad. My dad wasn't going to be home much because he'd have to fight a war.

Prior to September 11th, people in my neighborhood rarely knew what a Muslim was. Occasionally, people would ask my mom or older sister, Mariam, why they wore a headscarf over their hair. Mom and Mariam would explain that they were wearing a hijab and that it's worn for religious purposes. Now everyone in my neighborhood knew exactly what a Muslim looked like.

Following September 11th, the hijab became inexplicably linked to the World Trade Center attack because of the attackers being of the Muslim faith, leading to hate crimes against Muslim women. American Muslim women were suddenly taking off their hijabs, fearing to go out of their homes while wearing it, or becoming victims to this newly developed stereotype. Men belonging to the Sikh religion, who wrapped their heads in turbans, were commonly being mistaken for Muslim men and also became victims of hate crimes.

Considering how long it used to take for me to explain what a Muslim was before, I realize how powerful the hijab must have been at the time, and still is now. At the time, I no longer had to explain what a Muslim was; instead, I had to explain what Muslims were not, and we are not terrorists. Wearing the hijab was costing Muslim women their lives and it wasn't even being considered a hate crime.

I was only six years old, but my older sister, who was sixteen years old at the time, routinely wore the hijab. I can remember my sister coming back from high school feeling gloomy. Some of the students attending her high school were bothering her because she was Muslim. A student happened to have asked Mariam, "Aren't you a Muslim, like the people who crashed planes into the World Trade Center?" and that was enough for Mariam to come home sad. We were United States military dependents just like the other students living on base, for goodness sake; how could we be part of that attack? We were also sitting beside our classmates in the afternoon when teachers were relating this urgent news to us, how are we now affiliated with that attack? Well, because we are Muslim. People automatically assumed that *all* Muslims collectively were responsible for the attack, and this stereotype is wrong.

Although my older sister and mom continued wearing the hijab, I didn't wear one myself, which allowed me to keep my religious faith to myself, at least for as long as keeping my religious faith to myself could last. I didn't want to be judged on the basis of my religion, especially while sitting in my first grade class.

One week following the 9/11 attack, President Bush visited the Washington Islamic Center to address the recent violent attacks against the American Muslim community, and sometimes the non-Muslim Arab-

American community. While standing at the pulpit with the Imam and other community leaders, President Bush stated:

> *Both Americans, our Muslim friends, our citizens, our tax-paying citizens and Muslims in (other) nations were just appalled - could not believe - what we saw on our TV screens. These acts of violence against innocents violate the fundamental tenets of Islamic faith and it is important for our fellow Americans to understand that. The English translation is not as eloquent as the original Arabic, but let me quote from the Quran itself: 'In the long run, evil in the extreme will be the end of those who do evil. For that they rejected the signs of Allah and held them up to ridicule.' The face of terror is not the true faith of Islam. That's not what Islam is all about. Islam is peace. These terrorists don't represent peace -they represent evil and war. When we think of Islam we think of a faith that brings comfort to a billion people around the world - billions of people find comfort and solace in peace. And that has made brothers and sisters out of every race - out of every race. America counts millions of Muslims amongst our citizens and Muslims make an incredibly valuable contribution to our country: Muslims are doctors, lawyers, law professors, members of the military, entrepreneurs, shopkeepers, moms and dads and they need to be treated with respect. In our anger and emotion, our fellow Americans, we must treat each other with respect. Women who cover their heads in this country must feel comfortable going outside their homes. Moms who wear cover must not be intimidated in America. That's not the America I know. That's not the America I value. I have been told that some fear to leave, some don't want to go shopping for their families, some don't want to go back to ordinary daily routines because by wearing cover they are afraid that they will be intimidated.[29]*

September 11 truly impacted my family's lifestyle because my dad would be deployed to fight in the Middle East by the later half of 2002.

My house always felt strangely empty following September 11th, even when the whole family was there. Every evening when my family members came home, there was a feeling of disconnection between everyone. My dad was preparing for a deployment beginning the later half of 2002, the

---

29 "US BUSH 2." AP Archive, uploaded by APTN, 17 Sept. 2001,

http://www.aparchive.com/metadata/youtube/64b3224c6a68feebea1025c830c53242 [Accessed 9 Sep. 2019].

women in my family were facing the challenges of wearing the hijab, and my family members began neglecting their regular prayers, which previously was something that had always brought my family together.

I didn't feel comfortable with the isolation between my family members, but this was the beginning of what was called the "War on Terror". Although its purpose was to eradicate Al-Qaeda and other terrorist sects, it had started to feel like it was against an entire religious group called Islam, and my family practiced Islam. I faced my own challenges because a religion which once brought my family together was now being blamed for worldwide violence.

I used to feel bad when I'd watch *nembiro* walk toward the area containing the prayer mats, spread out her mat and begin praying. I didn't feel bad because *nembiro* was praying, but I'd feel bad because sometimes she'd pray alone. Sometimes we'd pray alongside *nembiro*, but other times, she'd try to call us to pray and everyone would look dazed. She'd look disappointed before continuing her scheduled prayers alone, but when I missed praying, I'd stand near her and pray.

The days grew colder and winter was rapidly approaching in Hanau, Germany. My first-grade teacher arranged a day for all the students to go outside and gather autumn leaves, to begin the arts and crafts activities for Thanksgiving. The teacher instructed all the students to prepare for the cool weather before going outside to gather leaves. My classmates and I hastily rushed to our cubbies so that we could grab our coats and gloves.

While putting on our gear, we re-enter our classroom and wait for all the other students to also grab their winter coats and gloves from their cubbies. Once we're ready to go outside, all the students line up at our classroom door and my first-grade teacher walks us out to the schoolyard to gather leaves.

Immediately after exiting the school building, I feel chilly.

Once my teacher reaches a good area for my class to search for leaves, she gives us permission to begin gathering leaves. I join some of my classmates in looking for unique shaped leaves to use for my artwork.

"This leaf looks like it's been eaten by an insect," one of the boys from my class says.

"Yeah! It does look like it's been eaten by an insect," another classmate replies.

"I'm going to use this one for my artwork," another classmate says while looking at another leaf with fascination.

I gather enough leaves for my artwork, which provides me enough time to explore other things in our school yard.

"Hey, look it's a worm!" one of my classmates exclaimed.

My classmates and I stand around the worm, watching it move along the soil. While the worm is squirming around, one of the children ask, "Did you know that worms won't die if they're cut in half?"

"That's not true! Worms do die if they're cut in half," one of my other classmates respond.

"Okay, I dare you to cut it in half, then."

My classmates and I watch as the worm is cut in half and the two halves begin crawling its separate ways. I couldn't understand how one worm could be cut into halves but still continue to live. We're all disgusted, but we continue to explore other things in our school yard. We begin looking for ladybugs and other insects crawling around. In the midst of exploring our surroundings, our teacher calls out, "It looks like everyone gathered leaves for their artwork, we can begin heading back to our classroom now."

We quickly follow behind our teacher, so that we can return to our classroom. After entering our classroom, my teacher hands everyone a sheet of construction paper, glue, crayons and scissors so that we could begin creating our artwork for Thanksgiving. When my classmates and I get done with our holiday artwork, we leave our items to the side of the classroom to dry. The teacher starts teaching lessons after we're done with our artwork. At the end of the school day, my teacher places all of our artwork around the class, displaying everyone's work.

As a six-year-old, seeing my artwork hung up alongside my classmate's work walls made me realize that there was room for me to belong within my community, but there wasn't room for my religious faith. I appreciated seeing my artwork near my classmates' artwork.

I was missing a closeness at both home and school.

Deep down, I was saddened by the disconnection within my family slowly growing at home, especially regarding our Islamic faith. At school, I was worried that being the only Muslim student in my classroom would leave me an outsider. I felt that there weren't many people who could relate to me and for whatever reason, I felt alone in the journey of being an American Muslim military brat.

Chapter Six: A Muslim Girl's Christmas

Thanksgiving slowly turned into Christmas season and teachers at Argonner Elementary School began planning Christmas activities for the children. Every day, my classmates and I were required to line up at our classroom door so that we could begin walking towards our school music room and practice for our upcoming school Christmas show. After entering the music room, the music teacher asks everyone to stand in their assigned positions. I was always considered one of the tallest students in my class, so I was commonly assigned to stand in the back of the choir.

The music teacher turns her radio on, and everyone begins singing along to "We Wish You a Merry Christmas". For the students who didn't know the lyrics, we were handed a piece of paper with the song's lyrics written out for us. Collectively everyone in my classroom sings:

We wish you a Merry Christmas
We wish you a Merry Christmas
We wish you a Merry Christmas
And a Happy New Year
Good tidings we bring
To you and your kin
We wish you a Merry Christmas
And a Happy New Year

My classmates and I go over the song's lyrics multiple times until our music teacher feels that everyone's voices are well-orchestrated for the school Christmas show. After going over the song's lyrics several times, the teachers give us a short rehearsal break. Students express their excitement for the upcoming Christmas show. Even I was excited about it.

My parents couldn't pick me up from school that day, so I walked home with the other parents who lived on New Argonner. While walking home, my classmates and I began singing aloud, "We wish you a Merry Christmas, we wish you a Merry Christmas, we wish you a Merry Christmas, and a Happy New Year!" from the top of our lungs. We sang the song until we reached the bridge which took us to New Argonner. After crossing the bridge, my classmates and I parted our separate ways and headed home.

I walk up to my apartment door, unlock the door, and enter inside my apartment. I take off my winter clothing and walk into the kitchen to grab something to eat. Then I place my leftover food inside a bowl and place the bowl inside the microwave to heat up.

Around the time I came home, my other family members were still on their way home from both work and school. Everyone finally enters the apartment and my parents decide that they want to watch the news channel. I walk towards the microwave, grab my bowl of food and sit at the dining room table to eat. My older sister is feeling sad because she's having another rough day at high school. I listen in to my older sister telling us about her school day.

My sister is down while explaining the conversation she had between her and her schoolmates about her headscarf. I'm still eating my dinner when I overhear the reporters on the news channel continually state that the 9/11 attacks were the results of Islamic Terrorism. My mom's hijab is also being questioned at work. When I finish eating my dinner, I walk to the kitchen, place my bowl into the sink, and decide it's best if I head to my bedroom.

While playing with the toys in my bedroom, I start singing aloud "We Wish You a Merry Christmas". I'm practicing the chorus for my school's Christmas show and I want my voice to synchronize with the voices of my classmates'. At some point, I get tired of playing alone in my bedroom, so I begin singing along to the Christmas song while walking into the living room, where my family is still sitting and watching the news coverage of 9/11. It's been months after the attack, but the memory of it is so strong amongst Americans, it could've happened yesterday. The news channels repeatedly cover documentaries and reports about the 9/11 attack.

"We wish you a Merry Christmas, we wish you a Merry Christmas, we wish you a Merry Christmas, and a Happy New Year!" I blissfully sing aloud.

My family gets quiet for a slight moment and then they turn to look at me. No one attempts to say anything to me at first because we're all still grieving September 11th. After a few moments of silence, Dad quietly says, "Julde, we don't celebrate Christmas, I don't want to hear you singing Christmas songs in the house."

"But I'm rehearsing for the school Christmas show," I say. There's an awkward moment of silence before I continue saying, "My music teacher wants to make sure everyone's voices are well orchestrated for the upcoming Christmas show."

"You won't be part of the school Christmas show because Muslims don't celebrate Christmas. I'll write a note for your teacher stating that we're Muslim, and you aren't allowed to practice for the school Christmas show. Tomorrow you'll hand the note to your teacher."

Dad searches for a loose-leaf paper and pen to write a school note for my teacher. I was saddened after hearing the news that I couldn't participate in my school Christmas show.

I sat down with my family members that evening to do my homework, and when I was finished doing my homework, I put my backpack away. I decided that I wanted to go on my computer to play some games.

I'd sit in front of my big white-boxed looking computer, located in our living room, and play all the virtual games on barbie.com. The online Barbie games I enjoyed playing included dressing up my virtual barbie, taking her clothes-shopping, doing her nails, and so much more. At 9:00 p.m., I got ready for bed so that I could go to school the next morning.

The next day, my first-grade teacher let everyone know that we were going to join other first-grade classes inside the music room for Christmas rehearsals. I waited in my classroom seat for my teacher to finish talking, before walking up to her desk and speaking with her privately. While walking towards her desk, I watched my classmates express enthusiasm for the upcoming Christmas show, and I honestly didn't know how to feel. I wasn't going to be part of the show.

I feebly hand her the note dismissing my participation in the school Christmas show rehearsals.

My teacher opens the note and then turns to look at me, "You cannot be part of the school Christmas show because you're a Muslim? It's okay, you can just sit to the side while the other students rehearse the songs inside the music room."

That same day, my classmates and I did other creative activities in preparation for the Christmas holidays. Before heading to the music room, my teacher wanted us to make a gingerbread house.

"But, I can't make the gingerbread house, my parents said I can't participate in any Christmas activities."

"It's okay Julde, it's just candies and cookies. When you're done making the gingerbread house, you can eat the different parts of the house. Grab some supplies and begin making your gingerbread house."

I walk over and grab the supplies to begin building my gingerbread house. I grab candy canes, mints, marshmallows, pretzels, graham crackers, cake frosting and other snacks to place on my gingerbread house. After gathering my supplies, I sit next to my classmates and get to work. My teacher tells us that we can use the frosting as our "glue" to stick various snacks on our houses. When we're done building our creations, we sit them aside and line up at our classroom door so that we can go off to rehearsal. My teacher turns off the classroom lights, and we all walk towards the school music room. My teacher immediately pulls the music teacher aside to tell her that I cannot participate in the school Christmas show because my parents wrote a note asking that I be excluded from the rehearsals. Afterwards, both teachers tell me to sit aside, while the other students stand in formation, practicing the Christmas songs. I can see some of my classmates start to wonder why I wasn't part of the school Christmas show rehearsal, but the teachers tell them not to be concerned with that; their main concern should be rehearsing for the school Christmas show.

When rehearsals are done, everyone head back to our classroom, and some of the students ask me, "Why weren't you a part of the Christmas show rehearsals, are you in trouble?"

Some students clearly thought that I was probably in trouble, which is why I was told to sit aside. To avoid any further confusion, I tell them that I couldn't join them in the school Christmas show rehearsals because I'm a

Muslim, and Muslims don't celebrate Christmas. Some of the students inquire, "What is a *Muslim*?"

"It's my religion," I try explaining to my classmates.

A few other students in my classroom knew what a Muslim was, but they referenced my religion to the most recent September 11th attack in New York. This was conflicting for me because my religion was frequently being cited as the doctrine that led to the attack of September 11th, even inside my first-grade classroom. I felt like an outcast following the Christmas rehearsals. I was the only Muslim army brat in my classroom. Now that the holiday season was approaching, the children in my classroom were being identified by their religious faiths in order to learn more about their respective holidays; but if it were some sort of competition, anything was better than being a Muslim.

I return home from school in the evening and my classmates are all singing along to Christmas carols they were practicing for the school Christmas show. I refrain from joining along with them because I was told not to participate in any Christmas activities. The parents are also joining in to sing Christmas carols, but some parents realized I wasn't singing along with them. "Why aren't you singing along to the Christmas carols?" one of the parents asks me.

"She doesn't celebrate Christmas," one of the children tells their parents.

"Oh, so do you celebrate Hanukkah or Kwanzaa?" the parent queries.

"No, I don't celebrate Hanukkah or Kwanzaa either."

"Oh, okay, so, which holiday do you celebrate?"

"I only celebrate Ramadan and Eid."

"Which religion do you practice?"

"I'm a Muslim."

There's an awkward moment of silence. In that moment, I just hope that no one else references my Islamic faith to the recent September 11th attack. However, none of the parents say anything afterwards, we just leave it at the fact I'm a Muslim.

We continue walking towards the New Argonner Kaserne and cross over the bridge. After crossing the bridge, everyone goes their separate ways as we normally did. I walk into my apartment building and as I make my way upstairs, I can smell the scent of freshly baked pizza overtaking the staircase. I continue walking upstairs, hoping that the scent was coming from my apartment door. The closer I got to my door, the stronger the scent. I open the door and my dad is in the house preparing cheese pizza and buffalo wings for dinner.

"Good Afternoon, Dad. Are you making pizza and buffalo wings?"

"Yes, I am! I bought pizza and buffalo wings at the supermarket on my way home from work, I'm just now baking them."

I take my homework out of my backpack and begin working on my homework assignment. Some of the problems are challenging, especially the math problems, because it required me to know multiplication.

My dad watches me struggle with my math homework and says, "Julde, how many times do I have to tell you that you need to memorize the times table in order to solve your multiplication homework? If you memorize your times table, you wouldn't have such a hard time."

I try to finish my multiplication homework so that I can go back to memorizing my times table afterwards, as suggested by my dad. After a while, my dad calls me into the kitchen to eat, and I grab a plate of pizza and buffalo wings. I carry my plate to the dining room table and start eating. By the time I finish eating dinner, all my other family members arrive home.

After eating, I decide to grab a prayer rug from the area where my family usually places them, I spread out my rug, and begin praying. I wasn't taught how to pray properly, but I attempt to pray like my family always did, anyway. After praying, I place the rug back to where it belongs and get ready to go to bed.

A couple of weeks later, my classmates and I were preparing to take a winter break vacation from school. Before leaving for winter break, all the students were given information they needed for the school Christmas show. I already knew that I wasn't a part of the school Christmas show, so I continued doing my classwork. My teacher also told everyone to take their gingerbread houses home before leaving for winter break. My parents had said I couldn't participate in Christmas activities, but I'd let them know that I was going to eat my gingerbread house.

Going home that afternoon, the winter air smelled like smoked wood, burning from chimneys. I relished the smell of smoked wood seeping through the winter air. My hands were cold, but I continued holding onto my gingerbread house while walking home. When I got home, I began eating parts of my gingerbread house. After my parents arrived, they saw the gingerbread house and threw it away. I didn't even get a chance to finish eating my entire gingerbread house. They told me that we didn't celebrate Christmas, nor did they want me to be part of any Christmas activities. I let my parents know that I was only eating the gingerbread house, but they insisted that Christmas is not our religious holiday.

I spent my winter break watching all the Christmas specials on Cartoon Network.

Sometimes I went outside to play with the other children living in my neighborhood.

During the Christmas break, my older sister Mariam, took off her hijab. January 2002, my older sister, Mariam would begin her school year without wearing a hijab. My *Nembiro* and Mom were the only women in our household wearing one.

Fall of 2002, I began my second-grade school year at Argonner Elementary School in Hanau, Germany. My second-grade teacher told my classmates and me, "Don't ask your military parent what they go through while they're away for war. You don't want to ask them a question which initiates a memory of something which happened at war."

During my second-grade school year, my dad was preparing to be sent to his first duty following the 9/11 attacks, nearly a year later. My teacher's advice remained with me for the rest of my life because I also took into consideration, "What if it truly disturbed my dad to ask him what war was like?" From when I was seven years old up until adulthood, I haven't asked my dad anything about whatever he may have experienced at war, and I still won't. I respect my dad's career and his experiences, so I rarely have a clue about what he does for work.

The first time my dad deployed was after September 11th, in 2002, and it felt like he was gone for nearly a year. My family waited on my dad's phone calls and tried our best to not miss his phone calls because if we did, it was difficult reaching him.

It was becoming difficult for me, thinking that something might happen to my dad while he was away at war. I'm grateful that nothing happened to my dad, but it's something I often worried about as a child. My family and I made sure to purchase items my dad loved so that we can send those items to him. We packed my dad's favorite items like candy, beef jerky, peanuts, T-shirts and socks. There were times while my dad was away for war when he couldn't get the same items he regularly enjoyed while he was home. It didn't feel right, but what choice did my family have? That was part of my dad's career.

My grandmother Halimatu Bah truly was our caregiver during this time period. My younger sister was two-years old and my *nembiro* would place my younger sister on her back and wrap her in the traditional African baby wrap. She'd walk around the house while my sister was on her back, rocking my younger sister to sleep.

Sometimes, my grandmother would take a break from watching the WWE wrestling matches and she'd watch Cartoon Network with me.

I couldn't understand why my dad had to leave for so long. I also barely saw my mom at home because she constantly worked to continue her goal of building a house for her family in Guinea.

As an adult, I finally understand that my dad left home because he had to take care of the family, but as a child, I wasn't trying to understand that. Of course, I love my mom with my whole heart, but I also love my dad in that same exact way. I felt a sense of confusion from the rapid change of my household dynamics; everything seemed to crumble during the period following the 9/11 attack.

That school year, the teachers frequently took the students to the school library. Now that we were old enough, the teachers often told us to check out chapter books which we could read at home. My favorite book series to read was *Little House on the Prairie*, by Laura Ingalls Wilder. As a seven-year-old, I loved reading books which discussed the past in the United States, even if it was fictional. Laura Ingalls Wilder's and Christopher Paul Curtis' books allowed me to explore the fictional and non-fictional past of the United States. Sometimes while reading their books, I forgot about what I was going through and I instantly felt like I was a part of their stories.

Christopher Paul Curtis wrote books which highlighted the lifestyles of African-Americans during the times of segregation. My favorite read from Christopher Paul Curtis was the book, *Bud, Not Buddy.*

I spent most of my days getting lost inside the stories of their books. It was the best way for me to forget about the terrible things that were happening around me. My dad being away at war, my mom working to support her family in Africa, me and my siblings trying our best to achieve academically. Most of my classmates similarly had to face watching their parents leave home to fight in a war. Some students at my school had it harder than other students because both of their parents were in the military.

Chapter Seven: Cona-Cry, Guinea

My parents wanted to take my grandma, Halimatu Bah, back to Guinea. At the same time, my mom also wanted to see the house that she was building for her family. The house wasn't completely built, but my mom wanted to see the progress that had been made.

The flight duration to Guinea, West Africa was about eight hours from Germany. When my family and I touched down in the nation's capital, Conakry, my mom's older brother Wurie picked us up from the airport. After finally making it into Guinea, the sun was setting, and the evening sky was approaching.

As we were making our way to his car, my mom told Uncle Wurie to show her the house that they were helping her build.

Uncle Wurie is a short, bronze complexioned man, with chinky eyes.

My mom's family had only accomplished building the foundation of the house. None of the walls were built, and there were no scaffolding. It was just solid foundation. My mom was really disappointed with the house because with all the money she had sent to Guinea, there should've been more progress to the house.

Since the house was not finished yet, we spent the night in a house my mom had been renting for her family until the new house was completed. The home my mom's family was renting was built with cheap materials. The roof was made of sheet metal, the walls were made of concrete and were never painted, there was no piping built in the house for running water, and there was no electrical wiring in the house for light.

When everyone got to the house, it was already late at night and my mom's family had numerous kerosene lamps lit around the house; my other family members were holding flashlights. The house was completely dark, except for the areas where someone was sitting near a lamp or holding a flashlight. My mom wanted to catch up with some of her family members, so she decided to stay up to speak with them. I didn't understand Fulani, but I sat next to my family members while they spoke.

As my family members spoke, I watch the flame flicker in the kerosene lamp. As it flickered, the lighting around the house constantly changed. After my mom finished talking about everything she wanted, we got ready to go to bed. My family prepared for us to go to sleep by placing a huge net over our bed.

"What is this huge net for?" I ask.

"To keep the mosquitoes from biting us during the night," my mom responds.

That night, it rains. The entire night, while I lie in bed, I can hear the rain tapping on the metal roof——*Clink, Clank, Bong*——The rain continues tapping on the roofing, only interrupted by loud bangs of thunder.

I slowly find myself dozing off to sleep. Several hours later, sunlight begins creeping through the window and hits my face. The weather is hot and some of the mosquitoes still managed to make it through the net which covered our entire bed.

"Cock-a-doodle-doo!" a rooster calls out.

In the morning everyone in my family sits out on the front porch. Guinea was the first place where I physically got to see and touch certain farm animals. A lot of people in the neighborhood raised their own animals for food. No one ate processed nor chemically injected meat, so their animals ran freely around the neighborhood, eating nearby grass and grains.

Out in the yard, you could see chicken running around; however, they all belonged to a family. People in the neighborhood would walk their sheep and cows around on a leash to eat fresh grass. Sometimes people held a long stick while following their farm animals around the neighborhood and if their animals walked out of line, they'd whip their animals.

I grew an attachment with one of the chickens my family owned. I told my family members that I wanted to keep the chicken as a pet, but my family members laughed at me.

My uncle helped me tie the chicken's feet to a bench, so that I wouldn't have to catch it every time I wanted to play with it. For the next three days, I was playing with the chicken tied to the bench. I grew such an attachment to it that I began feeding the chicken. It was easy for me to grow attached to animal like a chicken, especially since I was on the other side of a language barrier while visiting Guinea. Almost everyone around me spoke French, Fulani, or one of the other tribal languages of the region, but there were very few English speakers, and none of them were children like me. So, when my family members were busy or I couldn't easily communicate with someone, I'd go and feed the chicken.

On the fourth day, the chicken is missing. I'm devastated. I look for the chicken everywhere and it isn't in the same location that I left it. I go to ask my family members, "Where is the chicken?"

And Alfa replies, "I think they killed it."

"They killed the chicken that I have been playing with?!" I say back incredulously.

"I guess so," my brother responds.

I began sobbing and break down in tears. I look for the chicken everywhere. My eyes are filled with tears and I could barely look for the chicken, even if I wanted to.

My family simply tells me that the chicken ran away, but it would come back home. I really put my hopes into the chicken coming back, as my family claimed.

Later that evening, one of my aunts made a delicious chicken stew which we ate with a side of rice. At first, I was hesitant in eating the meal my aunt prepared, but I was starving, and hadn't eaten the entire day. So, I just hoped that this wasn't the chicken I was looking for. It was customary for everyone to share dinner on one huge plate, so if I didn't eat, everyone would end up finishing the food. When I was finished eating the chicken stew, my family members told me that I'd just eaten the chicken I was looking for. Then some of my family members laughed. In that moment, I felt betrayed.

I was no longer in the mood to deal with anyone or look anybody in the face. I couldn't believe I was tricked into eating the chicken that I took as a pet.

I spent three good days playing with that chicken and felt disgusted to hear that I actually ate it.

Some mornings, I 'd get up around the same time as my cousins and watch them get ready for school. My cousins would prepare something to eat for breakfast and then afterwards they'd walk for ten to fifteen minutes to get to school.

In the daytime, I often found myself bored because none of my cousins stayed home.

While at home, I began playing with a goat which my family owned. There was no need for me to grow an attachment with the goat because it could possibly become my family's next meal, but it helped relieve some of the boredom I acquired while my cousins were gone for school.

While playing outside with the goat, one of the neighbors calls out from their front door, "Julde!"

I turn my attention towards the neighbor after hearing my name. Instead, another girl responds to my name. In that moment, I didn't know how to feel that another person was responding to my name. I never remember meeting anyone else with my name. My family confirmed that the neighbor's daughter was also named Julde. Now I was curious because I was never told the root meaning of my name nor was the information about my name easily accessible online. I always pronounced my name to people I met, but had a hard time giving people the meaning of my name. The name Julde wasn't common in any place I've been except for Guinea.

Then I ask my family members, "Are there other people named Julde?"

"Yes, Julde is a Fulani name," my family members respond. This news comes as a surprise to me. Anytime I asked about my name while I was younger, I was never told that my name was of Fulani origin. And I couldn't believe that I was finally meeting another person with my name. That day, I'm told that my name is a unisex name, so a boy or girl could be named Julde. There are different variations of my name's spelling; for instance, Juldeh, Djoulde, or Julde. So, then I ask, "What is the meaning of my name?"

Then one of my family members says something off the top of their head, "Your name means precious." Later into my adulthood, I found out that this isn't the meaning of my name, but I'll explain how I discovered the true meaning of my name at a later time.

Now that we had eaten the chicken I was playing with, I began playing with the neighbor's daughter, Julde. We never understood each other, but we knew that we wanted to play with each other. Through my interactions with Julde, I began picking up a few words in Fulani. Later in the day, my cousins would return home from school and we planned to go around the neighborhood to hang out together. Before hanging out, my cousins had household chores that they had to complete. I watched my cousins do their chores, which was different from the chores I was used to doing in Germany. My cousins were required to pull buckets of water from a nearby well because there wasn't running water in their house. They'd hang their bucket onto a rope which was hovering over the well and then, lower their bucket into the well. When the bucket was full, my cousins would quickly pull the bucket up using the rope. After getting water into their bucket, they'd take the water and pour it into a barrel sitting in the house. When the barrel of water was full, the children would then use the excess water to wash dishes and hand wash their clothes.

While my cousins were hand washing their clothes, they'd use a washboard. They'd lather their clothes with soap and then continuously rub their clothing on the washboard, making sure to get all the stains out of their clothing. While the clothes were being scrubbed against the washboard you could hear the tin material on the washboard making a clunking sound as my cousins' knuckles glided past the board. When my cousins were done washing their clothes, they'd hang their clothes outside to dry.

Now we could go hang out in Conakry. The weather is warm and sometimes slight breezes come our way. While walking around the city, I see trees everywhere with fresh fruit in the progress of growing. Lots of children happily playing outside. Some children playing soccer, tag, hand games, and Chinese jump rope. There are lots of people selling items along the side of the street. Some items being sold are roasted peanuts, grilled corn, fried donuts, fresh fruits, fresh vegetables, and much more. My cousins and I pass by an area where people are selling frozen red drinks. One of my cousins, Adama, asks me if I want to try one of the red drinks.

"*Nam,* yes," I reply.

This frozen drink is tied in a small plastic bag. Adama opens a little hole for me in the corner of my drink bag, and afterwards she breaks a hole into the corner of her drink bag. We begin eating the frozen drink called bissap[30]. Bissap is a beverage made from boiled sorrel. The street vendors would make these beverages at home, freeze them, and begin selling them in the neighborhood. My cousin, Adama, and I start to drink the bissap beverages as it melts. Whenever we get impatient, we bite parts of the frozen bissap. My cousin finishes eating her entire frozen bissap and then she looks towards me. I'm still in the midst of enjoying my own bissap, savoring the flavor of the bissap drink because this was my first time trying the beverage.

Out of nowhere, Adama snatches the bissap out of my hand and bites a huge chunk of the drink. I'm just so disappointed at this point. My cousin and I begin fighting for the bissap, but during the fight, she's biting parts of my drink. She finally finishes my bissap and now I'm annoyed with her.

I was surprised that she'd snatch the bissap from my hand and eat it without asking my permission. Adama decided that she'd wanted to visit the house my mom was building, but she forgot where the house was located. I told Adama that I remembered where the house was located. This conversation took place in broken sentences and informal sign language because Adama barely knew English and I barely knew Fulani. Adama decided that she was going to trust that I knew where the house was located. My cousins and I began our journey in looking for the house and eventually, fifteen minutes later, we arrived. After getting there, my cousin was taken aback because I didn't grow up in that neighborhood; better yet I had only been there for a couple of days, but I was able to lead us in the direction of the house.

---

30 Bissap: a drink made from the sepals of a hibiscus flower, commonly known as sorrel. These sepals are boiled in hot water and then later cooled down to make a sweet beverage. This beverage is a tea, but is often referred to being a juice when it is sweetened and iced.

While looking at the house, we wanted to see progress, but it was in the same condition we had left it, just a solid foundation. When we got tired of looking at the foundation, we decided to head back to our family. On our way back to our family, it began raining massively. All the street vendors rapidly gathered their products from under the rain. Some street vendors covered their products with huge plastic coverings. People without umbrellas were running to reach for some sort of shelter to stand under.

My cousins and I start running home, but then, incredibly, the whole area begins to flood. People are swimming in the water, but I don't know how to swim. I find a little hill to stand on and stay there. Adama comes to take my hand and try to drag me off the hill. I attempt to fight her off because I didn't want to get off the little hill and drown in the water. Somehow, she still manages to get me off the hill and she drags me into the flooded water.

After finally getting to land, half of my body is soaking wet and at this point all I'm thinking about is how much I do not want to go out with my cousin anymore. I begin to think, Adama is too wild for me and I've had enough of her. Shortly after, the rain finally stops. It just so happens that Guinea doesn't have adequate water drainage systems, just in case there was a flood. In some areas there were large rectangular holes dug up on the side of the roads to act as water drainage, but sometimes that isn't enough. Even when it didn't rain a lot, the rain would gather into the streets.

When the rain stops, everyone returns to their normal selling activities. Far out into the clearing sky, a majestic rainbow forms. The colors green, blue, red, violet and orange appeared above in the beautiful clearing sky. I show my cousin the rainbow and she looks at it, but she doesn't even care. After we finally get home, Adama begins doing her homework for school the next day.

Right after arriving in front of my family's house, I see a stray dog. Knowing that every dog I have ever met in my life was friendly, I approach the dog. My family, all of whom are sitting on the porch, start screaming from the top of their lungs, "Julde, No! Do not go near that dog!"

Swiftly, I jump back and get away from the dog. I ask my parents, "Why can't I go near the dog?"

My parents say, "Some of the stray dogs in Africa have rabies. That dog especially has rabies." Some of my other family members also agree that it's common for stray dogs in Africa to have rabies. I didn't understand what rabies was at that age, but it sounded serious. From that time forward, I always tried my best to avoid stray dogs in Africa.

Some of my family members who lived in Guinea were able to communicate with me in English because they survived the Civil War in Sierra Leone. Sierra Leone is one of the West African countries which became a British crown colony. This meant that many of the people who lived in Sierra Leone knew how to speak English. English, as the national language, became the more widely spoken languages between people living in Sierra Leone, especially if two people were from different tribes. Although my family member's English was a blend of some French and Fulani words, I could still understand what they were saying.

The next morning, my cousin Adama gets ready for school. While my cousin is getting ready for school, I brush my teeth and take a shower. One of my family members helps me warm water, pulled from the well, on a firewood stove to take a shower with. Sometimes my family members would joke that Americans can only take a shower with warm water. For them, they rarely warmed water to take a shower.

When the water seems warm enough, they pour the water into a bucket and help me carry the bucket into the shower room. After dressing up, my family tells me that my cousin is ready to go to school, then they ask me, "Julde, do you want to go to school with Adama?"

I already had enough of Adama at this point, so I say no. My family insists that I accompany Adama to her school. Everyone including my parents, say that I'm going to enjoy attending this school located near Warindara, Guinea.

I end up following my cousin to her school.

There are several rows of tables in the classroom and each table has a bench chair which the students sat on. I sit near my cousin and her friends. At some point, I'm just excited to be in a classroom again, even though I had been dreading the idea of accompanying Adama.

At the school, the students are reading the Quran. Instantly, the teacher recognizes that I am not one of his regular students, so he asks me who I am. I really don't know what he's saying, so my cousin tells him that I was visiting from Germany, but that I'm American. The teacher introduces himself and speaks to me in the little English he knew. We speak to each other until the conversation could no longer proceed because of our language barriers.

The conversation quickly ends after an awkward moment of silence and the teacher begins calling the attendance of every student in his class. When the teacher finishes calling the attendance of all the children, he resumes his curriculum from the subjects the students were learning the prior day. The teacher writes out the work on the blackboard and all the children repeat after the teacher. A few minutes into the teacher starting the curriculum, a few students walk into the classroom late. The teacher takes a break from teaching, grabs a stick, takes the children outside and whoops them for coming into the classroom late. Some of the students start laughing at the children being whipped. It's a complete culture shock for me. The thought that immediately runs through my mind is, "Is this teacher allowed to whoop the children like this?"

The children come back into the classroom crying and the curriculum resumes like nothing happened. Two of the girls sitting in the front row of the class are talking to each other. The teacher continuously asks the girls to quiet down and repeat after him, but when the teacher had enough of the two girls talking, he takes out a stick and whoops the two girls.

Now my heart is racing.

I couldn't believe what was happening. I'm sitting in a classroom where the teacher is openly whooping the children.

At this point in my life, I have already attended two elementary schools and this type of disciplining never occurred. Suspension, detention, or timeout was common in the schools I attended, but never getting your behind beat. I just so happened to be sitting next to my cousin who already exhibited an out-of-control character. My cousin Adama wants to ask me several questions in the middle of her teacher's curriculum and I ignore her.

Now my cousin is laughing and carrying on in the area we are sitting in. I didn't know what was going on in the curriculum. The teacher comes to the back of the classroom and asks me to repeat the curriculum. I didn't hear any of the curriculum because my cousin was talking too much. I tell the teacher I cannot repeat the curriculum because I didn't hear him. Suddenly, the teacher grabs my hand and attempts to hit my hand. Sweat instantly emerges from the palms of my hands.

"I didn't come to school to get beat," I thought to myself.

The teacher laughs and tells me that he won't beat me because this was my first wrongdoing, but he'll beat me next time.

I count the hours for the school day to end. I knew that I wasn't coming back to this school, especially with my cousin. When the school day ends, my cousin and I start heading back home. On our way back home, I think about how children could get whooped by their teacher in Guinea as a means of discipline. I knew that I wasn't going to return to that school under any circumstances.

When my cousin and I get home, I feel the need to use the restroom. I start walking behind the house, so that I can enter the latrine[31]. Before reaching the latrine, I see a stray dog sitting in the path. All that ran through my mind was, this dog may have rabies. My parents already told me that some of the stray dogs in Africa have rabies and I didn't want to walk past this dog to enter the latrine. I decide that I'm going to call one of my family members to help me remove the dog. My cousin Adama decides that she will take me to the latrine, despite the dog sitting in the path. We start fighting each other until I nearly pee on myself. Finally, the dog moves out of the way on its own and I entered the latrine to use the bathroom.

The next day, my parents ask me if I wanted to go to school.

"No!" I shout passionately.

---

31 Latrine: a pit dug into the ground with the purpose of people using it as a toilet for defecation and urination.

Under no circumstances was I going to follow my cousin or attend a school where students get whooped as a form of discipline. I stayed home that day and enjoyed my time outside by myself.

After visiting Guinea for a few weeks, my parents let the family know that we were returning to Germany. My family needed to get back to New Argonner so that my dad could get back to work. I would need to return because I needed to return to school in Argonner Elementary School. By the time my family decided that they wanted to leave Guinea, most of the house my mom was building was done.

On the day that my parents were planning to head to the airport, they took away my older siblings' passports. My parents told my older siblings that they wouldn't be flying with us to Germany. Instead, Mariam and Alfa would now be staying with our family members in Guinea for a short period of time. My parents decided to enroll Mariam and Alfa into an all-American school in Guinea. Mariam and Alfa felt betrayed by my parents because they found out this news the day we were all supposed to leave the airport together and travel back to Germany. Mariam and Alfa joined us at the airport, but we'd say our farewells to them. This was the beginning of my older siblings adopting the nickname Cona-cry, to reference the city Conakry. My older siblings cried so much after being tricked into staying in Guinea, that they began calling the city Cona-cry.

A few months after returning to Germany, my dad receives a call from his family members in Virginia that his sister nearly passed away due to a health condition. My dad had to take emergency family medical leave to check on the health of his sister.

Chapter Eight: Westmoreland County

My parents book the earliest flight to Virginia. After arriving in Virginia, the first thing we do is meet with my dad's family to see how my aunt is doing. Our family tells us that my aunt is still admitted in the hospital to get medically treated. For privacy reasons, I will not expose my aunt's name nor her medical situation.

My dad, Bilal Bani Ball, knew that we were going to be in Virginia for a while, so he enrolls me in the same elementary school he attended as a young child, Cople Elementary School. Cople Elementary School is in Hague, Virginia, only a fifteen-minute drive away from my great grandmother, Mary Tolson Smith's house. My parents arrange to have a school bus pick me up from my great grandmother's house on school days, so that I can attend Cople Elementary School.

After my dad checks on his younger sister and my younger sibling and I are enrolled into school, he decides to take us to go see his family members.

Hague, Virginia is a beautiful country area. While driving to go visit our family members, I look outside the car window and observe large corn and soybean fields. Occasionally, I see a tiny house located far out in a large, green field. There are long driveways connecting the tiny houses to the main road. Not every driveway leading towards a house was made of pavement. Some driveways were created through the homeowner continuously driving on that part of the land, eroding into a driveway. Other driveways were made of gravel, forming the layout of the driveway. To visualize how country Westmoreland County is, there's lots of grass and trees; and if you want to go shopping, it would take several miles to get the main shopping area.

Mary Tolson Smith is my dad's grandmother, which makes her my great grandmother. My great grandmother has a total of eight children.

Not only did my great grandmother take care of my dad while he was younger, but she also took care of her other grandchildren.

Five minutes away from my Great Grandmother Mary Tolson Smith's house was my Grandmother Daisey Ball's home. Daisey Ball is my dad's mom, also known as Dickey Dee.

It was my first time meeting some of my family members since I was born. Grandma Daisey and my Uncle Dominic came to visit my family in El Paso, Texas; but, they were the only family members I knew from my dad's side of the family. Now I'm finally getting the chance to meet everyone else on my dad's side of the family. It was already difficult for me to meet my family members in general because my dad's military career made it difficult to live near relatives.

While my family and I were in Virginia, most nights were spent at my Great Grandmother Mary Tolson Smith's house. The few times that I left my great grandmother's home, Grandma Daisey would pick me up to go hang out in Tappahannock, Virginia. At all cost, Grandma Daisey spoiled me while we were hanging out. She purchased me any items that she could, whether it was toys, candy or clothing. Whenever we were done spending time in Tappahannock my Grandma Daisey would return me to my Great Grandmother Mary Tolson Smith's house.

The crickets are chirping, frogs croaking, and birds tweeting. I look out towards the road in front of my great grandmother's house and a single car passes by every thirty to forty minutes. Hardly anyone walks around my great grandmother's neighborhood because the houses are built too far away from each other. The sun begins to set while I enjoy the scenery and the beautiful sounds of the country. The cats living in the area make their way around my feet and they're delightfully friendly for strays. Knowing that some stray animals could be dangerous, I ask my family members, "Do these cats have *rabies?*"

But my family members respond, "No, you should be good. Go 'head and play wit 'dem."

The night sky arrives and it becomes pitch black outside. I look up toward the beautiful night sky. And I must admit, you never truly know how beautiful the country night sky is until you realize that the stars resemble diamonds. As I looked up towards the glistening stars, I think about how much I truly want to meet my aunt who everyone says is in the hospital.

"Julde! Come inside the house. You have to get ready for school tomorrow morning!"

I instantly stop what I'm doing and run inside the house to get ready for bed.

The next morning, my mom wakes me up for my first day of school at Cople Elementary School. I slowly pull myself up from the area where I was lying down and sit up on the edge of the bed. Once I feel more awake, I completely get off the bed and walk towards the bathroom to brush my teeth.

Before I get to the bathroom, my dad calls me back into the bedroom and tells me, "Julde, let me tell you something I learned while I was younger. While I was younger, my grandmother used to tell me that I should spread my bed immediately after waking up. Can you tell me why my grandmother would tell me to spread my bed immediately after waking up?"

"Yes, I know why you had to spread your bed," I tell my dad.

"Okay then, tell me why," my dad says with a serious look on his face.

"Did you spread the bed so that it could look neat?" I ask my dad.

"No," my dad responds. "I was told that if I didn't spread the bed, I wouldn't know if there were a snake hiding underneath the sheets when it was time for me to go to bed later in the night. I could accidentally jump into the bed, which had a snake in it, and not know. So ever since then, I always tried to spread my bed immediately after waking up."

"So, you only spread the bed because you wanted to make sure that there weren't any snakes hiding underneath the sheets?" I confirm with my dad.

"Yes, because if there's a snake hiding underneath the sheets, while they're spread, you'll instantly recognize the shape of the snake. Rather than having a messy bed and not knowing that there's a snake hiding underneath the sheets."

Then my dad helps me spread my bed before I continue heading towards the bathroom again, so that I could brush my teeth.

My Great Grandmother Mary is done making breakfast for everyone in the house. She lays the breakfast out on the dining room table for everyone to grab and eat. After eating breakfast, my dad walks me outside in front of the house to wait for the school bus heading towards Cople Elementary School.

"We are waiting for the cheese bus," my dad says.

"What is a cheese bus?" I ask my dad out of curiosity.

He laughs and says, "That's what people used to call the school bus while I was younger. We called it the *cheese* bus."

One of the stray cats living around my great grandmother's house begin circling around my feet and purring.

To me, it was weird that the stray cats living around my family's home in Virginia are safer than the stray dogs living in Guinea.

The cat continues moving around my feet in a slow motion, while purring its body around my legs. The school bus slowly approaches in front of my great grandmother's house, and after coming to a full stop, the bus doors open.

I knew that this day was coming again. The day that I'd have to begin second grade in a totally different classroom.

I nonchalantly begin walking towards the school bus door, but I trip over the cat which is circling around my feet. After getting the cat out of the way, I enter the school bus so that I can begin my first day of school. The bus driver immediately asks me for my name because I must sit in my assigned bus seat. I tell the bus driver that my name is Julde Ball. "Your name is Juldy?" the bus driver asks me.

"No, my name is Julde," I tell the bus driver.

Then afterwards the school crossing guard shows me my assigned seat and I walk over to sit down.

After beginning class at Cople Elementary School, I was lost in the curriculum. This is not where I left off in Germany. The students here were learning an entirely different curriculum from what I was learning in

Germany. While sitting in class, I nearly zone out because I couldn't understand the course material.

I only manage to make it through the school day because nearly all of my classmates are related to me. Shortly after realizing we're cousins, we'd also become friends. We begin talking to each other until abruptly the teacher pulls out a yardstick and slaps it against our classroom desk. I get nervous and look up towards the teacher in hopes that he wouldn't beat us, but he doesn't. The teacher just mentions that he likes slapping yardsticks against the desks of students who aren't listening. I'm suddenly glad that this isn't the same kind of disciplining I was witnessing while attending my cousin's school in Guinea.

The school day ends, so I go outside in front of Cople Elementary School to look for my school bus. After getting on the bus, I sit in my assigned seat and then the girl sitting next to me asks in an eloquent southern accent, "Are you a new student here at Cople Elementary School?"

"Yes," I reply.

"Yeah, I realized it this morning. Which area does your family live in?" she asks.

Then I tell her the street and area my family lives in.

The girl instantly recognizes the area and tells me that the bus driver will drop her off first. The girl looks at me with a smile, her eyes the color of jade gems and her hair a chestnut color. We chat for the remainder of the bus ride home.

The school bus slowly approaches a southern-styled home, when the girl asks me, "Do you see that house over there, you know, the one wit' all those horses?"

"Yeah, I do see the house over there with all those horses," I tell her.

"Yes, that's my house," she tells me. "And sometimes I ride those horses in the evenings after getting home from school. I'd like to invite you some day to come over, so that I can let you ride one."

Then the school bus comes to a full stop, the crossing guard gets off the bus with a long pole, and safely crosses the young girl to her home. Thirty minutes after dropping the girl off, the bus driver finally arrives my great grandmother's home, where I then get off the bus.

After going inside, I notice that the news network is playing on the television set and reporters are talking about Al-Qaeda. "This is a war on Islam," the reporter says.

This is absurd for me to hear because I am aware of the many Muslims who truly love the United States of America.

My mom, who still wears her hijab, is temporarily staying in a remote part of Virginia. There's hardly any exposure of Islam to the people living in this part of Virginia. So, when the news reporters reference Muslims to terrorism, especially to a community who is rarely in contact with Muslims, it's damaging. Many people living within this community are either Southern Baptist or part of another Christian denomination, but they're not Muslims.

The Easter holiday quickly approaches and nearly everyone on my dad's side of the family is preparing to host Easter activities at my great grandmother's house. I stay in the house to watch my older family members dye Easter Eggs and set up Easter baskets for the children. Other family members prepare food for us to eat during the Easter celebration. I already knew that I wasn't allowed to participate in Easter because I could barely partake in Christmas activities at my school. When my family members finish dying all the eggs, they set them aside so that later, the children could go Easter egg hunting.

I wait for my cousins to come over to my great grandmother's house for the Easter holiday celebration. After seeing some of my cousins arrive, I run outside to the front of the house and introduce myself to my family members. My cousins and I get wrapped up in conversation, and we play a few games outside before our family finishes getting all the Easter activities ready.

After everyone makes it to my great grandmother's house, the adults tell the children to go inside the house and wait until all the eggs are placed into their hiding spots. When they're done hiding all the eggs, the adults ask the children to come back outside and begin the Easter activities. I decide to stay indoors because I feel that my parents wouldn't let me participate in the Easter activities. My older family members begin looking for me because they realize that I'm not outside preparing for the Easter celebration. After finding me inside the house, they ask me why I'm not outside hunting with the rest of the children. I tell them that I can't participate in Easter egg hunting. So, they approach my dad and ask if I can join. To my surprise, my parents actually let me go Easter egg hunting with my cousins.

Outside in the yard, my cousins and I all try to collect as many eggs as we can and at the end, we count the eggs we gathered. Although I wasn't successful in collecting many eggs, I still had fun.

After the Easter egg hunt, we gather inside my great grandmother's house to eat dinner. Before eating dinner, one of my family members opens dinner by saying grace. Everyone links their hands, lowers their heads, and closes their eyes. Respectfully, we listen to the family member say grace before fixing our own plates for dinner.

Not many people know about the historical significance of Westmoreland County, Virginia, a history which I learned through visiting many of Westmoreland County's historic sites. My family decided that since this was my first trip to Virginia, they'd take me around the state and teach me a little bit of where I came from.

Westmoreland County, Virginia happens to be the same county where the very first President of the United States, George Washington, was born. Historically, Virginia made up one of the thirteen original British colonies. In fact, Virginia has a unique history in the United States because seven of our other presidents were also born there. In the Reader's Digest article, "Can You Guess Which U.S. State Produced the Most Presidents?" it states:

> *The state that produced the most U.S. presidents is Virginia. The eight men that were born there are George Washington, Thomas Jefferson, James Madison, James Monroe, William Henry Harrison, John Tyler, Zachary Taylor, and Woodrow Wilson.*[32]

---

32 Cutolo, Morgan. "Can You Guess Which U.S. State Produced the Most Presidents?" Reader's Digest,

https://www.rd.com/culture/most-presidents-born.

My family and I are on our way to visit the George Washington Birthplace National Monument to go see the replica of his original home. When we get there, we wait for a tour guide to explain the various areas of George Washington's birthplace. We enter the various living areas, including what could've been his bedroom, dens, and original plantation area. It's interesting how well the newly reconstructed monument is kept; its original building was destroyed in a fire during the late 1700s.

A couple of weeks later, my aunt felt better following her medical treatment in the hospital. She no longer ran the risk of dying and my dad began preparing to go back to Hanau, Germany so that he could return to work. My parents packed all our belongings and made our flight heading back to Germany.

Chapter Nine: No Child Left Behind

During the fall of 2003, my family and I were back in Germany preparing to relocate back to El Paso, Texas because my dad was being sent to Fort Bliss for his new duty station. I had to attend my third-grade school year at Argonner Elementary School for a couple of months before moving to Texas with my family. As usual, my parents took the time to thoroughly clean the apartment before handing it over to housing.

Mariam and Alfa had returned from Guinea the year before, only a couple of months after my parents had left them there. After finishing her final year in high school, Mariam left to go live in Washington, DC with an old relative. Alfa, on the other hand, was sent back to Guinea to start his sophomore year. The only people traveling to our dad's new duty station was my parents, my younger sister and me.

Now that we were back in El Paso, Texas, my younger sister and I began school at Bliss Elementary School.

Nothing is more difficult than transitioning from the curriculum I learned in Argonner Elementary School to the curriculum I was now required to learn in Bliss Elementary School.

After being introduced to my new third-grade school teacher, I was directed to take my assigned seat in the classroom. I sat in my classroom desk feeling lost in the curriculum, not knowing what was going on. I had to rapidly adapt to my new school's course material all over again.

My teacher pulls a projector out in front of the classroom and hooks the projector's plug into the outlet. After turning on the projector, she takes a transparency projection sheet and places it on the light. I pull out my brand new notebook and a pencil from my backpack and get in position to begin taking notes. While the teacher uses a dry erase marker to write on the projection paper, I begin following along with her in writing my notes.

I try to focus on what I must learn to take the upcoming Texas Assessment of Knowledge and Skills (TAKS) test. The TAKS test would determine my entry into the fourth-grade and although I recently moved from Germany, the teachers are still expecting me to pass this test. It's outrageous how my performance on a state exam would determine whether I could move forward to the next grade level.

Not only am I overwhelmed with the fact that I must take the TAKS test, but I'm also beginning my first couple days of school alone.

"I need to stop feeling shy and speak to my classmates," I think to myself.

Most students who previously attended Bliss Elementary School in 1999 had already moved away because their parents were now stationed on various military posts around the world. Now, it's the early months of 2004 and this is the moment where I'd have to meet new friends all over again. I'm a shy person, but life as a military child forced me to become more social.

Not only did the teachers at Bliss Elementary School take the time to teach us the course material, but they also taught us ways of "tackling" the state TAKS test. The teachers took time out of our class curriculum to discuss methods they thought could help students pass the state exam.

"If you're not sure about which answer to choose on a multiple-choice question, always pick the letter 'C', the letter 'C' would most likely be the answer."

Then the teacher would give us replica bubble sheets, to practice bubbling in the answer choices on the state exam. Slowly, the other students and I would completely shade in the replica bubble sheet and the teacher would walk around the classroom, critiquing the ways in which we bubbled them in.

"Listen up everyone! If you don't fill in the bubbles correctly, you'll get the answer wrong on the test. You cannot draw X's or scribble into the bubble sheet. You'll need to fill in the circle completely."

The teacher would then walk over to the chalkboard and demonstrate the correct method to shade in the bubble answers. Not only was I nervous about how to choose the correct answer on the state exam, but now I was also worried about if I'd shade in the bubbles correctly to receive my points.

I didn't know if choosing the letter C on a multiple-choice question was the best answer choice, but I also knew that I didn't want to fail the third grade. Whenever I had doubts about a multiple choice question, guess what letter choice I was choosing?

The *No Child Left Behind Act of 2001 (NCLB)* by President George W. Bush was signed into law on January 8, 2002. The United States was trying to find a solution to the failing education system since the Ronald Reagan Administration after the publication of *A Nation at Risk: The Imperative for Educational Reform* in 1983. From that point forward, the public school education in the United States was a central topic of debate. The NCLB Act would mandate local governments to provide assessments to students from grades 3rd to 8th and at least once in grades 10th through 12th. School districts operating under the local governments would have to make the assessment scores of their students public for everyone to view. Schools who refused to follow the mandate might have their funds eliminated from the federal government. Since each individual state was responsible for their K-12 testing, the federal government will only provide financial support by giving out grants as authorized by the *Elementary and Secondary Education Act (ESEA)*.[33] [34]

The assessments being provided to students would be timed, unless the student needed special accommodations for a disability. Schools that fail to meet the state assessment achievement goals after five consecutive years could be restructured by the federal government or all the school's staff could be replaced.

My dad decided that he no longer wanted to live on Fort Bliss and he began making plans to build his first house. My parents found an apartment complex off Fort Bliss that we'd temporarily stay in until our house was

---

33 Haretos, Chrisanti. "The No Child Left Behind Act of 2001: Is the Definition of 'Adequate Yearly Progress' Adequate?"

Harvard Kennedy School Review, vol. 6, Jan. 2005, pp. 29–46. EBSCOhost,

search.ebscohost.com/login.aspx?direct=true&db=a9h&AN=19737510&site=ehost-live. Accessed 3 October 2019.

34 "No Child Left Behind [Documentary Film]." YouTube, uploaded by Boondoggle, 7 April 2011,

https://www.youtube.com/watch?v=yiGN7kVyeaM.

done being built. After building our new house, I'd have to transfer my school documents to the nearby school belonging to that neighborhood's district. I tried to forget that moving into the new neighborhood would become another educational challenge; for now, I'd have to focus on Bliss Elementary School's adequate yearly progress (AYP).

I followed my parents a few times to discuss the interior and exterior design of our first house. I made sure to be there whenever they selected items for our new home. My parents carefully selected countertops, carpeting, doors, landscaping, etc. for our home. Before our house was completely done being built, my family and I routinely drove past the construction to see how much progress our house had undergone.

In the meantime, my parents were still working hard to provide my siblings and me a better life. Every day after school, my younger sister and I went to the YS (Youth Services) on Fort Bliss. The YS is an after-school center where older military children went to engage in numerous activities until their parents came to pick them up. Depending on how old a child was, they could travel to the YS on their own.

My favorite area in the YS to play in was the arcade room. If I had enough quarters to spare, I'd play the various arcade games such as car racing, Pac Man, etc. After running out of money I'd go outside and play in the playground area.

I run outside to join in on the activities that the YS staff members have set up for us. Today, the staff members are bringing out multi-colored parachutes for us to play with. All the children are holding onto different sections of the parachute while they're spreading it out. The YS staff member begins counting aloud to the number twenty before everyone collectively raises the parachute up into the air and then we quickly run into the parachute to sit down on the inside edges of the parachute. While everyone is sitting on the inside, until the parachute looks like it's about to deflate. The top of the parachute has a hole in the middle where the air is escaping. The parachute topples down and everyone rushes to get out of the parachute.

"Everyone, get out the parachute, but continue holding onto its ends. Now, let's begin shaking the parachute. Shake it fast! Faster! C'mon now, y'all can do better than that. Move your arms quickly!"

All of us shake the parachute as fast as we can until the material begins moving in every direction. We're all standing in a circle around the parachute and I can see the children standing across from me smiling. While we continue shaking, one of the staff members releases several multicolored balls into the middle of the parachute. Some of the balls begin popping up into the sky and landing right back into the parachute. Other balls pop up into the sky and completely bounce off. We continue shaking the parachute as fast as we can until the YS staff members indicate to us to stop. Everyone helps the staff members gather all the multicolored balls and fold the parachute before continuing to play other games in the playground.

I took the YS talent show seriously. All the children attending the Fort Bliss YS were preparing to showcase their talents in the gymnasium.

I joined a dance group in the YS who were learning the choreography to Usher's song "Yeah!"

Step-by-step, I, along with a few other children, tried to master the choreography weeks ahead of the talent show. After getting home, I'd continue practicing the steps to the choreography.

After about a month, all the military children gathered in the YS gymnasium to display our talents. Unfortunately, my group wasn't prepared to perform the choreography to Usher's song, so we didn't go.

"Children, get ready, we're going to the mosque for the Quranic studies class!" my parents scream aloud in our newly built house.

My parents rush around the house trying to get me and my younger sister ready for the Quranic studies class at the Islamic Center of El Paso.

While sitting in the passenger seat of my dad's red Nissan 240SX, I watch my dad constantly shift gears as he drives to the mosque.

The Islamic Center of El Paso is still located downtown in the same two-story house from years before, on the side of a steep hill. My dad continues moving gears on his stick-shift until he finally gets up the hill and parks his car.

As we walk to the mosque, I feel like I'm nearly falling down the hill. I press my body forward and take firm steps while walking up towards the mosque. The air feels dry and the sun's heat is beaming down on me. I'm thirsty, but I'll have to wait until I make it inside.

The Islamic Center of El Paso is collecting donations to build a more authentic looking mosque on the westside of El Paso, Texas. Since the current mosque was in a two-story house, only people familiar with our Muslim community was aware that the house was actually a mosque.

In my Quranic studies class, I sit alongside other Muslim students who are learning the translated meanings of the Quran. After going over the translations, my teacher goes on to discuss various deeds of Muslim prophets. We memorize letters in the Arabic alphabet. Then, afterwards, the Islamic studies teacher assigns us homework which is due by next weekend.

Dhuhr prayer signals the end of our Islamic weekend class.

The Imam begins calling the Adhan through the microphone and all the children promptly pack away their homework, make wudhu, and run into the prayer area in preparation for Dhuhr prayer. Some of the girls begin helping each other fix their hijabs. Some boys begin rolling their pants above their ankles. Other children are reciting the Quran as we wait for the Imam to begin Dhuhr prayer.

Although I am eight years old, I feel complete after praying. Prayer felt like the antidote to whatever was missing from my life. If I was having a hard time, I knew that I could turn to Allah and wish for times to get better. I prayed just as I prayed long before, when my family prayed after enjoying our family nights. Prayer is good for the soul and it has always been my way of connecting with Allah. To me, prayer held more importance than playing video games or watching television.

After Dhuhr prayer, I walk outside and wait for one of my parents to pick me up. The teachers hand all the students chips and Capri Suns. After eating our snacks, we run outside tirelessly, only stopping occasionally to gasp for air. My hijab is getting messy and so are the hijabs of the other girls running around. Occasionally, we stop running around to fix our scarves. As time goes by, parents gradually come to pick up the children they left for the Islamic weekend class, the area begins falling silent, and then my dad comes to pick up my younger sister and me from the mosque.

Our newly built home had a three-door garage, three living rooms, two dining rooms, four bedrooms, and a huge backyard. My family and I were excited to finally own our own space, especially in comparison to what we were used to having in military housing. My family and I went around our new neighborhood introducing ourselves. Some people living in our neighborhood were military members, police officers, medical workers, or corporate workers. We exchanged contact information and if the neighbors had kids, they'd let me know that we could play outside within a visible distance from the home.

My family and I purchased new furniture for our new home.

One of our living rooms was purely for decoration. My parents said that no one was allowed to sit in that living room except if they were as important as the President of the United States of America. Our second living room was a common living room. That was where most people sat upon entering our house. Our third living room was the entertainment room. The entertainment living room was located on the second floor. This room had surround sound effects, a big screen TV, and we normally watched movies together in this room.

After decorating the house, my family had more time to spend with each other. Within a couple of months of us settling into our new home, we found out that my dad had to go back to Iraq for deployment.

Before my dad leaves for Iraq, my parents sign me up to attend fourth grade at Barron Elementary School. Thankfully, by that time I had passed my third grade TAKS assessment at Bliss Elementary School, which allowed me to move forward to the fourth grade.

Passing my third grade TAKS exam was a major accomplishment considering that I attended two different elementary schools for my third grade. Such are the difficulties of being a military brat transitioning schools within a single school year, but you're still expected to follow laws mandated by the federal government.

Third grade also happened to be the grade that the NCLB Act went into effect, so I did fairly good for my third grade assessment.

While driving to Barron Elementary school, I look outside the car window and admire the various landscaping in my new neighborhood. Some landscaping consisted of simple grass lawns and others were made of rock schemes. Fencing designs varied from each home with some consisting of concrete wall, brick, and wired or wooden fencing.

El Paso, Texas is a desert climate, so you can tell which neighbors took care of their grass. While driving toward the elementary school, I'd notice one front lawn with healthy, green looking grass and another lawn with yellow-dry patchy looking grass.

My parents turn off of our neighborhood street and head down the main road towards my elementary school. The land consists of almost nothing other than golden-beige sand. Different plants like marigold and golden barrel cacti are scattered throughout the landscape. My family and I finally arrive at Barron Elementary School, park our car, and head towards the school's main office to begin the school registration process.

After registering me for school, we receive information about which items my younger sister and I should bring for our first day of school. As usual, I'm told which vaccinations I had to get before starting school.

A couple of weeks later, my mom and I are sitting in the waiting area of the doctor's office so that I can get my required vaccinations to begin the school year.

Having Tricare medical insurance made my doctor visits affordable and possible. Tricare is the military's medical coverage for active duty, retiree, and dependent family members. Barely being denied medical coverage meant that I could always get the required medical check-ups I needed while also visiting the doctor for preventive care.

"Ms. Ball, are you ready for your shots today?" the doctor asks me while leading me into the exam room.

"Yes, I'm ready for my shots," I nervously tell my doctor without knowing for sure if I am, indeed, ready.

"Alrighty then, if you say so," the doctor replies.

I realize I really wasn't ready, but I take a deep breath and flinch a couple of times before finally letting my doctor give me my shot.

During this point of my childhood, I required eyeglasses to see. I began wearing glasses while I was six years old, but I didn't always put them on. Now, I was a little bit more dependent on eyeglasses for vision, so we made an appointment to go see an optometrist and get prescription eyeglasses.

On my first day of fourth grade, my parents walk my younger sister and me to wait at the school bus stop. After getting to the bus stop, we join a crowd of other parents and children waiting for the school bus to arrive.

When we see the yellow bus turn onto the street, everyone exchanges their goodbyes, and the students board the bus.

After arriving at Barron Elementary School, all of us get off the bus and head towards the school. I try to find out where my class is located and wait for my teacher so that she can begin teaching us the curriculum for the day.

For me, I'm simply happy that I made it into the fourth grade. With hard work and dedication, I was capable of passing the third grade Texas TAKS test.

Shortly after, the school administrators get on the loudspeaker and announce the school program for the morning. When the school administrators near the end of their announcement, everyone is told to get up from their chairs and stand in position for the American Pledge of Allegiance and the Star Spangled Banner. The entire class stands up, faces the American flag, and places our right hands over our hearts.

We begin our fourth grade class curriculum. I feel a sense of loneliness. I feel tired of always starting over, but that's part of being a military child; that's part of my family's constant moving process. Now that I'm in a new school, I'll have to start over in building a relationship with everyone. Sometimes, even having a teacher who watched me grow academically could've been nice because they could evaluate my progress in school, but as a military child, teachers can only determine that I was progressing after taking the required state test. Going to Barron Elementary required me starting from scratch again. The curriculum that I needed to learn at Barron Elementary School was necessary for the fourth grade level TAKS state exam.

Textbook producers like Pearson Education began capitalizing off the education of students because they began signing contracts with states to develop our state exams. When we have textbook producers like Pearson, McGraw Hill, or Cengage developing contracts with state public systems, not only did we read their learning material, but we'd have to take tests developed by them. The public school teachers or school administrators that we interacted with daily had no clue what material textbook producers would place on their exam and teachers could only guess that it'd be similar to the material we read regularly in their textbooks. NCLB Act served as an advantage to these corporations while teachers worried about their merit pay and students worried about making it to the next grade level. [35]

A few months into attending Barron Elementary School, my dad was given orders to leave home for several months and deploy.

As he was leaving for Iraq, my dad wore his United States Army uniform. My dad's uniform was camouflaged in the colors brown, beige and tan. The luggage in which he packed his belongings matched his uniform.

My dad's uniform name tag read, "Bani Ball". Military personnel wear their last names on their military uniform. While on duty, everyone calls their peers by last name. "Bani" literally means the "children of" in Arabic. "Ball" is my dad's family last name. "Bani Ball" literally means, the children of the Ball family. My dad adopted the "Bani" prefix after converting to Islam in 1993 and filing for a name change.

My dad's backpack is humongous and appears heavy in weight, but he puts it on anyway. After putting on his backpack, everyone walks outside to

---

35 "Texas-Sized Nepotism." Utne Reader: The Best of the Alternative Press, no. 169, Jan. 2012, p. 21. EBSCOhost,

search.ebscohost.com/login.aspx?direct=true&db=a9h&AN=69979040&site=ehost-live. Accessed 8 October 2019.

the van while holding my dad's military items, so that we can take him to the airport.

It would be nearly a year before my family got the chance of seeing my dad again. Commonly, my dad left with a group of other U.S. Army soldiers at the airport. Before my dad leaves us for several months to go to Iraq, we say our last goodbyes.

There's a lot of foot traffic in the airport. Everyone is rushing around trying to get their ticketing information and check in their luggage.

My dad says his goodbyes to everyone else before approaching me last. He kneels down, gives me a huge hug, and looks me in the eyes before saying, "Julde, I love you and I'm going to miss you."

"I love you and I'm going to miss you, too," I respond to my dad.

My dad slowly walks off towards a group of his colleagues, leaving our family behind. They greet each other with smiles and they're happy, as if they're not about to head to war. I couldn't understand why they were happy; perhaps it was the fact that they felt united with each other, or had grown a bond with each other. But, I'm scared. I wasn't going to a war but I'm sad because I won't get to see my dad for a long time. In this moment, I realize that my life only meant constantly leaving people I cared about the most.

My dad continues walking alongside the group of Army soldiers until they enter the airport terminal. I keep looking back at them until I could only see them from a distance. I begin to cry while watching them leave.

Chapter Ten: Telephone Line

For the next year, my siblings and I are home with my mom, Khadijah Barrie, while my dad is gone for Iraq. I continue attending Barron Elementary School, but after school I begin selling items to people around my neighborhood. Of course, my parents had enough money to take care of me, but I enjoyed the independence of earning my own money. Without having financial independence, I always have to ask my parents for money and wait until their obligations are met before they could give me money. On the other hand, when I made my own money, it was there whenever I needed it.

I used to stay home, mix Kool-Aid powder with water, and then freeze the Kool-Aid juice inside disposable shot glasses. The next day, I'd go out into my neighborhood and sell frozen Kool-Aid popsicles to children playing around my neighborhood. I engaged in the common childhood entrepreneur ideas because I was obviously too young to get a regular paying job.

Whenever it seemed that the children were getting tired of purchasing my frozen Kool-Aid popsicles, I'd go out to the neighborhood and do car washes for my neighbors. I especially knocked on the doors of my neighbors whose cars looked dirty.

"*Knock, knock* ——Do you need a car wash?" I'd ask.

If the person replied, "yes," I'd grab my bucket, soap, sponge, towel, and car vacuum to get ready and clean their car.

I didn't charge a fixed rate for washing my neighbors' car. I let my neighbors give me any money that they could afford for my car washes. Some people would hand me a five, ten, or twenty dollar bill for washing their car. Sometimes I went with other children in my neighborhood to do car washes. In a large group, we'd all make between 120 to 200 dollars a day by washing people's cars. Depending on how many of us washed cars together, we'd split the money amongst ourselves evenly.

As a child, I always embraced working hard. Everyone in my neighborhood was welcoming, we knew each other, and nearly all the children in my neighborhood attended the same school as me, Barron Elementary School.

One day my family and I were driving around El Paso because my mom had to make a few stops and run some errands. While looking outside the window from my passenger seat, I read out the words "Can Bank" on a machine.

"What does can bank mean?" I ask.

"A can bank is a machine where you recycle cans and earn money."

"So, you recycle cans and get money back for recycling them?" I confirm.

"Yes."

That became the beginnings of me not only selling frozen Kool-Aid and doing car washes around my neighborhood, but also recycling cans.

I was regulating the recyclables in my house. I told everyone in my household that we now had a designated area for our recyclables and everyone should separate the items accordingly. My mom, Khadijah Barrie, went to the Post Exchange with me to purchase another trash bin which would be used specifically for the recyclables. We placed the recyclable bin next to the garbage bin, in the kitchen. My mom promised me that whenever the bin got full, she would drive me to the can bank so that we could recycle my cans.

I needed a container where I was going to hold my money. I found an empty Royal Danish cookie container and began placing all the money I made from selling frozen Kool-Aid, doing car washes, and recycling cans, inside of it.

My mom worked at the Fort Bliss commissary, so other Muslim military spouses frequently watched my younger sister and me on the weekends. The majority of the Muslim military spouses were women and their husbands were also away fighting the war in Iraq. Sometimes while my mom was at work, they'd take me and their children to the nearest Wal-Mart and go shopping.

"Okay kids, after we're done shopping at Wal-Mart, we're going to stop at McDonald's, eat our meals, then we'll go to the newly built mosque on the Westside," one of the mothers tells us.

As usual, these mothers aren't blood related to me, yet I considered them my aunts. It's weird because as military children, we often formed family members through the military families we met in life. Especially since these family members were our caretakers whenever our parents were working or in the absence of our relatives.

We get in the car, go shopping at Wal-Mart and my military aunts decide to purchase me a few items.

"Hey, Julde, how do you like this shirt? Do you want me to buy it?" I'm unsure if I should accept their offer, but I say yes anyway.

After purchasing all our items at the Wal-Mart checkout counter, we head towards the McDonald's food court inside Wal-Mart and begin purchasing our meals. My military aunts ask me which meal I'd like to eat and I order a McChicken sandwich, french fries, and Sprite. The aunts give me my meal and we sit down to enjoy our food.

After eating, we head to the other side of town to visit the new mosque. Following months of collecting donations, the Muslim community in El Paso had finally built a nicer, traditional-style mosque on the Westside of El Paso. The white two-story house would no longer be used for mosque services and the Muslim community displayed excitement for our new mosque.

My military aunts lend me one of the additional hijabs they have stored in the trunk of their car. After quietly entering the mosque, we sit in the women's prayer area and listen to the Islamic lectures. When the mosque service finishes, everyone gathers in the dining area to eat together. I'm still feeling full from the meal I ate at McDonalds, but the Muslim sisters are insisting that I eat the meals they cooked for us. After eating, we head back to one of my aunt's home, so that my mom can pick me and my younger sister up after work.

Other days, my mom takes me to her Nigerian or Ghanaian friends to watch my younger sister and me on the weekends. My mom especially loved being around the company of her Nigerian or Ghanaian friends because it reminded her of being back home in Sierra Leone. Although my mom's friends aren't from the same countries as her, they still enjoyed each other's company. The majority of my mom's African friends were Christian, but they were also military spouses and they too were my military aunts. They took me places to hang out while my mom had to work. Although the cultures and customs in each of their countries were different, they found those differences amongst each other interesting.

My mom gets ready to go over her friend's house to watch African movies and talk about their experiences growing up in their countries. While sitting beside my mom, I hear my mom speaking English creole to her friends. The English creole in Nigeria and Ghana sounds different from Sierra Leonean English creole; however, they appear to understand each other.

While my family and I are living in El Paso, Texas, my older sister, Mariam, gets married and moves into an apartment complex with her husband fifteen minutes away from our home. Occasionally, Mariam comes over our house to spend time with the family. Alfa is still living in Africa since the last time our family left him there, but my parents are planning on purchasing his plane ticket to meet us here.

My parents finally commit to purchasing Alfa's airplane ticket so that he can join us. Alfa arrives in Texas after staying in Guinea for over a year. He explains his experiences in Guinea and we catch up with each other because it's been a long time since we spent time with him. Now that Alfa is back in Texas, he needs to get registered for high school. My mom schedules a day to register Alfa to a high school near our neighborhood.

After arriving at the high school, the administrators want to place Alfa two grade levels behind because he attended high school in Africa. My mom insists that Alfa take the school exam to assess that he shouldn't be pushed back. My mom couldn't get the school to give Alfa the assessment, so she arranged to meet with the Texas State Board of Education (SBOE). Finally, Alfa is granted permission to take the state exam and he passes with flying colors. The school administrators are amazed that a student coming from Guinea, an African country, was capable of passing the exam at a higher margin than most students in El Paso.

"When Alfa was in Guinea, he attended an American school," my mom continues explaining.

Alfa's high score on the exam made it possible for him to begin his intended grade level when starting high school.

My family often waited for my dad's phone call home, so that he could let us know how he was doing. Sometimes, if I was at school, my mom would get the chance to speak with my dad. Then later, she'd relay any words that my dad had for me. Due to our time differences and my attendance in school, it was common for me to miss my dad's phone call.

I wake up one school morning and begin searching for an outfit that I can wear for school. While searching for an outfit, I couldn't help but wear my African outfit that a tailor customized for me while visiting Conakry, Guinea. I missed Guinea and wearing my African outfit reflected the Fulani part of my identity. After putting on my outfit, I walk downstairs from my bedroom and my mom asks me, "Julde, are you wearing that African outfit to school?"

"Yes," I reply.

"Why?" my mom asks.

"Because I like this outfit," I say.

I finish whatever I'm doing at home before beginning my walk to the school bus stop. The other children standing at the bus stop are surprised to see me wearing my African outfit.

"I really love your outfit, Julde. Where did you get it?" they ask me.

"I got this outfit in Africa," I respond.

"In Africa? You've been to Africa before?"

"Yes, I've been to Africa before. My mom is an African."

"Oh, I didn't know that your mother is an African," they exclaim. "I thought your mom was Jamaican."

"No, my mom is an African," I confirm.

I go about the rest of the day receiving multiple compliments from my classmates and people continually ask me where I got my outfit from. I tell everyone who asks that I got it in Africa. My classmates are amazed to hear that I've ever been there.

Then one of my classmates makes one of the most offensive remarks.

"How is your mom African and you're light-skinned? Are you light-skinned because your dad is light-skinned? Because Africans are *really* black."

"No, there are light-skinned Africans. There are different shades of black people in Africa," I reply.

"So, do Africans sleep in trees?"

"No, they sleep in houses."

Oftentimes, people think that Africa is an uncivilized continent, but that's because they are unaware of the advancements in Africa. Yes, there's corruption taking place in Africa and it's also true that Africa is being drained of all its natural resources, but it's also horrible that there is a colorism against African people. People think that Africans who are of a lighter complexion are either mixed with another race or they're bleaching their skin, and this isn't always true.

"Africans sleep in houses, they own cars, they wear clothes," I respond to my classmate. "Africans also come in different skin tones. My mom is light-skinned and she's an African."

"Oh, she must be mixed then," my classmate says.

I do feel sad about the exchange, but I decide to disregard the incident and go about enjoying the rest of my day with my friends.

On another school day, the teacher sets up various activities in our classrooms. My favorite activity required everyone to sit beside each other and wait for the teacher to whisper a message into the ear of one student. Each student was told to repeat that message to their neighbor. The teacher would ask all of the students to quiet down before beginning the game.

The classroom quiets down and the teacher whispers in the ear of the first student. Each student whispers the message to the person sitting to his or her left until the message reaches the last student. After reaching the last student, the teacher asks that student to shout out the message they received from their neighbor. Sure enough, when the student shouts the message out, it's different from the one the teacher began with.

Everyone in the classroom is confused. We look at the teacher in disbelief and say, "That's the message that you told us!" Some students disagree that this is the message she began with, while other students agree that we received the teacher's message.

The teacher says, "No, that's not my initial message, I began with another message, but someone down the line changed the meaning."

At the end of the game, we found out the specific student who changed the message. The teacher explains that she purposely had us doing this activity because she wants to show us how a message can be distorted.

"This is how rumors begin. I told the student this message and by the time the message reached the last student, the message changed."

The student who changed the message looked embarrassed, but the teacher told him not to worry; she was demonstrating why preserving a message is important.

Chapter Eleven: Dad is Coming Home

After nearly a year of him being away to Iraq, my dad is finally coming back home. The morning of my dad's arrival, my mom assigns everyone in the house chores to complete before my dad's arrival. Mariam no longer lives with our family, but she comes over to our house to help clean for my dad's arrival, anyway.

Some of us are responsible for cleaning the first floor of the house, others are responsible for cleaning the second floor.

On the first floor, there are a lot of areas to be mopped and I can hear my family members wringing water into a bucket. The entire second floor is carpeted, so you can hear someone running a vacuum. We set up signs and balloons all over the house for my dad's homecoming.

My mom cooks her famous meals for my dad's arrival. As usual, we're having jollof rice, chicken and salad, but my mom cooks additional dishes as well. Everyone helps to set up the dining room table.

There are multiple dishes of food set up around the dining room table, the house is clean, and the air smells like citrus. After cleaning the house, everyone avoids walking around the house because we do not want a single crumb falling on the floor before my dad gets here. Our routine for my dad's arrival home never really changed. It's always been the same routine for as long as I can remember.

Later that night, my family and I attend the convention where my dad and the other servicemembers would arrive back home to their families. The families sit in the stadium while waiting for the homecoming ceremony to begin.

At the start of the ceremony, one of the soldiers comes out to give a speech to all the military families. The soldier begins by greeting all the families, and then he says that despite our excitement, he needed to speak with us.

He addresses the fact that although we're all excited, we should be aware that the soldiers have just returned from a combat zone. There's a chance that the soldiers no longer look the same way they used to due to amputations or other accidents which could have occurred in these combat zones. Sometimes the military members do not tell their family members about their amputations or other accidents because they don't want to add that agony to their family's lives.

I begin breaking down in tears immediately after hearing soldiers can actually keep their amputations a secret. My family members begin asking me why I'm breaking down in tears and I tell them that I hope dad doesn't look different.

Now I'm anxious to see my dad. It never crossed my mind that my dad could have secret amputations. The soldier finishes making his announcement, he walks away and the background begins moving.

As the background moves, we see the soldiers standing in rows, the lights shining brightly onto them, and they begin smiling when they see all of us. Everyone is excited to finally see their families again.

The soldiers are standing in formation, in nice, even, straight lines. I start walking down the bleachers to find my dad. Everyone is wearing the same uniform, so it's difficult for me to locate where my dad is. I keep searching for my dad within the formation. Other family members are also searching through the formation. Meanwhile, the formation slowly breaks apart as families are reunited. Husbands and wives rush towards each other for hugs and kisses. Mothers and fathers embrace children they haven't seen in ages. The more the formation breaks apart, the harder it is for me to find my dad. The lighting should've been good enough for me to see him, but I'm just a little girl roaming around in a crowd of tall adults.

My dad spots me right at the moment when I think I've found him. We thought we saw each other so my dad does a double-take and glances at me once more before approaching to greet me. After all these months we finally get to see each other again. I immediately give my dad a huge hug.

It was late at night; all the families begin walking out of the stadium so that they could head home. Everyone is happy to finally reunite with their family. I look up towards the night sky and the stars sparkle, each star taking their own turns to shine, glowing their own colors. The stars make the dark night sky beautiful, with each glowing with radiance.

"How much longer would I live a life of constant moving, starting all over, and trying to adapt to my new surroundings? How much longer?" I think to myself.

My family and I get inside our green van and drive back home.

My dad enters the house to see the surprise my family and I made for him. For the next several months, my dad is home from Iraq and my parents begin planning weekends for us to all hang out.

Chuck E Cheese's was a family favorite, especially since my younger sister and I play all the arcade games while my family sits at a table eating pizza and chicken wings.

Before entering Chuck E Cheese's, everyone gets their hands stamped by one of the workers, and then we stand in line to purchase a Chuck E Cheese's family package deal. My parents evenly split the Chuck E Cheese's coins between me and my younger sister.

"Let's see who is going to get the most tickets," I tell my sister before running to play in the arcade.

I already knew which of the prizes I wanted before finishing my coin credit, so I make it my goal to earn a certain number of tickets. In between playing arcade games at Chuck E Cheese's, I run back to my parents' table to see if there is food at the table. The savory scent of freshly baked pizza brushes past my nose as I pass the tables of other families in Chuck E. Cheese's. It's getting difficult for me to get back to my parents' table because there is a lot of congestion in Chuck E Cheese's. I try to dodge between people and excuse myself through the crowd.

I make it to my family's table where I see pizza. I take a slice and down it fast so that I can get back to playing games in Chuck E Cheese's. I sip some soda to rinse down the pizza because I'm nearly parched from thirst. When my younger sister and I are done playing games, my parents walk us over to the prize counter.

This is the moment when I'd find out if I earned enough tickets to get the prize I wanted. I rarely got the prizes I wanted from Chuck E Cheese's because they required getting thousands of tickets, which I could never accomplish.

Since my dad was back from deployment, he buys himself a motorcycle. The motorcycle, a Suzuki GSX-R1000R, is customized to read "Bee" and there's a bumble bee sticker placed on the motorcycle. My dad's nickname is "Bee" because his name is Bilal Bani Ball. The colors on the Suzuki are blue, white, and black. My dad finds a motorcycle club and so starts the beginnings of my dad's motorcycle riding hobby. My dad used to join other bike riders and ride motorcycles all around El Paso, Texas during his free time.

My dad likes explaining all the trips he takes on the highway with his bike. On occasion, my dad offers to take my younger sister and me on motorcycle rides. My younger sister enjoys riding my dad's motorcycle more than I do. The part that I dislike the most about riding is when my dad makes any turns into streets. Every turn that my dad makes tilts the bike to one side, and I feel like my knee is nearly touching the street. Although I never fall off the motorcycle when my dad makes turns, I always decline from riding on the back of his motorcycle.

My mom, Khadijah, is hardworking. During this time, my mom is working hard to improve the living conditions of her family back home in Guinea, West Africa. My mom happens to be the only child my grandparents have in the United States. My mom did whatever she could to relieve her family from poverty.

My mom often reflects on the life she lived as a young girl in Sierra Leone, especially since her home is no longer the same after rebels destroyed the land for diamonds.

"I heard that my neighborhood is not the same," my mom tells me. "The rebels broke some of the houses down in my neighborhood down to gather the diamonds. They sold the diamonds so that they could afford more weapons."

Most of the land that was destroyed in my mom's neighborhood, Kono, was the land that her dad purchased through hard labor. My mom and her siblings were supposed to inherit that land but now, the family is too scared to return to that area of Sierra Leone. It brings back flashbacks of all the horrors they witnessed while trying to flee the civil war.

Chapter Twelve: Bye, Bye Lone Star State

I was getting ready to graduate my fifth-grade school year at Barron Elementary School. Right around that time, my family found out that my dad needed to relocate to a new duty station. He was given the choice to decide between going to Hawaii or Alaska. After some consideration, my dad decided that he wanted to go to Hawaii. My dad had just graduated from Warrant Officer School in Georgia and he would move to Hawaii as a CWO1 in the United States Army.

My family began planning to leave El Paso, Texas and my parents didn't want to rent our house. Most of the time, people who rented their homes in our neighborhood had tenants who didn't take care of their property. My parents feared that if we rented our home to a tenant, they too wouldn't keep up with our property.

When we were ready, we placed a "For Sale" sign in front of our home. The process for moving was beginning all over again, but this time, my parents also had to worry about selling our property.

My family and I began packing up our belongings into boxes so that we could begin shipping our items to Hawaii. After one week of packing, my parents called the moving company to pick up our household goods. The moving company arrived with huge wooden crates.

When everything was done being packed into the crates, my family began cleaning our home. As usual, we made sure to clean the house thoroughly. In the meantime, my parents found an apartment complex we could stay in temporarily. We were hoping to sell the house immediately and didn't want to occupy the house while we were in the process of showcasing it.

I always wondered about the glowing bright star that was located on the Franklin Mountains. What did the star represent and why did this huge star sit atop the mountains overlooking El Paso? So, one day, I ask my Dad, "Why is that star on the mountain?"

My dad tells me, "That bright star represents Texas because Texas is called the Lone Star State."

For the first time, I learn that the bright star which stood above El Paso is called the Lone Star, therefore representing Texas as the Lone Star state.

It doesn't take long for my parents to find an apartment complex for us to stay in, but now we didn't have furniture for our apartment. My family and I head to the nearest Wal-Mart to purchase three air mattresses to sleep on until it's time for us to leave for Hawaii. After buying the air mattresses, we return to the apartment and begin setting them up.

"Julde, where's the pump for the air mattresses!"

"The pump is over here!"

My mom begins pumping air into the air mattresses. When they're full, we spread them with sheets and blankets.

"Good night, children! Go to sleep so that you can go to school tomorrow morning."

I get on my air mattress and fall asleep. Gradually, my air mattress begins deflating ——*PSSSHHH!* In the middle of the night, I wake up lying on the ground, with nothing between me and the floor but the deflated air mattress.

The days of sleeping on air mattresses became the worst days of my life.

"Mom, Dad, can you please buy me a new air mattress?"

"If you weren't hopping on the air mattress the other night, it wouldn't have popped," my parents reply.

"But, I barely got on the air mattress and it already began deflating!" I exclaim.

My family and I try everything we can to seal the hole in the air mattress, but we never find where the air was escaping from.

It's only a few more weeks before the end of my fifth-grade school year at Barron Elementary School. My parents begin collecting all the necessary documents they'll need for my school in Hawaii. My older brother, Alfa, is graduating from his high school in El Paso.

Before leaving for Hawaii, my parents wanted to take my older brother, Alfa, to the University of Houston, where he would begin college.

My parents decide that it's best for us to take a road trip from El Paso, Texas to Houston, Texas, to help my older brother move his belongings to the University of Houston. We're going to pack all the cars with his belongings instead of getting a moving company. The road trip also gives my parents the opportunity to see the school that my older brother was going to attend.

The trip from El Paso to Houston is excruciatingly long. It takes us about two days, and that's just travelling within one state. My family stops along the way to stay in a hotel before finally reaching Houston.

In the meantime, I'm so excited about moving to Hawaii. I always heard about Hawaii, but I'd never been there. This was my chance to finally see Hawaii as I had always seen it on commercials. After getting to Houston, my dad booked a hotel room at the Marriott hotel.

The next day, my family and I visited the University of Houston campus. After about a week of being in Houston, we leave our brother Alfa behind while we take our flight to Hawaii. Mariam stayed behind in El Paso, Texas with her husband and baby.

Chapter Thirteen: Home Sweet Hawaii

My family and I finally land in Oahu, Hawaii. The weather is brilliant, and the people are friendly. I always thought of Hawaii as being one island, but now I learn that Hawaii consists of several islands.

The first thing that my family does after arriving in Hawaii is rent a car. My parents had left their green van with my older sister in El Paso and the red Nissan with my older brother in Houston. After getting the car rental, we drive towards our new home on Schofield Barracks, an Army post in Wahiawa.

We'll have to wait a month before receiving our furniture in Hawaii because it's still being shipped. In the meantime, my family and I utilize the air mattresses we bought from the Wal-Mart in El Paso, Texas until all our furniture arrives.

Our housing unit on Schofield Barracks is a two-story duplex. The first floor of the duplex has a kitchen, dining room area, living room, laundry room, guest bathroom, and master bedroom. The second floor of the duplex has three bedrooms, an office and a full bathroom. There's a driveway in front of the house which leads to a one-door garage, and at the back of the house we have our own fenced backyard.

The moving company finally brings our furniture and helps us open the crates to begin unloading all our belongings into the house. I dislike the entire moving process, especially since it's been taking my family weeks to unpack all our belongings into our new home.

Although we've just moved to Hawaii, my dad already has to work. My mom is in the process of transferring her paperwork to the Pearl Harbor Commissary so that she can also begin working.

My parents gradually unpack their belongings every day after getting off from work. While my parents are at work, my younger sister and I do our part by unpacking all our belongings into our bedrooms. When there's nothing left to unpack, I go outside to meet other children living in my neighborhood. It's the summer of 2006, and I start learning about my new neighbors on Schofield Barracks.

Although I used to have to be home by dusk, after moving to Hawaii, my curfew changed. The children and I play various games in the neighborhood, even past midnight.

In preparation for the upcoming school year, my parents enroll me to attend Wheeler Middle School, located on Wheeler Army Airfield. My younger sister will be attending Hale Kula Elementary School, located on Schofield Barracks.

Wheeler Middle School doesn't look like a traditional middle school building; it's more of a campus layout. The hallways of Wheeler Middle School are outside. There are gardens in certain areas of the school hallways. The gardens are watered weekly by school custodians. Sometimes, the rain does its natural job of watering the garden through the open parts of the school hallways.

Wheeler Middle School has two floors. The second floor of Wheeler Middle School has balconies surrounding each parcel of the garden from the first floor.

My parents sign me up to catch a school bus from Schofield Barracks to Wheeler Middle School every morning.

Every morning I wake up to the sunlight beaming through my window curtains. In front of my duplex home, there's a large tree and the birds perched on begin every morning by chirping in various melodies —— *Chirp, chirp, tweet, tweet-* and mesmerizing flows, taking turns calling the morning to the neighborhood.

I finish getting ready for school and walk towards the school bus stop. On my way there, the morning sun shines glamorously down onto the street, causing the trees to cast shadows on the sidewalk. I listen blissfully as the birds continue to sing in harmony.

I walk past the neighborhood playground and decide to take a shortcut towards the bus stop. While walking on the sidewalk leading towards the shortcut, I start hearing a constant buzzing sound. I search left and right to see where the sound is coming from. Then I look up.

"Oh, my, goodness," I say quietly.

There's a gigantic beehive hovering above my head. As the bees fly in every direction, I feel my blood run cold with fear. I freeze for a moment as I wonder what I should do next. Should I run? What if that agitates the bees even further? Should I walk instead to keep them calm?

After that morning, I deliberately start avoiding that shortcut to keep from being stung by bees.

Every day, after my school mates and I boarded the bus, the bus driver would turn on the local radio station for everyone to enjoy. Sometimes students would sing along to the songs for the duration of the bus ride. After getting to Wheeler Middle School, everyone would get off the bus and go to their classes.

The majority of the students attending Wheeler Middle School were dependents of military members. Every branch of the military maintained a presence in Hawaii. The Navy, Army, Air Force, and Marines all had their own bases and installations on the island, and even the National Guard, and Coast Guard service members had dependents who attended school here. I knew most of the students attending my school because they also lived on Schofield Barracks.

Like most schools, outside of the regular common core curriculums such as math, science, social studies, and English; the students and I had other class requirements like physical education, arts, sex education, and home economics. Our school day was divided into eight ordinary class periods.

I became familiar with a few other Muslim students at my school; however, we didn't hang out with each other. We all had our own group of friends while attending school; but, for Jummah, we would speak to each other. None of the Muslim students attending Wheeler Middle School were identifiably Muslims; you could only sometimes guess that we're Muslim because of our names. Most of the time the Muslima students didn't wear a hijab at school, so other students weren't aware that we were Muslim unless we told them.

Academically, I was an average student in Wheeler Middle School. Achieving average work had nothing to do with me trying my best either. I simply didn't push toward my highest potential. I was good at absorbing information in class, but I also enjoyed hanging outside after school with other children in my neighborhood. I met a few friends on Schofield Barracks who I enjoyed spending the whole day with, walking all over base.

Schofield Barracks is very big. Walking to another neighborhood within Schofield Barracks can range between ten to thirty minutes, depending on which neighborhood I'm visiting. Sometimes after getting late, I contact one of my parents to pick me up from my friend's neighborhood. If my parents couldn't pick me up, I'd let my friend's parents drive me home.

One morning, after continuously observing other students in my neighborhood crossing under the beehive, I ask them why they aren't afraid of walking under the tree. The students tell me that if bees don't feel threatened, they won't bother you. There's a chance of learning something new every day because once I start crossing under the beehive, to my surprise, the bees never come after me.

I had a few Muslim friends who lived on Schofield Barracks and sometimes I'd spent weekends over their house, hanging out. One of my Muslim friends was named Danisha. Sometimes my family let me sleep over Danisha's house. I believe both of Danisha's parents had converted to Islam. Her parents are African-Americans who grew up in the United States. Danisha's dad also served in the United States Army, just like my dad. Most of the time, we hung out in Danisha's neighborhood, a twenty minute walk from my neighborhood. Whenever I wanted to go over Danisha's house after school, I'd catch her school bus and get off at her bus stop. Not only did I have the opportunity of chatting with Danisha about Islam, but we also did other things like play video games, watch movies, or dance to music.

One day Danisha and I decide that we're going to join the Wheeler Middle School talent show. Danisha and I agree that it would be nice if we danced along to "Cater 2 U" by Destiny's Child. We begin choreographing steps to the dance in her house and sometimes, Danisha's mom helps both of us with some of the choreography.

After choreographing all the steps to our song, we apply for the Wheeler Middle School talent show auditions. Danisha and I dance our hearts out for the talent show auditions, but unfortunately we don't make it past the auditions.

One week later, Wheeler Middle School holds the Talent Show while I sit in the audience, feeling a little crushed that Danisha and I didn't make it at the auditions at the talent show.

Some weekends, the Muslim military members on Schofield Barracks would arrange a Halaqa to discuss for the week. Some of the discussions for the Halaqa were in relation to the prophets of Islam. The parents would discuss how the prophets lived, some questions about common practices in Islam and they discussed various matters in the Quran. When the Halaqa finished, everyone discussed other events occurring in the proceeding weeks.

Following the Halaqa, the parents would arrange a movie night for the children. Parents pop popcorn and hand out juice boxes to all the kids. While we watch the movie, parents sit in the back of the room, talking and eating some of the food families brought for the Halaqa. When the movie finishes, some families walk home, while other family members get in their car and drive to their neighborhoods.

Muslims living on Schofield Barracks adopted a highway through the Hawaiian Adopt-a-Highway Program. This made it our responsibility to clean any trash people threw out their car window; but, first, we had to schedule a day to clean the highway.

On the date chosen to clean our highway, the parents hands everyone attending our mosque a bright orange shirt reading, "Adopt-A-Highway," and we're asked to put them on. Afterwards, everyone is provided gloves and trash bags. Some people given rakes to gather the leaves on the ground. After raking all the leaves into a pile, everyone puts the leaves into trash bags.

At some point, the highway looks clean enough, so the children start exploring other parts of the highway. The other children and I begin finding things like empty shells. We look at the shells to see if they're nice enough to take back home. After finding a shell that looks nice, I wrap it in a napkin and keep it.

The parents take one last look around to make sure everything looks relatively clean, and then decide that it's time to go home. Cleaning the highway in Hawaii made me realize the responsibility Muslims have to the environment. As Muslims we not only have an obligation to our creator, but we also have an obligation to God's creations. It became our social responsibility to clean that highway from that point forward, whenever it needed to be cleaned.

I felt good about my Muslim community, and I also felt good about myself. It meant a lot for me to be part of a community which was making a difference, even if it means renting a highway which we were frequently obligated to clean.

Chapter Fourteen: My First Ramadan

I began my first Ramadan when I was twelve years old. Danisha and I were participating in physical education class together while we were fasting. I fasted most of Ramadan, but from time to time I had to break my fast. There were days when I couldn't handle fasting. I was still trying to grasp an understanding of the practice.

In my first few days of fasting, I still had much to learn. My parents told me that I couldn't eat or drink the entire day from sunrise to sunset. So, the first couple of days of Ramadan I adhered to my parents' advice. I didn't eat or drink the entire day, but I was chewing different flavored gums. I chewed to get all the flavor out of the gum. I'd purchase all the sweet flavors such as berry, orange, and watermelon. I honestly didn't know that chewing gum while fasting was forbidden, too I thought it was fine. I mean, was chewing gum forbidden while fasting? I commonly saw Muslims chewing on miswaks throughout the entire day of fasting and I thought the concept to be similar. Besides, chewing gum couldn't *really* be that different from chewing miswaks, right?

One day my mom catches me chewing gum and gets angry.

"Julde, aren't you fasting!?" my mom asks with fury.

And without understanding my mom's anger, I reply, "Yes, I'm fasting."

"Then why are you chewing gum?"

I sincerely didn't know chewing gum was impermissible while fasting. I hadn't acquired that knowledge of what's required of me during Ramadan.

I decide to complete fasting for the rest of the day because I committed an honest mistake, which I knew only God could forgive.

Then there was a day where I was truly wrong for breaking my fast because I did so with my friend Danisha during our physical education class. After running laps around our Middle School basketball court, Danisha and I decided to break our fast. First, we drank from the water fountain because we were thirsty and I personally nearly felt like passing out, then afterwards we shared a Red Vine candy, but I wasn't going to let my parents know I broke my fast.

Later that day, after returning home, my parents ask me, "Julde, are you fasting today?"

"Yes," I reply.

I didn't understand why my parents were asking me whether I was fasting. I was too ashamed to face my parents and let them know I wasn't fasting, and I felt that my parents shouldn't be worried about this matter because they couldn't save me from the punishments of Judgement Day. In Islam, Muslims believe whether we're friends or family, we're all responsible for our own deeds and actions.

My parents decided to confront me, "Danisha's parents already called us earlier and told us that you two broke your fast in school." I was shocked. I wasn't expecting my parents to find out that I broke my fast. As an adolescent, I often found myself being disorderly in terms of my religion. It was hard for me to focus on Islam, especially while having multiple temptations revolving around me. I was reaching my teenage years and this is the time where most people fall into making ridiculous mistakes. I wasn't proud of my stance as a Muslim at the time; I really felt that I needed to get my Muslim practices together.

I deeply believed in a Creator while I was younger, but I also didn't know what to consider a "true" religion, amongst all religions. There are too many religions in the world and every religion has followers who all believe they are following the "true" religion.

So, what's the "true" religion?

This is a serious question which I had while I was younger, especially since everyone persistently debated on reasons why their religion is free from all fallacies. This question led me to think deeper about my own religious belief, Islam, and ask myself, "Is Islam *really* the true religion?"

I used to walk across the street from my house, go to the park, sit on the slide and reflect on the meaning of life. I spent time thinking about the possibilities of a Creator. I tried making sense of life's existence.

"What's the meaning of life?" I questioned myself.

The meaning of life is a twisted subject. It's the foundation of philosophy, and it's also a serious question that I had. It doesn't make sense to me that humans are born into a world solely as a drawn-out result of the Big Bang Theory. Do you mean to tell me that we just exist? We just evolved from being animals, once upon a time? No, I didn't want to accept evolution as simple explanation for the existence of life. I must admit, I was confused. I was confused with my life as a Muslim, confused with religion, life, and I definitely didn't believe the Big Bang Theory. Who was really alive to witness our Creator or the Big Bang? There are documentaries of how the Big Bang occurred, but no one was there to even see if those graphic visuals are accurate.

Sometimes my thoughts got so deep, I'd think about how God looked or what his character was like. I wondered what God wanted from creating the universe or life in general. If there was a God or if the Big Bang really occurred. I just wanted to know why.

I couldn't understand life because I thought that its very existence was too complex. At some point, I didn't understand that these deep thoughts of life were also forbidden in Islam. Muslims aren't supposed to think nor imagine how our creator looks. God's image can never be grasped inside a human's imagination. No matter how hard I tried to think of how God looked, I was never going to imagine his correct image.

However, Muslims are allowed to make sense of life. We are allowed to assess our knowledge about the complexity of life when it pertains to Islam, especially when this assessment of life motivates us to seek knowledge. There's nothing in Islam which prohibits a Muslim person from seeking knowledge in the first place.

Later that day, after speaking to my mom, I find out that it's forbidden to imagine or think how our creator, Allah, looked like.

My mom yelled, "Julde, you're not supposed to imagine or think about how God looks! We have numerous hadiths and Qurans in this house, and all you do every day is to go outside and play."

The next day, my mom made it mandatory for me to read a little bit of the hadiths and Quran every day before going outside to play. My mom realized that there was a lot for me to learn about Islam. Sometimes people focus so much on memorizing the Quran and getting the correct tajweed[36], but they don't have much knowledge of the hadiths. Don't get me wrong, tajweed is very important in Islam. While reading the Quran, you must hit every vowel and syllable correctly because mispronunciation in the words of the Quran can change the meaning of the text, but *understanding* the meaning of the text is even more necessary in Islam. The Quran is not merely a melody, it's guidance for a Muslim's life, and a commandment from the Creator. As for me, I didn't know how to recite many chapters in the Quran, but I did have recordings to listen to. It didn't matter how many times I listened to the Quran, it wouldn't increase my knowledge of Islam if I didn't pick up the Quran and read the English translation.

Knowledge of the Quran and hadith is important because as a Muslim, you'll understand what you're required to follow as it pertains to Islamic practices, and you'll be happier while practicing Islam.

I sit in the living room and look outside the window. The sun's rays glare past the living room curtains and I feel the need to be outside. I understand that the only way I could go outside is if I follow my mom's instructions and read parts of the Quran or hadiths. I approach my family's collection of hadiths. The books had accumulated dust from sitting on the shelves in my family's living room. I slowly begin reading sections of the hadiths. It's taking me a while to understand what I am reading; it's as if the English was translated during the time of Shakespeare.

The hadiths discuss many Islamic practices such as how a person should perform prayer or the ways Muslims are supposed to live. I begin acquiring a new insight into Islam and its teachings. After an hour of reading hadiths, I finally go outside and play.

---

36 Tajweed: rulings which control the correct letter and vowel pronunciation within the Quran because mispronunciation of the Arabic words can misinterpret the meaning of the Quran.

The Eid celebration in Hawaii rapidly approached, signaling the end of the Holy Month of Ramadan. The Muslim families living on base agreed that we wouldn't pray our Eid prayers on base; instead, we'd join the Eid festivities at the mosque located off base. The parents made plans for where we'd meet and when. One of the parents went to the Muslim Association of Hawaii to find out the prayer time for Eid. We all knew that we didn't want to be late for prayer, especially since praying on Eid is the most important part of the celebration. Eid 2006 took place on a school day, which meant that my parents had to write a formal note excusing my absence from school. Schools almost never took off for Muslim holidays, so as a child, I often missed a lot of school material by the time I returned to school from a religious holiday.

While attending Wheeler Middle School, I tried placing myself in extracurricular activities to keep myself busy. First, I tried out for the school basketball team. I had difficulty understanding the concept of playing basketball. After my basketball team's devastating loss against another middle school team, I gave up on playing basketball and decided to change sports.

Then, I tried out for the Wheeler Middle School track team. For a while, track was a decent sport for me to commit to after school because it provided me with all the necessary exercise that an adolescent needs. The tryouts for the school track team was exciting. Wheeler Middle School had a vast green field, where the coach held the tryouts for track.

The coach draws a chalky white line in the grass and instructs all the students to begin running at the sound of his whistle. The weather is warm with the occasional light breeze. My classmates and I are wearing our track uniforms and stretching to get warmed up for tryouts. Immediately after hearing the coach blow his whistle, we all take off running. I run as fast as I can to the other side of the field, trying as hard as I can to keep up with my classmates.

"I need to make it on the track team," I think to myself.

After the tryouts, the coach announces which of the students he chose to be on the track team. I'm honored to be placed on the Wheeler Middle School track team.

Although I was on the school track team, I wasn't one of the main students who ran track at our school games. I was mainly invited to participate in our track meets, but during the school games, I sat at the bleachers. Impatiently, I gave up on track. I didn't like sitting on the sidelines while watching my teammates run without me. Sometimes, I wasn't even invited to come along to the games, so I left the track team.

Afterwards, I decided to join the Wheeler Middle School volleyball team. Sometimes playing volleyball was difficult, especially if it were a hot day. My teammates and I were constantly running around the court, trying to get our hands ready to catch the volleyball. The sun's heat never gave up on piercing down on our necks. Sweat seeped out the pores of our skin and not long after, our skin glistened in the sunlight. By the time I was done with volleyball practice, I'd feel exhausted. All I wanted to do was find the nearest water fountain.

At Wheeler Middle School I had a small group of friends. I never really enjoyed hanging out in large groups. I was fairly well-known around school, but I liked maintaining a small circle.

Naturally, I was slightly different from the other kids attending my middle school. First off, with a name like Julde, people either had a hard time pronouncing my name or had never heard of my name. Second, some of the students were aware that I was Muslim, even though I didn't wear a hijab. Most of the time, I kept within my small circle of friends because I also thought it resulted in less drama. Some girls felt threatened that I'd take their crush as my boyfriend, even when their boyfriend had never crossed my mind.

"He isn't even all that," I'd tell the girls in my school, because sometimes they'd make a *big* deal about boys who really *weren't* all that.

I began riding bicycles with one of the girls attending Wheeler Middle School, named Vanessa, to and from school. Riding my bicycle to school really had to do with me being late to the bus stop nearly every morning. If I missed the school bus, I'd have to go back home, get my bicycle and ride it to school.

My bike rides to and from school gave me the opportunity to absorb the beautiful landscaping on both Schofield Barracks and Wheeler Army Airfield. Some of the residents living on both bases took the time to plant massively beautiful gardens in front of their yards. The homes with the most beautiful landscaping earned a sign placed in front of their home, awarding their beautiful lawn.

On the main street next to my neighborhood, palm trees had been planted down the median that separated opposing traffic, each tree evenly lined up behind the other. Near the roadside were large fields of grass with exotic tropical plants spread throughout. While riding past the field, I'd breath in the pleasant scents from the tropical plants. I'd always take time to look at the beautiful scenery, even while riding my bike in a rush to keep from being late to school.

By the time I reached Wheeler Middle School, I'd feel sweaty, hot, and tired. I'd lock my bicycle at the bike rack so that no one stole it, and then rush into my classroom.

On my way back home, I'd ride my bike with Vanessa; however, she lived in a different housing area from me. Every day we'd pedal our bikes speedily on our way home. Occasionally, we'd choose a day to stop at the Burger King on Schofield Barracks to order a Whopper Jr., value fries, and value drink. We'd finish eating our food in the food court before continuing our bicycle ride home. My friend knew much more about Schofield Barracks than I did. I enjoyed my bicycle rides with her because she'd take me on different routes on the base that I'd never take on my own.

Chapter Fifteen: Foundation of Economic Autonomy

Once again, I began investing more time into selling products. Sometimes there were items in my room which I no longer wanted, and I'd sell those items. Selling items gave me my own financial independence, although it wasn't an official job. I loved proving to myself that I was hard-working, and I loved enterprising.

I took time making Icees, just as I did in El Paso. I'd mix Kool-Aid powder with water in a juice container and make sure that the flavor was just right.

I tried having a variety of four to five Icee flavors that my customers could choose from. Before freezing the Kool-Aid juices, I'd place them in the disposable shot's cups. After several hours of freezing the juices, I'd take the juices out of the freezer and sell them. I'd go into my garage, pull out my wooden table and carry it across the street from my house to the neighborhood park. I'd go back into the garage, get my small wooden chair, and then sit on my chair while waiting for my customers. I always placed a sign of the item I was selling in front of the table. There was nothing fancy about my signs, they were normally handwritten by me on a white poster saying:

```
Icees For Sale
25 cents Each
```

By the end of the day, I'd make between forty to sixty dollars by selling Kool-Aid Ices in front of my neighborhood park.

On the days I didn't sell frozen juices, I'd take my bicycle around Schofield Barracks to collect recyclable bottles from my neighbors' recycling bins. I'd go around doing that every day and on the weekends, I'd go to the Schofield Barracks Commissary parking lot to recycle all my bottles for a reimbursement.

I hand the recycling workers a full bag of plastic bottles and cans for them to weigh. After weighing the bag, the workers figure out how much money to reimburse me.

After saving enough money, my friends and I would go to the Schofield Barracks PX to hang out.

Roughly between the years 2006 and 2007, the Schofield Barracks PX underwent renovations to make more space for vendors to set up shop. Vendors would rent those spaces for their little shops outside of the Post Exchange. Sometimes, my friends and I would check out items being sold by the vendors.

At the time, the Schofield Barracks food court was adding a Starbucks coffee shop near the other vendor shops. Some of my friends said that they already tried Starbucks coffee before moving to Hawaii. They began speaking positively about Starbucks coffee; but I'd never tasted Starbucks coffee before. I was looking forward to trying Starbucks after they had their grand opening.

The food court at the PX was spacious and there were plenty of tables and chairs for restaurant purchasers to enjoy their meals. My friends and I chose restaurants that we liked eating at inside the food court, before deciding which table we were going to sit at. There were multiple restaurant selections at the Schofield Barracks food court, but oftentimes I'd get something from either Anthony's Pizza, Jamba Juice, or Panda Express. After getting food we wanted to eat, we'd sit together and enjoy our meals. Everyone had their own meals to eat from; but, periodically, we'd ask to taste each other's food. After finishing our food, we'd clean our area before leaving the food court and hanging out.

The Post Exchange sold games I frequently enjoyed playing. I'd search through the gaming section to find games I'd be interested in playing at home. I owned a Nintendo DS and decided to purchase the Sims game compatible for my device.

Another popular game that nearly every child in Hawaii had during the time was the Tamagotchi. The Tamagotchi toy is a miniature egg-shaped toy in which you virtually take care of a creature.

On a nice warm day, my friends and I would sit outside and discuss the progress of our Tamagotchi creatures.

"My Tamagotchi finally hatched from its egg!" one of my friends exclaims.

"Wow, let me see how your Tamagotchi looks!" another friend says. They exchange Tamagotchi devices to see the newly hatched Tamagotchi.

Nearly all the children living in my neighborhood wanted a Tamagotchi and some of them collected multiple Tamagotchi toys. I frequently used the money I earned through recycling bottles and selling frozen Kool-Aid to buy myself Tamagotchis from the Post Exchange. A Tamagotchi cost me nearly sixteen dollars to purchase.

It felt good buying my Tamagotchi because I'd purchased it with my own money. I always felt good about the items I purchased on my own. In fact, the items I purchased on my own carried more value than items my parents bought for me. Sometimes my parents would purchase me things and find them laying around in the house.

"You have your Heelys shoes laying around in the house? It's because I bought these shoes for you with my own money," my parents would scold me. "I don't blame you, I blame myself for buying you those Heelys!"

By the time I was twelve years old, my mom wanted me to learn how to manage my own money. My mom believed that the best way for me to learn how to manage my own money was by opening a bank account for me. My mom discussed her plans to open an account with me and then, the next day, my mom contacted the bank. I was now an owner of a joint bank account that I shared with my mom. It took me approximately two weeks to receive my new debit card and personal checkbook in the mail. After arriving in the mail, my mom educated me on how to make purchases with my debit card and personal checkbook.

At twelve years old, not only did I get in the habit of earning my own money, but I was also in control of how I spent my money. Making purchases no longer meant spending cash that I kept in a Danish cookie container; now I could deposit my money in my checking account and use a debit card instead. My mom taught me that getting used to various financial habits could make me better at handling my own money in the future.

One day, I went to the Post Exchange to buy myself personal hygiene products like deodorant, lotion, and body wash. Before entering the PX, I had already decided that I was going to purchase my personal hygiene products with my personal checkbook. Once I was inside, I grabbed a shopping cart and began placing the products into my shopping cart. After I got all the items I wanted to purchase, I headed to the cash register.

The cashier asks me for my military ID card upon arriving at her register. I hand the cashier my ID and wait for her to give it back to me. Upon receiving my ID card back, I open my checkbook and start writing out my check to the Post Exchange.

"Who I should write the check out to?" I ask the cashier.

The cashier looks down at me confused, before asking me, "*How old are you?*"

"I'm twelve years old," I reply.

"And you're writing out a personal check?" she questions me.

"My mom wants me to learn how to manage my own money," I tell the cashier.

"That's very smart of your mom. I didn't know how to write out a check until I was a young adult," the cashier admits.

It takes me three tries before I finally write out my check properly. The first two checks were no longer valid and the cashier told me to write "VOID" across the first two checks so that no one else can use them. Finally, I inscribe my signature on the check, the cashier processes my payment and then, afterwards, I walk home from the PX with all my belongings.

I felt empty whenever I was home because my dad was always deployed for war. My parents were married, but my mother was the main parent actually taking care of me and my younger sister on her own. Whenever my mom was at work, my younger sister and I would go outside and play with the other children in my neighborhood.

There were numerous things on base children occupied themselves with. There was a swimming pool, youth center, community center, and

146 | P a g e

sometimes people within our neighborhood organized events for everyone to enjoy.

Before moving to Hawaii, I didn't know how to swim, so whenever I went to the pool, I'd stay near the shallow end. Swimming classes were offered weekly to family members living on Schofield Barracks. My mom enrolled my younger sister and me for swimming classes at the Schofield Barracks pool.

For the next few months, I attended the Schofield Barracks' swimming pool regularly to learn how to swim. Promptly after learning how to swim, the children in my neighborhood frequently arranged days for us to go to the swimming pool. When I joined them, I no longer wanted to stay in the shallow end of the pool. The swimming classes gave me confidence to play in the deep end.

As I walk to the deep end of the pool, I feel accomplished. I still remember the days I couldn't join the other kids at the deep end. Those days were now all gone and I can finally join the other children and have fun.

The air is warm and smells of chlorine. I walk over to one of the benches to spread out my towel. Some of the children jump into the pool, making a huge splash around the pool patio. Some of the water also splashes on me and it feels cold. I already know that I'm going to have a hard time adjusting to the cold temperature of the water, despite the warm weather.

As the sun bathes my skin, I first dip my foot into the pool before finally lowering my whole body into it. The other children are already playing various pool games like Marco Polo. I'm still trying to adjust to the cold water, so I hold off on joining the pool games.

While I'm enjoying the pool water, I overhear a kid shout out, "Who's going to jump off that tall diving board?"

"Which diving board?" another one asks.

"The tallest diving board near the swimming pool. Who's going to jump off it?" the first kid persists.

When I overhear the two children from my neighborhood asking who's going to jump off the tallest diving board, I immediately avert my gaze to avoid any eye contact with them. In fact, at all cost, I try to mind my own business. I just learned how to swim, and nothing was going to make me climb all the way to the top of the tallest diving board and jump into the deep end of the pool. Some of the children begin climbing to the top of the diving board and jumping off. Others climb to the top, but get scared and climb back down.

Then another kid had the nerve to ask me, "Julde, are you going to jump, too?"

I give the child a humorless look before saying, "Nope, I'm not going to jump off that diving board."

I just learned how to swim and hadn't become a professional swimmer overnight.

While all the other children climb up the ladder to the highest diving board and jumping off, I go to the shortest diving board and gently jump into the water.

One of the boys climb up to the top of the diving board, laughing. Then he spreads his arms out wide and jumps off the diving board, maintaining his arms and legs like the letter "X".

Flop! The water splashes high as the boy hits the surface of the water.

Just after splashing into the water, the boy comes out of the pool in pain. The boy says that his stomach hurts, and he feels he needs to throw up.

Who gave this boy the bright idea of jumping off the tallest diving board to do a belly flop in the first place? Afterwards, the children decide to take a break from the diving boards and we returned to playing Marco Polo.

Chapter Sixteen: Establishing Military Families

I didn't always stay on Schofield Barracks. Whenever I did go off base, I hung out with either my family or friends. While spending time together, we'd visit a multitude of attractions in Hawaii.

One of the places my family frequently visited was Honolulu. Honolulu has a beach called Waikiki which runs along the length of the southern shore and there are multiple shopping centers which people commonly shopped at. I preferred swimming at Waikiki because the water there is shallow, and the waves weren't as vicious as other beaches on Oahu.

At Waikiki, the waves gently sway side to side and the air smells of sea salt. The seawater is aquamarine and unbelievably clear, as if you're looking through a blue crystal. While standing inside the water, you can see tiny fish swim around your feet.

My family and I normally stayed at the beach for an hour to relax under the hot sun before exploring more of the city. Before leaving the beach, each of us would go to the free-standing showers to rinse the sand and salt off our bodies.

The shopping centers in Honolulu were surrounded by green tropical foliage. The many trees, majestic and staggering in size, served as shade on a hot sunny day.

The shopping centers located in Honolulu had a medium flow of foot traffic. If you were lucky, you could find Hawaiian hula dancers in various areas of Honolulu performing for money. Crowds of people would gather around to watch the hula dancers move their bodies and hips, side-to-side, performing traditional Hawaiian dances.

On Kuhio Avenue, one of the three main streets of Waikiki, a person spray painted in gold from head to toe stands astonishingly still on a golden platform.

I ask my family, "Is that a statue?"

"Yeah, I think so," my Mom replies.

"*Sooo*, why does it look like the statue has hair?" I'd ask. "Wait! Oh wow, it looks like the statue's hair is blowing in the wind."

I am confused about whether I'm *really* looking at a statue because the *"thing"* is standing still; yet, I see "*its*" hair moving every time the wind blows. It's possible that a talented artist sculpted a golden statue with realistic human hair. *Right?*

A tourist drops money into the jar in front of the golden statue. Soon after, I'd learn that the golden statue is actually a human, standing incredibly still. The "gold statue" suddenly breaks into a dance routine, expertly pop-locking and doing the robot while blowing through a whistle. While watching him dance, I'm fascinated that a person could stand still for so long until money is placed inside their jar to begin dancing. Other tourists begin crowding around the metallic-golden person dancing on the sidewalk. After dancing for a few minutes, the dancer slowly gets back into their original statue position, and the crowds of people break into applause before finally dispersing in different directions.

Not far from Waikiki is Pearl Harbor. My family and I drive to Pearl Harbor to view the Pearl Harbor memorial. My visit to the Pearl Harbor memorial was the first time I'd ever learned about the Pearl Harbor attack during World War II.

First, my family and I waited in line to watch the Pearl Harbor documentary at the memorial. We stood in line for about ten minutes before finally entering the theater. My family and I sat throughout the entire documentary and watched a portrayal of the ordeal American Sailors had faced during the attack on Pearl Harbor. Some clips were actual video footage from the attack, but other clips were reenactments of what occurred.

I learned that prior to the United States' entry into World War II, tensions between the United States and Japan had been steadily rising. Hawaii was the closest state to Japan and of great strategic importance to the United States due to our large naval presence there. Realizing that launching a preemptive strike would potentially give them the clear advantage in the coming conflict, Japanese pilots flew to Hawaii and attacked Pearl Harbor, releasing bombs and torpedoes from their aircraft. The video footage showed the Japanese dropping bombs on United States ships.

After watching the documentary, everyone was granted the opportunity to view the remains of the USS Arizona, which lies forever at the bottom of the harbor. The staff working at the memorial preserved some other items which were bombed during the attack, for them to be viewed by memorial visitors.

Other places that my family and I visited in Hawaii was the Dole Plantation. The Dole Plantation is a well-known pineapple plantation in Hawaii. It's funny to admit, but I always imagined pineapples being grown on trees. All it took was for me to visit the Dole Plantation in Hawaii to learn that pineapples were *actually* grown underground. At the Dole Plantation, nearly every food served in their food court was made of pineapples. My family and I tried different variations of pineapple food, walked around the pineapple maze, and took a train tour around the Dole Plantation.

After getting more familiar with Hawaii, my dad was being sent back to war. This time, he would stay in Iraq for approximately six months. A lot of the other families in my neighborhood were also experiencing their military sponsors preparing to be sent away for war.

My neighbors at Schofield Barracks became people I continuously socialized with daily. After school, I'd complete any necessary homework and chores so that I could go outside and hang out with the other children living in my neighborhood.

The spouses living on Schofield Barracks formed support groups with each other. Groups formed either because their military partners shared a command, they were neighbors, or they shared common interests with each other. Despite the reason for their support groups forming, the spouses needed each other, especially while their partners were away for war. These groups allowed military spouses to develop and grow relationships with each other. I watched military spouses struggle with the fact that their husband or wife had to go away to a war for multiple months. They wouldn't know their military spouse's fate and that was difficult for them. They'd wonder if their spouse would return from war or God forbid if they would ever see their spouse again. Many military families maintained their informal family relationships. Children were calling parents within the neighborhood aunt or uncle if their parents had a close-established relationship. Sometimes other children from these parents were now your cousins, who you weren't even blood-related to.

I similarly watched many military children experience struggles with the wars their parents were fighting in. These were the challenges that I often had to battle with myself as a military child. Some people seem to forget that military family members also face life changes. It takes a lot for a soldier to fight in a war, and part of that is their support system back at home. People shouldn't forget that there are also families involved in this process who are worried about the outcome of the war.

It's important that people understand the social challenges of military dependent children. As kids, we constantly move around to several schools, neighborhoods and sometimes countries. Yes, we're young and gain exposure to various parts of the world, but where are the enriched long-lasting relationships you could've developed with the people from those parts of the world? That's the problem; as a military brat, there are no long-lasting attachments to any one place. You begin to wonder, where exactly are you from? Where do you call home? It's easy to get lost in trying to identify with or belong to one place, when you've lived in so many locations. As a military brat, this only worsens the feelings of emptiness you may get, having a military parent who's constantly away at war. Despite living a comfortable middle-class lifestyle; relationships, bonding, getting to know your community, and being able to genuinely call somewhere home, also matters more than anything At least that's what I believe.

When people want to remember their childhood, they normally feel better after visiting that childhood place and reliving the moment: seeing the old grocery store, pharmacy, mom-pop restaurant, playgrounds or parks. As they visit their old stomping grounds, they can relive their past, even if it's just for a moment. They can reconnect with some of the people they knew when they were younger; people have aged and become parents or grandparents. As military children, it's difficult going back to the places you grew up to relive your past. Even if you go back to those locations, most of the people that you knew no longer live in those places. It's important that we too try to remain connected, especially if we plan on speaking with each other again in the future.

The children also benefited from the social groups which were formed between military spouses. The parents organized family gatherings within the neighborhood so that they could bring their children along and connect with other families. There were remarkable gatherings in my neighborhood which I also wanted to be a part of; however, I wasn't invited to attend every gathering. My family and I never knew the family members who organized some of those gatherings. I used to hang out with children who were always discussing the upcoming get-togethers their parents were organizing.

One family group formed simply because the parents lived within the same cul-de-sac and they maintained a close network with each other. The "Cul-de-sac Group" had one of the best activities organized for their children, in our neighborhood. Sometimes I would've liked to join the Cul-de-sac Group for their events, but they always said that their events were only funded for their own families. The parents in that group put money together to setup remarkable events. Considering how much money it required for them to set up their events, they didn't want to invite every child living in our neighborhood.

One notable event that the Cul-de-sac Group set up was an outdoor movie night for their families. The mothers and fathers who lived in that cul-de-sac purchased a huge outdoor movie screen, a film projector, popcorn, a whole bunch of candies, and multiple outdoor folding chairs. In the evening, the families blocked off the entrance to their cul-de-sac and began setting up equipment in preparation for their outdoor movie night. Mothers and fathers prepared the popcorn while other parents got the other necessary snacks ready for their children, and everybody else placed their chairs and blankets in front of the movie screen in preparation to watch the outdoor movie. Sometimes if there was extra popcorn, the parents were nice enough to give it to the other children living outside of the Cul-de-sac

Group's circle. While the parents prepared for movie night, all the children living outside of the cul-de-sac discussed how much we wished we lived there.

"Can we please join your family and watch the outdoor movie with you guys? Please!" we'd ask the children living in the cul-de-sac.

On one movie night, those parents and their children were watching a Snoopy & The Peanuts Gang film. I don't remember exactly which Snoopy film they were watching, but I knew they were watching a Snoopy film. I rode my bicycle through their cul-de-sac and the Hawaiian night air was warm with breezes brushing past me every so often.

While enjoying the breeze, I lean toward the front of my bike to watch segments of the Snoopy film. The night sky is navy blue, and the stars shine like diamonds. I look up towards the night sky to watch each star sparkle in its luminosity. I can't help but notice that each star has its own shine, its own color, but together, they all light up the heavens in the most breathtaking manner. After looking down from the sky, I look back at the movie from a distance, appreciating the Cul-de-sac Group's togetherness. A togetherness which I lacked my entire childhood.

I always had people around me during different phases of my childhood; nevertheless, the moments I shared with those people never continued. My family was always on the move, constantly adapting our lifestyles around my dad's career, which is the reason why I barely got to know people for a long period of time.

As I glance over to the Cul-de-sac Group watching Snoopy on the big screen, some people have blankets wrapped around their bodies. Everyone sitting in the cul-de-sac is unbothered and comfortable. After watching a few more minutes of the Snoopy film, I ride my bicycle back home.

My mom had a culturally diverse set of friends which she hung out with on base. My mom's friends consisted of military spouses who were Muslims, Africans from various countries, Black Americans, and Asian Americans.

The Muslim military spouses had a great support group, especially for us Muslim children who were hugely impacted by our parents being away for war. As Muslim children, we also occasionally fell victim to stereotypes revolving our Muslim faith. It's challenging to have Muslim parents who not only value their jobs because it means taking care of their families, but it also means sacrificing their lives to protect the United States of America. Despite our Muslim parents putting their lives on the line to protect our country, they still bear the stereotype that all Muslims are "terrorists." Of course, the stereotype isn't true because our Muslim parents wore the United States military uniform every day to fight terrorism. At some point, as Muslim military brats, you're drawn between two ceaseless stories: the unheard stories of American Muslims getting up daily to protect the United States of America and the story of Muslim extremists who get media attention for suicide bombings. Unfortunately, the story which receives exponentially more news attention is the story of Muslim extremists. It's sad to admit that there's inadequate coverage of pleasant American Muslims. In fact, it's the daunting reality which many American Muslims face, especially for us who live and work in U.S. military communities. It's as if we do not exist.

I found it necessary to have military dependent friends who were also Muslim because I could talk to them about what it felt like being a Muslim military brat. It's true, I confided in them. I needed reassurance of my faith. Slowly but surely, I was becoming ashamed of my religion. I began feeling a disconnect with Islam entirely and I felt like much of it had to do with the way society was treating American Muslims.

As an adolescent, I constantly found myself questioning Islam. Sometimes the company of other Muslim children helped me reconnect with my Islamic faith because I no longer felt alone in my journey to self-discovery.

American Muslims are constantly condemning the acts of Muslim extremists; but, on the other hand, another attack promptly follows. It's frustrating because Islam doesn't belong to a specific country or culture, Islam is a religion.

Those people who lost their lives on the day of 9/11 were my people, the American people. Whenever attacks occur on U.S. soil, it's not only an attack on American people of other faiths, it's also an attack on the American Muslim population. It's even more frustrating that Muslim servicemembers are fighting for the United States of America and they go unrecognized. The news media will air attacks done by a single Muslim extremist for an entire month; then, make sure to bring it up multiple times within the year while also directly pointing a finger at Islam. That attack has nothing to do with Islam; that attack has to do with that particular individual, despite what ridiculous rhetoric he or she may spew.

When would the news media cover the good Samaritan Muslims from their local communities? It seems like never. When would someone develop a documentary about Muslims in the U.S. military, so that they too can air it on live television? It doesn't seem like anyone is trying to provide that exposure. That's the problem: the American Muslim community is diverse, yet there isn't any concern about highlighting our diversity within the United States.

As a young girl, I didn't want to walk out of my front door while wearing a hijab. I'm not proud to say I was ashamed of my hijab, but honestly, I didn't want my neighbors seeing me wear one. I was completely ashamed of myself, my identity, and of being a Muslim.

Whenever I played outside with other children on base, I didn't openly tell them that I was a Muslim. I only brought up my Islamic faith after they began noticing that I didn't attend the local Church; I didn't celebrate St. Patrick's Day, Easter, Halloween, or Christmas. After a period of time, other military brats began questioning me, "Julde, which church do you attend or why don't you celebrate holidays?"

I'd explain to them, "I don't attend the local church or celebrate those holidays because I'm a Muslim."

Their facial expressions would instantly light up in shock.

"You're a *Muslim*?" they'd ask me. "I didn't know this entire time that you're a Muslim. You're *too* nice to be a *Muslim*."

Sometimes upon hearing the news that I'm a Muslim, I could feel that our friendship was beginning to fade away.

"Yeah, well that's because not every Muslim is a bad person," I'd reply.

"Well, how come you don't wear that scarf other Muslim women wear?"

"Because I don't want to wear that scarf," I'd respond.

These children had been playing with me the entire time. Sometimes we'd play with each other for months, but now they were finding out that I'm a Muslim. They already knew that I'm a nice person, so it's not my character which is the issue in our friendship; rather, it's my Islamic faith.

I kept my religion hidden from friends because I wanted them to judge me solely on the basis of my character, rather than my religious faith. Some people remained my friends upon hearing news that I'm a Muslim; however, I noticed other children becoming distant with me or behaving differently afterwards.

Muslim military parents would take all the children to social gatherings organized by the Muslim Association of Hawaii in Honolulu, Hawaii. The Muslim Association of Hawaii would rent a huge space for special occasions, so that we could get to know each other and establish additional relationships with Muslims living off base.

My mom's Asian American friends were pleasant people. I learned a lot about their cultures through my mom. When I'm talking about culture, I'm mainly referring to their food. Every now and then, they would cook one of their well-known cultural dishes for my mom. After getting home, Mom would bring these meals home for everyone to try. Some of my mom's friends were Koreans, Filipinos, or Japanese; my mom also had some Polynesian friends. Polynesians are believed to have migrated from Asia and Australia. Some researchers claim that Hawaiians have Asian roots, that somehow Hawaiians travelled from Asia and settled in Hawaii. That could be a false theory because no one was physically present to witness the first Hawaiian settlers travelling to Hawaii, but this theory does make sense. That theory was developed after people questioned the origins of Hawaiian people on these islands, which are largely isolated in the middle of the Pacific Ocean.

The first time I ate shark, my mom's Hawaiian friend had prepared shark filet, baked in coconut milk. At first, I was hesitant to eat the shark dish. The immediate thought which crossed my mind was, "Sharks are carnivores, how could anyone be comfortable with eating an animal that eats other animals?" Afterwards I decided to give the dish a try. The shark dish was pretty good, and I didn't mind the flavor. The coconut milk was a nice element to the shark filet. My mom tried to imitate the dishes her Asian and Polynesian friends prepared for her and for the most part, my mom's dishes closely resembled her friends' dishes.

Workwise, my mom said her Asian friends were the best people she worked with at the Pearl Harbor Commissary. The people that my mom worked with were cool and down to earth. Most of my mom's co-workers were Asians because Hawaii has a huge Asian population.

About six months of my dad being away at war, he finally returns home. By this time, I was approximately eleven years old. My family made sure to visit more nice attractions in Hawaii so that we could spend valuable time with my dad. My family and I decided to visit Hawaiian Waters Adventure Park and by this time, I was an experienced swimmer. The swimming classes I took at the Schofield Barracks truly paid off. After getting on many rides at the Hawaiian Waters Adventure Park, I was impressed at how well I was swimming.

My family also visited many Luaus following my dad's return from war. A Luau is a Hawaiian party where guests enjoy a series of Hawaiian entertainment. At the Luau, you can watch men and women perform various Hawaiian traditional dances. The Hawaiian dance performance is the main attraction of the Luau because everyone eats dinner while watching the hula dancers. After watching the show, you have the option of either taking pictures with the hula dancers or resuming your dinner.

If you decide to take pictures with the hula dancers, they'd place a lei[37] around your neck before the photographer took the picture. When they placed the lei around your neck, the flowers felt slightly heavy. The more leis around your neck, the heavier it weighed. I believe it had much to do with the water weight inside each of the flowers. My family and I decided to

---

37 Lei: A lei is a necklace made from fresh Hawaiian flowers. The flowers are placed on a string or plastic wiring. There are different kinds of flowers that are placed on these leis.

take pictures with the hula dancers for memories. After taking pictures, my family members settled around our table to enjoy each other's company.

Tiki torches are lit up around the Luau area, workers are assisting the visitors in getting their meals and drinks, and people are drawn into their side conversations. The night air is warm and occasionally, hula dancers pass by people seated at nearby tables. People get up from their seat to ask hula dancers, "Hey, do you mind taking a picture with us?" Without hesitation, the hula dancers would agree to take pictures with the Luau visitors. Just before leaving the Luau, visitors are provided with the option of paying for the professional photographs taken by the photographer at the Luau.

Everyone on the Schofield Barracks is like family which is why whenever people hear about the deaths of family members, everyone feels the impact. Hearing that a man returning from a 15 month deployment at the same time as my dad and dying in a motorcycle crash one week after returning hurt everyone living in my neighborhood. We grieved that the soldier made it through 15 months of war and only one week after reuniting with his family, he passed away. That death really hit to the core for many families living on base. We similarly grieved the loss of other family whenever a soldier passed away, it became the reason why we try not to take each other for granted even though we weren't relatives and we're informal military families.

Chapter Seventeen: Read Girl, Read!

My family kept up with all the activities of other Muslims living on Schofield Barracks. Our common gathering place was the mosque located on Schofield Barracks. Just like many of the other military bases I lived on, this mosque wasn't in an obvious location. Our mosque was a small room located behind the other Chaplain offices on base. While we were attending our local mosque, our parents decided to prepare a day out at the beach. We arranged that our day out would be a barbecue because the beach had a grill we could use. As usual, parents began mentioning dishes and meats they'd bring to the beach. After getting clear on which items our parents would bring, we'd all go our separate ways home.

While sitting in class at Wheeler Middle School, one of my teachers starts ranting about Muslims.

"All Muslims are terrorists! Muslims just go around with the mission of killing everyone! When Muslims partake in suicide missions, they're viewed as a hero. The Muslim people are enemies to the American public," my teacher fumes.

While sitting in the classroom, I feel overwhelmed. I'm not wearing a hijab, which means the teacher probably isn't aware that I'm a Muslim. After having enough of my teacher's anti-Muslim rant, I speak up and said, "I'm a Muslim. I wouldn't partake in any suicide missions nor am I an enemy of America." Instantly, my entire classroom becomes quiet, and I express disgust towards my teacher's speech.

"I wouldn't blow up this school!" I yell.

My teacher looks at me wide-eyed, and sarcastically says, "Of course not, Julde, you wouldn't do that," making sure to draw out each word.

The narrative of Muslims is so tightly controlled that people can flip a Muslim person's words. My teacher looks up at the class with a blank stare for a few seconds before continuing on with her lesson. People commonly say Muslim women are oppressed by the religion, but I feel that we're really oppressed because of the growing stereotype of "Islamic Terrorism."

Some students felt bad for me because of the debate; however, other students thought it was funny and began giggling. Some of my classmates were just learning that I'm a Muslim.

"Julde is a Muslim?" some students murmured.

Yes, I'm a Muslim, and this discovery would be one of the many reasons why some of my schoolmates would begin to slowly distance themselves from me. Some students who used to hang out with me, would begin hanging out with me less.

It was a lonely feeling.

There's nothing worse than being a military brat who feels lonely because of your religious practices; that other military brats would cut you off because you're Muslim. I had a few friends who didn't care that I'm Muslim. They kept in touch with me and hung out with me, however there were others who left me alone.

Every time I turned on the news channel, there was always a new story discussing a "Muslim terrorist." At this point, it's clear that if the criminal is identified as a person of Muslim faith, they were instantly a terrorist; if the criminal identified with other religious faiths, they were probably mentally ill. That's the social norm for identifying criminals on news networks.

News anchors spoke about Islam as if they knew everything that they were talking about.

"Yes, those poor Muslim women, they're oppressed because they have to wear the hijab. They don't have any say over their own bodies..." They'd speak on the behalf of Muslim women with confidence, as if they could answer for us! That's a form of oppression itself- to answer on the behalf of Muslim women instead of giving us the chance to communicate our choices to the public. "The Islamic terrorists go on suicide missions, so that they can go straight to heaven where they'll meet 72 virgins," the news anchors continue on to say.

I was so puzzled about my religious faith. I wanted to wear the hijab, but I didn't because I was scared of being mistreated by members of my society, not because I was oppressed. In my awkward stage of adolescence, I was worried about fitting in, which is why I neglected the hijab, not because of oppression. Rather, I was oppressed to not wearing the hijab. As a Muslim girl, I was never taught that a Muslim who carried out a suicide mission would get 72 virgins upon entering heaven. None of my Imams taught me this fallacy the news anchors spoke of. Why would any man be fascinated with the idea of having 72 virgins? This is a sickening purpose for any person to commit acts of violence against entire communities, especially in the case that these extremists were committing suicide.

Where were these "professional" news anchors getting these "Islamic" sources from?

I was learning that Muslims were criminals at my middle school, and the news anchors narrated a felonious image of Muslims; but, at home where I'm part of a Muslim military family, we saw Islam as a positive part of our lives. The problem was, why would everyone constantly deliver this description of the villainous Muslim if it wasn't true? I realized that there were only a few homes surrounding me which believed Muslims to be good people.

Around this time, my family was also slowly pushing away from their basic Muslim obligations. It was good that we had a Muslim community to visit because if it weren't for those community members, we would've been far worse. At home, my family prayed whenever they wanted, we listened to music, and we were less active in reading Quran. I have to admit that we weren't completely off-track with Islam, but we also didn't follow the complete guidelines of Islam either. I'm glad that my parents kept in touch with other Muslim families on base because they too saw the pleasant image of Muslims. Those Muslims were the only other people which brought the positive image of Islam in my life. My family was non-traditional Muslim whose commitment to Islam was slowly fading. We were well associated with Muslims within our community; but, I felt that we didn't have anything to show for it.

I began thinking to myself, "Why am I Muslim?"

My question of faith became the beginning of my withdrawal from the entire Muslim faith. I still believed in the existence of one God, but I was skeptical about Islam. My family wasn't putting their entire effort towards

Islam. This made me withdraw from Islam because I felt that I couldn't connect to it no matter where I was at. On television, the narrative of Muslims remained that we were terrorists. At school, there were hardly any Muslim students and when Islam was taught, a negative portrayal of Muslims was told. At home where my family members were Muslim, everyone was doing their own thing and occasionally, we'd link up with other Muslim families. I gave it serious thought before yelling out to my mom, "I don't want to be a Muslim anymore!"

My mom quickly grabbed her cellphone to call my dad, who wasn't home at the time, to tell him that I didn't want to be a Muslim anymore. I was unsure of which religion I'd turn to because I believed in the existence of one God, but I had enough of being Muslim.

"No one in my household takes Islam seriously, so why am I still obligated in following its religious practices?" I thought to myself.

Later in the evening, after my dad returned home from work, my parents held a meeting with me about my decision to leaving Islam. While discussing this matter with my parents, I honestly didn't know how to feel. "Should I be happy that I don't want to be a Muslim anymore or am I making a serious mistake?" I contemplated to myself.

My parents decided it was best for me to begin attending Islamic weekend school at the Muslim Association of Hawaii.

It's the Saturday morning following my conversation with my parents, during which I expressed my decision to potentially leave Islam. The sunlight shimmers past my window curtains, and I can hear rustling downstairs. My dad runs upstairs to the second floor of our house to wake both my younger sister and me up for our first day of Islamic school. We were told that we'd begin classes at the Muslim Association of Hawaii that very morning. My siblings and I used to attend Islamic school in the other places which we lived; however, after moving to Hawaii, my parents didn't enroll my younger sister and me for Islamic school. Now that I was renouncing my Islamic faith, my parents found it necessary to enroll my younger sister and me into the Islamic school located in Honolulu, Hawaii.

After getting ready, my dad, younger sister and I get into my dad's silver Infiniti G38S and drive off towards the Muslim Association of Hawaii. The drive towards the mosque gave me enough time to think about my parents' willingness to pay for my younger sister and me to attend weekend Islamic classes. Yes, my parents were imperfect, and were slowly drawing away from Islamic practices, but they did try their best to keep me in contact with the community. My family did try to maintain our connection with other Muslim families. I was just confused about my faith and needed to take a step back to evaluate my religion, to get to know it through a brand new perspective.

While riding in my dad's car, I pull my Muslim attire out from my bookbag and begin to slowly put on my hijab and abaya[38] over my regular clothing. After I'm done, I refasten my seatbelt and wait until we reach the mosque where I'd attend my first day of Islamic studies class.

My dad reaches the parking lot of the mosque, parks his car, and walks my younger sister and me into the mosque. The first thing that we do upon entering the mosque is wait to meet our Islamic studies teachers. I'm informed of who will be my new Islamic studies teacher. My teacher and classmates welcome me into the classroom. I tell everyone my name and settle down to join the class lesson. My teacher asks me which Surahs I knew in the Quran[39]. I was twelve years old, and had only memorized four out of the 114 Surahs from the Quran. At the time I could only recite Surah Al-Fatihah, Surah An-Nas, Surah Al-Falaq, and Surah Al-Ikhlas; all of which I learned by reading the English transliterations of the Arabic text. After telling the Islamic teacher I only knew how to recite four Surahs, the Islamic studies teacher tells me to recite the four Surahs I know. She wants to confirm that I know how to recite the four Surahs properly before moving on to learn how to recite new Surahs. I recite the four Surahs, then after

---

38 Abaya: A large cloak or over-garment that is worn by Muslim women to cover the shape of their bodies or figure.

39 Muslims are required to memorize chapters in the Quran, also known as Surahs. The goal is for Muslims to memorize the entire Quran to preserve the authentic verses therein, knowledge of the Quran can benefit a Muslim in the afterlife (level of Heaven they're granted), and chapters are used to complete prayers.

hearing me recite, the teacher tells my classmates and me about the Prophet Muhammad (peace be upon him) who was told by the Archangel Gabriel (*Jibril* in Arabic), "IQRA[40]!"

I ask my Islamic studies teacher, "What does Iqra mean?"

My teacher proceeds to tell me, "Iqra means read. The Archangel Gabriel commanded Prophet Muhammad (peace be upon him) to read, but Prophet Muhammad didn't know how to read because he was unlearned. Prophet Muhammad expressed to the Archangel Gabriel, 'how could I read if I am unlettered'. This conversation between the Prophet Muhammad (peace be upon him) and the Archangel Gabriel became the beginning of the Quran's revelations to the last Prophet (peace be upon him)."

In Surah Al-Alaq of the Holy Quran, the Surah writes:

> *Recite in the name of your Lord who created -*
> *Created man from a clinging substance.*
> *Recite, and your Lord is the most Generous -*
> *Who taught by the pen -*
> *Taught man that which he knew not.*
> *No! [But] indeed, man transgresses*
> *Because he sees himself self-sufficient.*
> *Indeed, to your Lord is the return.*
> *Have you seen the one who forbids*
> *A servant when he prays?*
> *Have you seen if he is upon guidance*
> *Or enjoins righteousness?*
> *Have you seen if he denies and turns away -*
> *Does he not know that Allah sees?*
> *No! If he does not desist, We will surely drag him by the forelock -*
> *A lying, sinning forelock.*
> *Then let him call his associates;*
> *We will call the angels of Hell.*
> *No! Do not obey him. But prostrate and draw near [to Allah].*

Muslims know that Prophet Muhammad (peace be upon him) was illiterate, however he was advised by the Archangel Gabriel to read. I believe

---

40 Iqra: an Arabic word which means read.

that by my Islamic studies teacher explaining Prophet Muhammad's encounter of illiteracy with the Archangel Gabriel, she was trying to spread words of encouragement to me. The Prophet (peace be upon him) indeed couldn't read, but he accomplished memorizing all 114 Surahs in the Quran.

The Quran is special considering that it literally translates into meaning the "Recitation" or "read aloud" in Arabic. Before the Archangel Gabriel was sent to reveal the Quran to the Prophet Muhammad (peace be upon him), the pre-Islamic Arabs living in the Arabian Peninsula during the time regularly retained parts of their history through oral traditions. Arab societies were heavily nomadic and they commonly used poems to chronicle their history throughout the generations. Many of their poems were told in first person and the Arab nomad tribes living between the 6th and 8th centuries used to gather around in the marketplaces of Mecca to share their poetry. Seven of the most prominent pieces of poetry were selected from amongst the greatest Arab poets of the time and hung up on the Kaaba in what was called the *Mu'allaqat,* or "the Hangings." A prominent pagan poet named Imru' Al-Qais is thought to be the originator of the *Mu'allaqat* before he was later exiled into leaving Mecca. [41] [42]

When Prophet Muhammad delivered the verses of the Quran to the people living in Mecca at the time, he let the people know that these verses weren't poetry, but words sent from God as a reminder of monotheism as previously presented to the Jewish and Christians. Many of the people were slowly breaking away from the directives written within the Torah, Psalms, and Gospel by worshipping statues, which were pagan practices.

These verses reconfirmed that the Torah, Psalms, and Gospel are revelations sent from God, but some of their verses were altered by man. The earliest Arabs who accepted Islam were already used to their pre-Islamic

---

41 Cooper, Paul. "The Ancient Poems that Explain Today." BBC Culture, 21 August 2018,

http://www.bbc.com/culture/story/20180820-the-6th-century-poems-making-a-comeback.

42 Levin, Gabriel. "On the Hanging Odes of Arabia." Parnassus Poetry, Vol. 30, Nos. 1 & 2,

http://parnassusreview.com/archives/408.

oral traditions so it was easier for them to memorize the verses of the Quran orally. The verses of the Quran were continually recited aloud by the early Muslims. The early Muslims were corrected if they mispronounced words in the verses. Prophet Muhammad would verify the verses of the Quran with the Archangel Gabriel before going to the Muslims who'd actively write out portions of the Quran. However, the Quran wasn't compiled into its formal book until nearly a century after the prophet's death. [43]

Many of the verses in the Quran nearly parallel verses written in the Old and New Testament. After finding verses that parallel, it becomes apparent that there is no way an illiterate prophet can nearly replicate all the verses. Not to mention, the Quran has mention to scientific evidence that the Muslims during the prophet's time wouldn't be able to know such as the oceans which don't touch, the importance of bees, and the trimesters of a woman's pregnancy. There are countless other scientific evidence which hasn't been confirmed until the 20th and 21st century that would be impossible for anyone illiterate to coincidentally construct as verses coming from a higher power.

At twelve years old, I wasn't proud of saying that I was only capable of reading four Surahs. Honestly, I was ashamed of myself. I sat alongside classmates who were all younger than me, but this was the reason why I was in that class. I was already disliking Islam because I didn't know much about it.

All I knew was that someone had to be telling the truth about Muslims; whether it was the news media or the entire Muslim population. Everyone couldn't be right or wrong in this matter. It doesn't make sense that everyone was claiming the truth about Islam and the truth was unclear to me. As an adolescent girl, I was trying to discover who was right about Muslims, my initial identity.

My teacher gave me a brief explanation of the four Surahs. My teacher mentioned that everything I needed to learn about the Surahs would be written within the coursebooks being used for our Islamic studies class. I

---

43 "The Origin of the Quran." Why Islam, https://www.whyislam.org/quran/originofquran/.

was told that my dad needed to purchase these coursebooks in order for me to successfully learn the course material in that class. My coursebook would ironically be published by a company called Iqra. In the meantime, I'd read along with other students who already had the coursebook.

My teacher began her lesson that day by teaching the students how to recite Surah Al-Kafiroun. Surah Al-Kafiroun is the 109th Surah in the Quran and it means "the disbelievers" or "those who reject faith." The teacher's explanation of Surah Al-Kafiroun was that during the Prophet Muhammad's (peace be upon him) time, there were many people who rejected Islam as their religious belief system. Forcing any individual to accept Islam is strictly prohibited. Surah Al-Kafiroun's translation reads as:

> *Say, "O disbelievers,*
> *I do not worship what you worship.*
> *Nor are you worshippers of what I worship.*
> *Nor will I be a worshipper of what you worship.*
> *Nor will you be worshippers of what I worship.*
> *For you is your religion, and for me is my religion."*

Learning this Surah was significant to me because I was already beginning to reject my faith as a Muslim; that was the reason why I was sitting in that class in the first place. I was assigned to practice reciting that Surah for the night. After getting home, I began studying the recitation of Surah Al-Kafiroun.

The next day, my teacher made all the students continuously recite the Surahs we were learning aloud. It's customary for Muslim students to learn how to recite the Quran by reading the verses aloud. It took a lot for me to learn a single Surah in the Quran because I couldn't read in Arabic. Not only was I not used to reading Arabic, but I was studying the Surahs by using the Arabic transliterations.

Later that week, I went to my neighbor's house which was literally four doors down from my house. That military family also happened to be Muslims. My parents arranged for me to begin going to their house regularly to learn how to read in Arabic.

I walked over to their front door, knocked, and then after waiting a couple of minutes, someone came to open the door. The family welcomed me into their home. The wife of the Muslim family was in the U.S. military. She mentioned that she was originally from Kenya. Her husband was supportive of her military career. They recently had a baby girl and the husband helped to take care of the baby while the wife worked. I cannot remember exactly how many children they had, but I do remember them having twin boys who also attended Wheeler Middle School and a daughter attending Hale Kula Elementary School.

The husband was going to begin teaching me how to read Arabic during the week; this way, I'd be able to read Arabic text from the Quran. I went on my computer to find a printout of the Arabic letters. After printing it out, I began reading aloud, "alif, ba, ta, tha, jeem, ha, kha..."

My neighbor went over the Arabic letters with me several times and sometimes, his children would join in and assist me in memorizing the Arabic alphabet. I had a difficult time learning the Arabic alphabet and it was frustrating because I wanted to learn the letters faster than it was taking me; however, I realized that everyone in the community was already doing everything they could to teach me how to read in Arabic. By the end of the day, I had learned how to read the entire Arabic alphabet. I was not going to leave their house until I learned how to say the entire Arabic alphabet and I was proud of accomplishing that.

At twelve years old, I finally learned how to read the Arabic alphabet because a military spouse took the time to teach me. I certainly felt behind in learning many things as a Muslim girl. This was the disadvantages of me constantly moving around and traveling due to my military childhood. It was unfortunate that whenever I did move to a new location, the students at the weekend Islamic schools I attended were following a different Islamic curriculum. Now that I finally learned the entire Arabic alphabet, I felt that it was now my responsibility to continually visit my neighbor's house to learn how to read out the linked-Arabic words.

I arranged which days during the week to go over my neighbor's house to learn how to read the Arabic vowels, and then I continued my Arabic classes on the weekend.

A couple of weeks into learning new things about Islam, my parents asked me if I still felt like converting from being a Muslim. While my parents were waiting for my response, I noticed the look of concern written all over their faces. I knew that my parents cared about me and they were interested in knowing if I still had a connection with Islam. I did feel much better that people from our community were trying to teach me everything I needed to know about Islam. I knew some basics of Islam as a child, but I didn't believe that my knowledge of Islam was in-depth.

I knew that if whatever the news channels were uttering about Islam was true, I'd have to renounce my affinity for Islam. I continued taking my mother's advice of reading the hadiths located in the living room everyday before going outside to play. I wanted to seek answers about Islam by reading the hadiths. This is a serious question which I had in mind, "Would Muslim men really receive 72 virgins by committing an attack on innocent people?" I wanted to know the answers to the questions I always had about Islam.

While sitting in my weekend Islamic studies course, I told the Islamic teacher that I didn't know much about Islam. The Islamic teacher told me, "Part of being a Muslim is being able to seek knowledge." From what I understand, it's good to seek Islamic knowledge from people who've become scholars in Islamic matters, but always seek your own knowledge from the Quran and hadiths themselves. It's possible that while people are listening to Islamic scholars, they too can make innocent mistakes. It's highly encouraged that Muslims seek their own knowledge about Islam, even after hearing a lecture from a trustworthy religious leader.

I followed my teacher's advice and began researching information I needed to know about Islam on my own. I became more familiar with Arabic terms used in Islam and I never found any reference of someone receiving 72 virgins because they committed an attack against innocent people.

On occasion, I'd go outside to play with other children living in my neighborhood. Some children told me that they heard that I'm a Muslim. "Oh, is that the reason why we never see you attending church services?"

"Yeah, I don't attend church because I'm a Muslim."

"So, where do you go then?"

"I attend mosque services on base."

"Really? How come I never knew there was a mosque on base?"

"It's not an official mosque, we pray in a room located behind the chaplain offices."

Shortly after the conversation, other children and I began playing outside. It was easy for the children to sometimes forget that I'm a Muslim. That day, the other children and I played outside at the park located in front of my family's house. We ran around the park playing tag, discussing various topics, and when we were bored, we'd catch the geckos which commonly crawled all over the playground equipment.

During the next several weeks, I finally learned how to read out Arabic, reading the Arabic text at a steady pace to process each letter I was reading. At times, it was challenging to read in Arabic and I'd nearly feel like giving up; other times, I'd recognize my improvements of learning how to read in Arabic and keep going. It took me a great amount of reviewing to get better. As they say, "Practice makes perfect."

My dad left Hawaii for a few weeks to go on vacation. While my dad was out of Hawaii, he went to visit various parts of the Eastern Coast of the United States. One of the places he travelled to was to visit some family in New York. Considering I was already questioning my religious faith, my dad purchased several books and DVDs explaining topics in Islam. A couple of weeks later, my dad returned to Hawaii. One of the first few things my dad did was hand gifts out to everyone in my family and finally he gave me the Islamic resources he had bought me.

I'd use these new Islamic resources to study the parts of Islam which I questioned, hoping to gain answers which were building because of the misconceptions being presented in the media. I'd look at the material from an unbiased standpoint, but this was becoming increasingly important to me now that I wasn't just looking at Islam as something which brought my family together; I was looking at Islam from a standpoint of truly connecting with the religion on a personal level. Some people say that you're born into a religion and that's why you're likely to stay a worshipper of the religion. On the other hand, I was looking to see if I could evaluate the media's misinterpretation of Islam.

Chapter Eighteen: Farewell Aloha State

By 2007, I was attending Wheeler Middle School for my seventh-grade school year. My seventh-grade course schedule consisted of taking Math, English, Social Studies, Science, Sex Education, Physical Education and Dance.

The four main courses required in my curriculum were Math, English, Social Studies and Science. Those four courses were important because students were obligated to take the state exam and passing before moving on to the eighth grade. The other courses I took at Wheeler Middle School consisted of electives or courses important for basic life, knowledge, and skills.

In the sex education class, teachers went over the risks of having sex. During my seventh-grade school year, I was twelve years old and considering most of my classmates were within my age group, we were all adolescents. Some adolescents are known to engage in sexual behavior without knowing the consequences of having sex. The teachers taught the students how to prevent underage pregnancies and the risks of contracting sexually transmitted diseases without using protection.

Some students attending Wheeler Middle School were either abstaining from sex, close to engaging in sex, or were already having sex. Sex education class was an informative class for students because it provided all the knowledge we needed to know before engaging in those activities.

In my physical education class, students were required to purchase navy blue exercise shorts with the school logo. The logo was the Spartans, our school mascot, with the words Wheeler Middle School imprinted above it. Our physical education class didn't use a gym and opted to meet outside instead.

The other students and I would change into our exercise outfits prior to our class meeting by going into the school locker room adjacent to the outdoor basketball court.

After getting dressed for our physical education class, we'd run laps around the outdoor basketball court for nearly three minutes until the coaches blew their whistles, signaling us to stop running. We'd gather around the coaches to begin warming up for the subsequent exercises. While warming up, the coaches directed us on which stretches to do before engaging in the day's more rigorous exercise routines.

Sometimes the coaches gave students jump ropes, hula hoops, basketballs, soccer balls and other equipment to free-play and run around the basketball court. Some students would grab gym equipment they wanted their group of friends to play with.

In our Wheeler Middle School dance class, students learned various Hawaiian dances. The students customarily referred to the dance instructor as Kumu. In the beginning of the class, all the female students were required to grab a hula skirt from the area where the teacher kept all the dance equipment. Every female student would wear her hula skirt, then afterwards all the boys and girls stood in position to begin learning our new hula dance routine. Step by step all of us learned the choreography to various Hawaiian songs. The dance room had carpet, so some of us would take off our shoes and dance in our socks.

Kumu would teach us about the different Hawaiian harmonies and tunes that we could gently move our bodies to. In the beginning of her class, she'd usually play slow paced Hawaiian tunes; towards the middle of her class she'd start playing fast-paced melodies. I'd enjoy the rhythm of the Hawaiian songs as we followed along with Kumu's choreography. Through Kumu's choreography, my classmates and I learned the stories of how some Hawaiian dances came into existence. Some of us were already fascinated by the dances that we viewed at the Luaus with our families. I can remember wanting to dance like the hula dancers at the Luaus.

After learning dance moves for nearly an hour, the school bell rang. We all rushed to get dressed for our next class, despite being disappointed about dance class being over. The Hawaiian dances Kumu taught were very engaging.

After learning some of the Hawaiian dances at Wheeler Middle School, I realized that I was devoted to dancing. I previously danced at the Bliss Elementary School talent show, the youth services talent show, and I formed a dance group with my two other Muslim friends for the Wheeler Middle School talent show auditions.

About a couple of months after my dad returned from war, there was a Father-Daughter Ball being held on Schofield Barracks. My dad, younger sister, and I, along with our neighbor and his daughter, were all getting prepared to attend the ball. My dad wanted to take my younger sister and me to find nice dresses to wear for the occasion. We drove to Honolulu so that my younger sister and I could search for dresses at a few boutiques. After several stops, I finally found a cute black dress with halter straps, a line of rhinestones down the center of the bust, and a voluminous, full-length skirt. After finding my dress, my younger sister chose the dress she wanted to wear.

About a week after getting outfits for the occasion, it was finally the day of the Father-Daughter Ball. The ball was scheduled to begin late in the evening. For most of the morning, my younger sister and I were focused on getting our hair and nails done for the occasion. My dad took us out to the nail salon to get detailed manicures and pedicures. The nail technician painted intricate designs on our nails and added gems on a few of them as a finishing touch. I had begun getting my hairstyle ready the night before, so the only thing I needed to do was curl the tips of my hair before going out to the ball. After getting home from doing our nails, my younger sister and I curled our hair into the styles we wanted. We planned to go to the ball with our neighbor, so once we were dressed, we gave them a call to let them know we were ready to leave for the occasion.

Before leaving for the ball, the five of us took a group photo outside on our front yard. After taking our pictures, we drove to the community center on Schofield Barracks.

As the location of the Father-Daughter Ball, the community center room had been well decorated, with freshly polished hardwood floors and a multitude of round, formal dinner tables, exquisitely set up to seat up to 10 people. All the fathers who walked into the ballroom were dressed in suits or tuxedos.

The daughters ranged in age, from infants to full adults. No matter their age differences, all of the daughters still looked their best. Everyone was dressed so fancy and glamorous that we could've walked a red carpet before entering the ballroom. We looked absolutely stunning.

At the ball, I run into some more of my neighbors. I nearly cross paths with my neighbors without greeting them because we could barely recognize each other. Some of the girls from my neighborhood are wearing makeup, which makes them nearly unrecognizable.

The Father-Daughter Ball was hosted by other military members. The hosts begin the evening with an opening ceremony. Everyone is called to silence until the host was finishes his opening speech, then the beautiful night finally begins, with everyone sitting at their tables, waiting for the first course. The servers roll our meals out onto serving carts, making way to each table and handing everyone their meals.

Everyone receives their meal and starts to eat. After finishing our meals, servers come out to collect our dishes and wipe off our tables.

After every table is clean and the dirty dishes are out of the way, the host comes back out to get the party started. The DJ starts playing music, but at first, everyone is hesitant to get up and dance. It takes a while before people steadily make way to the dance floor. It's a beautiful sight, watching girls of all ages enjoy this evening with their dads. Most of the dads attending the ball were not only fathers, but were also active duty service members of the United States military. Other dads attending the ball had committed to supporting their wives who were in the service. Despite the fathers' reasons for coming to the ball, they had come to enjoy this beautiful evening with their daughters.

The excitement in the ballroom gradually elevates as the evening goes by; more fathers and their daughters approach the dance floor. When I feel there are enough people on the dance floor, I also get up to dance.

After I get done dancing, a lot of people come up to tell me, "Wow, Julde! You can really dance!"

Some people were unaware of my dancing skills, for whatever reason, and they couldn't picture me knowing how to dance.

The Father-Daughter Ball ends rather late that night. Everyone begins saying their goodbyes making their way to exit the ballroom. Once outside, the warm Hawaiian air greets us with a slight breeze. The palm trees, croton plants, and lusciously green grass around the community center are wet with dew. The moonlight beams down on everyone standing outside the ballroom, phasing into the lights coming from the community center. People remain outside to talk before saying their final goodbyes. My dad, younger sister, and I walk toward the car so that we could drive home. While my dad drives home, I listen to the music playing in the car and look up toward the night sky. I notice the stars competing in their brilliance. Each star shines in different colors at different times. One star looks gold, while the other looks silver. After arriving home, I tell my mom everything that happened at the Father-Daughter Ball. I try to fill her in on all the great details.

Since my dad was back in Hawaii, he got back to doing his regular extracurricular activities. The blue, white, and black Suzuki GSX-R finally ended its six-months long hibernation in our garage. For the first time in six months, my dad got up early in the morning to wash the accumulated dust off his "Bee" motorcycle.

After the motorcycle was cleaned, my dad would take my younger sister or me on rides around the base. As always, I didn't care too much for riding on his bike, so most of the time he would go with my sister.

My dad would take two helmets out of the garage, place one helmet on my younger sister and put the other helmet on himself. They would ride the motorcycle a couple of rounds around the base before my dad ventured off base by himself.

My dad is part of the Kappa Alpha Psi fraternity. My dad joined the Kappa Alpha Psi Fraternity group while he was attending college in El Paso, Texas to become a Warrant Officer in the United States Army. My dad's home office contained every form of Kappa Alpha Psi memorabilia you could think of.

Now that my dad was back from war, he could spend more time with his Kappa Alpha Psi brothers and catch up on activities he missed while he was away for war. The Kappa Alpha Psi held an event in Hawaii and my dad invited the entire family. He wanted to introduce us to the members of his fraternity.

This event would be the first time I'd witness the Kappa Alpha Psi brotherhood. At the event, the Kappas were going to perform a series of their signature step dance routines.

At the beginning of the Kappa Alpha Psi step show, I immediately notice that all the men are holding white canes wrapped with red tape. The lights in the room begin to dim with only a lone spotlight focused on the brothers. Then the steppers shout out, "*KAPPA ALPHA PSI*" and start the step routine. They call out each Greek letter with intensity, especially emphasizing and stretching out the, "*Psiii!*"

Then everyone in their group struts and steps with confidence. The fraternity members twirl their canes, each stepping in unison. No music is needed in the room, but the audience feels the energy of the step performance. People smile and admire the routine as they stand along the sidelines.

Some children in the room start to pretend that they too are part of the step performance. Their tiny feet mimic the movements of the fraternity members. Watching the Kappa Alpha Psi performance is especially exciting because this is the same year the movie *Stomp the Yard* was released. The movie cast Chris Brown, Ne-Yo, Brian J. White as well as others, and was representative of black college fraternities and step performances. The Kappa step team in front of us could have stepped right out of that film, they were so good.

Towards the middle of my dad's step performance, the steppers begin stepping to actual music and bring out their signature red and white canes again for the finale.

At the end of the performance, everyone gives the steppers a big round of applause. The performance was so good that they receive a standing ovation, with everyone maintaining their applause for a full minute. When the applause finally ends, one of the hosts gets up to make an announcement. The host wants to announce their fraternity's selected winner for the scholarship they would be providing to a college student. After everyone applauds, the college student is awarded with their scholarship, and we all settle down and enjoy the rest of the event.

*　　*　　*　　*　　*

One morning, my mom wakes up to a phone call downstairs in her bedroom. It was probably around 4:00a.m. in the morning. My mother receives news that one of her brothers passed away. My mom barely likes running upstairs to the second floor of the house, but she's so sad that she runs upstairs, crying, screaming from the top of her lungs.

My mother runs into my bedroom, wailing, "My brother died!"

I was in shock, waking up to my mom's crying with the news that her younger brother had passed away. I follow my mom through the hallway as she cries from despair. It had been a while since my mom visited her family in Africa and it was tragic to hear that someone in her family passed away. My mom ends up making her way back downstairs and slumps onto the kitchen floor, sobbing uncontrollably. "My brother Thierno [Cher-NO] passed away," my mom manages to say between sobs. I empathize with my mom but I can't recall which uncle of mine it was. My mom tries to see if I remember who passed away, but I just can't remember who she's talking about. The fact that I don't remember him shatters her completely. I only stayed in Africa for one month when I last went and most of my memories were formed around my cousins, especially my cousin Adama. I couldn't remember the uncle that she was speaking about because I was probably busy playing with the other children in the neighborhood.

I may not have remembered Uncle Thierno, but my family later told me more about him. Out of all my siblings, Alfa knew him the most from the year and a half he spent in Guinea. Alfa told me that Uncle Thierno was one of the most honorable, honest, and respectable people he had ever met. He had been a fantastic university student, a devout Muslim, and hands down was one of the nicest people you could ever meet. Uncle Thierno would take Alfa on adventures all over Guinea, teaching him the lay of the land to the point that after a while, Uncle Thierno would joke that Alfa now knew it better than him. During that time, they became like brothers, even sharing a room. He took care of all of his cousins and was quickly becoming the apple of my grandfather's eye. There was no doubt in anyone's mind that he would be the future patriarch of my mother's family. Tragically, he passed before he had the chance to fulfill that future, only in his twenties.

"Julde, you don't know which uncle I'm talking about?"

Honestly, I didn't know. Our stay in Africa was brief.

My dad comes into the kitchen to try and calm my mom down. My dad tells my mom, "Khadijah, you can mourn the loss of your brother, but it's too early in the morning and the kids have school." My dad didn't want us to be too tired for school so he tells my younger sister and me to go lie back down in bed.

As soon as morning reached, both of my parents took emergency leave from their jobs to attend the funeral. This was a very significant t death to my mom because that was not only her younger brother, but also one of her favorite siblings altogether. At one point she had been looking into helping him come to the states so he could earn a scholarship and go to college. It had also been a while since my mom visited her family and she wanted to catch up with her family before God forbid she lost another.

As a military spouse, she didn't always have the privilege of seeing her family like she wanted, and her whole family lived on an entirely different continent. The first thing that my dad did was buy the earliest tickets to Guinea. Both of my parents went to Africa for two weeks to visit my family. During those two weeks, my mom left my younger sister and me home with my older brother, Alfa.

My neighbor Ms. Shanice normally had countless children who came over to her house to play. Ms. Shanice turned her garage into a game room. There was a sofa, a television, a television stand, a game box and other items which the children in the neighborhood played with. During the day, her garage door stayed open. The children in my neighborhood walked directly into the garage to join the other kids playing video games. The game I enjoyed playing the most was Grand Theft Auto. For the few weeks that my parents left for the funeral, I grew empty inside. I began to think about how much I didn't actually know my family. I only knew my nuclear family; which included my dad, mom, older sister, older brother, and younger sister. I didn't really know my extended family living in Africa or Virginia.

After two weeks, both my parents returned from Africa. My parents went back to work and on occasion my family and I would go out to Honolulu to spend quality time with each other. My family began going out to places like Dave and Buster's. We'd enjoy our time more in Dave and Buster's than Chuck E Cheese's. At this point, both my younger sister and I thought we had outgrown Chuck E Cheese's. I'd always order the same items from the Dave and Buster's menu: buffalo wings with a side of fries. While waiting for the food, my parents would hand me my Dave and Buster's play card, and I'd run off to play some games.

I tried scoring the most points I could while playing the arcade games because depending on how many points I earned, I could pick out a prize at the Winner's Circle, or point redemption store. About twenty minutes into playing the arcade games, I'd see food at my family's table. While sitting down at our table, the smell of buffalo wings sweeps past my nostrils. Instantly, my stomach grumbles due to hunger. I sit down and wait for my parents to verify that we got everything we ordered. While waiting, I can see the steam escaping the hot wings and my dad says, "Everybody can eat."

I say, "Bismillah[44]," to myself before eating my meal.

On other days, my family and I would go to the beach so that we could spend our entire day by the ocean. When we were ready to leave the beach, we'd use the free-standing showers to rinse the sand and salt off our bodies. After getting most of the sand off our bodies, we'd dress up and go to the nearest Hawaiian restaurant to eat dinner.

One time, I ordered a meal that was cooked with peanuts and it was supposed to be eaten with white rice on the side. I didn't like the peanut sauce at all. There were whole peanuts in the sauce, sesame seeds, and other

---

44 Bismillah: a phrase that means "in the name of God" in Arabic. Muslims say it as a prayer before many acts, including eating.

This word starts every chapter in the Quran except for one chapter called Surah At-Tawba (aka Surah Baraat).

stuff that made the peanut sauce crunchy. I didn't like the crunchy texture of the meal, so my family ate their meals while I sat quietly at the restaurant table.

The state of Hawaii was holding the 50th State Fair and my dad wanted to take my younger sister and me. At the 50th State Fair, there were carnival rides and lots of very fun games. There was also a concert being held by Soulja Boy. Soulja Boy had a lot of songs that people really enjoyed during that time. Two of the songs he performed were "Crank That" and "Yahhh!".

That was the first concert I ever attended.

After three months of my parents being back from Africa, my parents made an announcement to my younger sister and me that they no longer wanted to be married to each other.

My parents were getting a divorce.

My parents expressed that they were no longer felt happy with each other and thought it was best for them to move on. I never thought in a million years that my parents would get a divorce. It seemed that my parent's marriage together would last an eternity.

Honestly, following my parents announcement of filing a divorce, home never felt the same. Everyone in the household became more distant from each other, and I didn't want to get into my parent's problems nor pick sides. I tried my best to be neutral because I loved my parents equally. After a while, though, I began to realize that the issues my parents were facing regarding the divorce were beginning to weigh down on me as well. My mom decided that since her and my dad were getting a divorce, she'd move to New York because she wanted to open her own business and begin life on a new slate. Throughout my dad's career, my mom had dedicated her time to taking care of my siblings and me while also working several jobs to support her family in Guinea, so she never got a chance to obtain a college degree. My mom, younger sister and I got everything packed to begin our new life in New York.

Part Two: Army Brat of Separated Parents

Chapter Nineteen: Hot Melting Pot

Upon arriving in New York City, my mom, younger sister and I temporarily stayed at my aunt's house in Brooklyn until we could find our own place. As mentioned earlier, my mom is the only child my maternal grandparents have that resides outside of Africa. My aunt living in Brooklyn is not my mom's sister; she's really my mom's first cousin, but for Fulani cultural purposes it's not customary for me to call her by name.

In the meantime, my mom and I searched for public schools that my younger sister and I could attend around my aunt's neighborhood. It was already late at night when we arrived in New York, so my mom told me that we'd get up first thing in the morning to begin searching for public schools. When morning approached, my mom and I ate a huge breakfast.

My mom's car was still on its way from Hawaii at the time, and my aunt didn't own a vehicle. Being that New York City is well-known for their extensive transit system, driving a car wasn't necessary for us to find a public school. My mom and I found the closest middle school in my aunt's neighborhood, called Middle School 61- Dr. Gladstone H. Atwell.

We entered Middle School 61's administrative office to begin the application process. They requested all the transfer documents they needed from Wheeler Middle School and my mom provided them with those documents. I was told that I needed vaccinations before beginning school and I waited a couple of weeks to begin my eighth-grade school year.

After beginning my first day of school at Middle School 61, I experienced that uncomfortably familiar difficulty of adjusting to my classroom's curriculum. The curriculum at Middle School 61 didn't properly trail the curriculum I learned at Wheeler Middle School in Hawaii. Once again, I was tremendously confused during my first few weeks of school. I opened my notebook to begin writing down the course material I was being taught in an attempt to begin catching up with New York City's school curriculum. Although I didn't understand the concepts being taught, I tried my best to follow along with the lecture and take notes.

Not only was it difficult for me to follow along with the curriculum, but I also had a hard time with my classmate's slang. New York slang is different from any other slang I've heard in other parts of the world. Nearly every place I lived had their own slang or vernacular, but New York's slang was difficult for me to understand. While listening to my classmates speak, I noticed that much of their words were spoken out of its correct context.

One of my classmates suddenly shouts out, "I'm MAD HAPPY!" while smiling.

"Like, huh? How does that make any sense? Did my classmate just say that they were mad happy?" I think to myself.

Logically, I couldn't understand a person being emotionally mad and happy at the same time. Normally a person experiences either mad or happy emotions; but, if someone is experiencing both of those emotions, chances are that they're struggling with an emotional disorder.

I became worried about my classmate for a slight moment because I couldn't understand why anyone would be smiling after they mentioned they were *mad happy*. But by the end of the day, I had heard around ten other students *also* saying they were *mad happy*. It was at that point I started to realize that this must be one of New York's unusual instances of slang phrases.

Clue: Mad Happy= Very Happy

I noticed that most of New York's slang words couldn't be found in an official English dictionary. Yes, I must admit, I did frequently check the English dictionary to figure out words being used in New York slang. It's true that the students at M.S. 61 spoke English just as I did, but sometimes the context in which they spoke English caught me off guard.

While observing two of my classmates arguing, one of the students stood up in fury and shouted out to the other student, "Are you dead ass!?" which in their context, means, "Are you serious!?" And I'm dead ass that this is what the phrase implies.

Middle School 61 was more culturally diverse than any other schools I attended as a child. The cultural diversity in Middle School 61 was invigorating and uplifting. New York is known to be a melting pot and most students were either first-generation or second-generation immigrants belonging to different nationalities across the globe. Majority of the students attending Middle School 61 were either Black, Latino, or Arab; but, within those ethnicities their original nationalities varied.

The principal and office administrators at Middle School 61 made an announcement over the loudspeaker every morning. Sometimes the announcement included a motivational speech, the major programs of the day and any other additional information which students and staff benefited from. To conclude the morning announcement, the staff would play, "Greatest Love of All" by Whitney Houston over the loudspeaker. All the students in my classroom sang along to the lyrics of Whitney Houston's "Greatest Love of All" and when the song ended, the teachers would begin their lessons.

Previously, I was used to beginning my school mornings with the "Pledge of Allegiance", "Star-Spangled Banner", or "America the Beautiful." Middle School 61's morning schedule was dissimilar from previous schools I attended. I experienced culture shock at Middle School 61 after realizing that we wouldn't be saying the traditional American allegiances every morning.

While attending Middle School 61, the housing market crashed. The economy in the United States was falling into recession and I was living in a horrible situation of watching both my parents going through a divorce. I really couldn't believe the divorce was happening in the first place. As a teenager, I felt like my life was taking a full 360-degree turn. While my mom was an Army wife, she never sought to obtain a college degree because she mainly supported my dad's career.

After a couple of months living in New York, my mom found an apartment for all three of us to live in. My mom found a three-bedroom apartment so that everyone could get their own bedroom, but it was very expensive. Despite it being expensive, my mom said that she wanted everyone to have their own bedrooms and feel comfortable within their own spaces. My younger sister and I were always used to having our own bedrooms while growing up and my mom didn't want to change that because of the divorce.

Our apartment was farther from the schools my younger sister and I were attending. Some mornings my mom dropped my younger sister and me off at a corner close to our schools so that we wouldn't have to walk a long distance. Other mornings, we walked all the way from our house to our schools; which was nearly a 35-minute walk. I didn't like walking around Brooklyn because men tried flirting with me, regardless of me saying I was fourteen years old. Sometimes a boy around my age group would try to shoot his shot, but I'd find it weird when older men, sometimes with grey hair, tried talking to me.

Frequently, guys would say, "Lemme get your AIM," if they wanted to get to know me further.

AIM, or AOL Instant Messenger, was commonly used by people at the time to chat with their friends or family. By the time I reached Middle School 61, at least four different men approached me with an attempt to be my boyfriend, get my phone number, AIM or MySpace information.

I learned most of my course material at Middle School 61 between two main teachers. On occasion, my teachers would escort my classmates and me downstairs to do art activities. When afternoon approached, all the students would go downstairs to the cafeteria for lunch. All the students lined up in front of the cafeteria door and waited in turn to get their school lunch. When we finished eating our lunch, we'd go outside for recess.

The air was cool, and some of the red, yellow and orange leaves were scattered throughout the school yard pavement. This was my first time having recess in a school yard without any grass. Right behind the school yard were numerous apartment buildings. Far off past the corner of the school yard were fast food restaurants, laundromats, lawyers' offices, churches, and dollar stores.

Some of the students playing would grab jump ropes; to either jump rope by themselves or play double dutch with their friends. Middle School 61 was the first time that I ever saw children playing double dutch. The students jumped in between the ropes while dancing. Two other students turned the ropes, with one student jumping inside the rope. The student jumping double dutch would turn around, drop it low, and even hop out of the ropes without getting hit by the ropes or messing up the rhythm of the turners. I was impressed by the students who played double dutch; however, I wasn't successful in learning how to do it myself.

Other students grabbed basketballs and played basketball in the court. The same students played basketball *every* recess.

Just in general, I noticed that the same students engaged in the same activities every day for recess.

My friends and I didn't do anything sporty during recess. Most of the time, my friends and I walked around the schoolyard, discussing various topics.

Other students snuck out the school yard to go to nearby restaurants and purchase food. Students weren't allowed to leave the school grounds during school hours, but they found ways to leave anyway.

If it were a rainy day, we weren't allowed to go outside for recess. Instead, the cafeteria staff folded all the cafeteria tables and placed them on one side of the cafeteria. The students would stay indoors and do a New York City styled dance called *lite feet* or "get light." All the students would collectively clap a distinctive beat, and students who knew how to dance *lite feet,* would jump inside a circle of students to show off their dance moves. While everyone stood outside of the circle, we'd clap our hands and chant, "get light, get, get, light!" until our lunch period ended.

After lunch, everyone returned to their classrooms and continued their lessons. Occasionally, I'd have difficulty learning in my classroom because I was accustomed to classes where teachers were the only person speaking. Much of the time, whenever teachers taught course materials at Middle School 61, students held their own side conversations. My classmates at Middle school 61 were bold and didn't care if the teacher was looking at them while they were talking. I could barely hear the teacher's lesson.

While living on base, students rarely spoke while the teachers were teaching the class. I must admit there were times, in my previous classrooms, where I'd hear murmuring or a little chitter chatter in class but immediately after the teacher tells the students to be quiet, the students would be quiet. At Middle School 61, students were more daring.

I eventually learned how to tune out the noise of my classmates and give my full attention to the teacher. Whenever I tuned out the noise of my classmates, I was capable of completing my homework in the evenings. The days I let my classmates' noise disrupt me, I'd have a hard time with my homework.

There used to be a boy in my eighth-grade class who always bothered me. Part of the reason why the boy bothered me was because I didn't have a native New Yorker accent and my English sounded strange to him. I still spoke with a southern accent and occasionally, he'd mimic the way I spoke. For whatever reason, the boy thought it was funny hearing me speak.

One day, the boy was bothering me and I told him to stop. The argument escalated, and the boy said, "I'm going to cut your ass." I was uncertain of what the boy meant, whether he intended in taking a knife and cutting me; but, regardless of what he meant, I replied by saying, "Sure."

The boy immediately began laughing and then, left me alone.

I was startled when the boy laughed but didn't stab me. Of course, I should be grateful that the boy didn't stab me, but why would he laugh in the first place? Especially after making that sort of threat.

Later that day, I explained the situation to one of my friends, about the boy mentioning he'd cut me in the middle of our argument. I told my friend that I defended myself by saying sure, however, the boy didn't grab a knife and stab me. Instead, he just looked at me and laughed. Immediately after telling my story, my friend bursted out laughing. I was expecting my friend to have empathy for me, especially considering the confrontation I had with the boy saying he'll cut me. Then I started to think everyone in New York was nuts because they all seemed to laugh about the most dangerous stuff.

My friend told me that whenever a person in New York says they're going to cut your ass, it doesn't necessarily mean that they're going to stab you; rather, the person is implying they're going to make a joke about you. So, instead of a New Yorker simply stating they're going to tease you or clown on you, they say, "I am going to cut your ass." In that moment, I felt a rush of embarrassment because I began understanding why my classmates laughed after hearing the situation. This incident made me realize how much I needed to learn New York slang in order to survive my eighth-grade school year.

It took me nearly two months to adapt to New York City's lifestyle. My first couple of months living in New York, I only made friends from my middle school. I never made friends from within my neighborhood because I didn't feel safe hanging outside there. New York City is a different environment from what I was previously used to. In Brooklyn, drug dealers stood on every corner, people smoked weed in parks and I wasn't used to living in a state which was that fast-paced. So, my initial friends were all students I met while attending Middle School 61.

Some students attending Middle School 61 were fortunate to have parents who owned local mom-and-pop stores around the neighborhood or parents who were homeowners. The success of their parent's businesses made them a little bit more well-off than some of my other classmates attending school. Some of the stores which my classmates' parents owned included restaurants, hair salons, clothing stores, discount stores, furniture stores, and other service businesses around our neighborhood.

On the other hand, some of my classmates lived in poverty and faced the challenges of calling a shelter their home. Others had parents who were selling drugs for a living, were living in a single-parent household or had at least one parent in jail.

I realized that the students in my classroom belonged to different socioeconomic backgrounds, even though we all lived within the same neighborhood. For the first time, I took notice of differences in students' living conditions. This was a major difference from all the previous public schools I attended. In the other states I lived in, students attended schools according to their district. If you belonged to a certain zip code, you'd be required to attend a specific school. Some students who lived near wealthier zip codes wouldn't get a chance to meet the less fortunate students. Students' schools are paid for by the taxes received in the neighborhood, so wealthier neighborhoods provide better resources for their school's districts. In New York, you sometimes see a variety of students belonging to various socioeconomic statuses studying in one classroom.

Before moving to Brooklyn, most of my classmates lived in comfortable conditions, where none of their parents were dependent on selling drugs for income, and it was less common for students to have a parent in jail.

Most of my previous classmates were United States military dependents and we rarely worried about being homeless, or living in a neighborhood with drug dealers, crimes, and poverty. Even the poorest military families were better off because the United States government provided for them.

As military dependents, we lived in decent neighborhoods, attended decent schools, had Tricare healthcare benefits, and if we lived on base, it was essentially a gated community.

For me personally, the greatest struggle I faced as a military brat was constantly moving around to new places, losing connections with people I met, not being able to grow up around my extended family, and never being able to spend time with my dad because he was always away for war.

By the time I was 14 years old, the thing that mattered to me the most was having a relationship or bond with someone. I was less concerned about the societal struggles of a person. Sitting in my classroom at Middle School 61 provided me a perspective I'd never had before. This gave me the chance to understand the lives of my classmates and broaden my outlook in life, especially because I was personally watching both of my parents go through a divorce. My dad gave my mom money every month to take care of my younger sister and me. My mom used most of the money to make sure my younger sister and I lived the way we did as military brats. But, sometimes, it was hard for my mom to maintain our old lifestyle because she didn't make enough money to provide that.

This made me sympathize with other students who also lived in single-parent households. I'm grateful that existing under different circumstances left me open-minded about life in general. I understood what it was like to live with opportunities, and then later, have those opportunities lessened. I realized that despite my classmates' backgrounds, their dreams were always the same as any other ordinary student, but their dreams were dependent on the few resources they had access to.

Many students attending Middle School 61 were unaware that I recently moved from Hawaii at the time. Some students made fun of my English accent and if I was in a good mood, I didn't pay them any mind. The only time I was easily offended by their jokes was if I were already having a bad day.

I avoided telling other students I moved from Hawaii because it's a very expensive state to live in, and I'd have to explain that my dad is in the military. If I told them that my dad is in the military, the students might've asked to know every place I've ever lived. I understood that some students probably never got the chance to leave New York and if they did, it wasn't to as many places I went as a child. I moved around many times and my parents could always afford family vacations. Knowing that some students probably didn't get those same opportunities, I wasn't interested in boasting about my life.

Towards the end of the eighth-grade school year in New York City, students would start to search for high school preferences by using a catalog. Every student was provided the option of looking through this catalog, or making an appointment to sit with an advisor to discuss which potential high schools they were interested in attending. Some high schools had specialized programs which catered towards specific career paths students were interested in. I was interested in pursuing a career in business at the time, so I looked through the catalog to find which of the high schools' programs replicated my interests in a corporate career. While looking through the catalog, I kept in mind that I didn't want to attend a high school with high rates of violence, crime, metal detectors, gang members, etc. I wanted to make sure I'd be entering a safe learning environment.

Eventually, I chose The Urban Assembly School of Business for Young Women as my number one high school choice. This high school had recently relocated near Wall Street, an affluent neighborhood. I wouldn't have to worry about walking past drug dealers every morning, at least not to my knowledge, since admittedly, there are people from affluent backgrounds who are professional drug dealers. The school had no history of violence or gang members. I thought that the high school had a satisfactory learning environment. I was unclear if I'd be accepted into The Urban Assembly School of Business for Young Women, but I'd find out toward the ending of my eighth-grade school year.

A few months after everyone spoke with advisors, students completed their applications and submitted them. We patiently waited months before finding out which high schools we were selected to attend.

In 2008, the United States was due to elect a new president to relieve George W. Bush after his second term in office. The election of 2008 was a significant moment for many people living in the United States because it was taking place during the recession and the housing market crash. The American people were looking to elect someone who would relieve the burdens of the economy.

The 2008 presidential election was down to two men, Barack Obama (Democrat) and John McCain (Republican). Most faculty and students at Middle School 61 were rooting for Barack Obama. Most of the residents living near our school were Democrats, so it made sense we wanted Barack Obama to win the election. Whenever Obama delivered speeches, I fell silent and tuned into whatever he was saying. Obama was masterful at capturing an audience's full attention. Every time he spoke, you knew whatever he was addressing was important.

If Barack Obama were to win the election of 2008, he'd become the first African-American president of the United States of America. Since the forming of our nation, every person who became president of the United States of America had been a white male. Barack Obama's presidency would become a historical moment in the United States, but we'd have to wait and see if he could defeat John McCain.

In the meantime, my parent's divorce was getting expensive. My dad was giving my mom money every month for retaining custody of my younger sister and me, but the cost of divorce was still eating up every last penny of my mom's funds. My mom worked   part-time, which limited her income, and received partial support from my dad, but she also had to financially support my younger sister and me as a single-parent. I quickly realized that whenever my parents disagreed on matters regarding their divorce, they always called lawyers and lawyers meant more money. The divorce was not only impacting both my parents; it also impacted me and my younger sister. Sometimes I tried expressing what was hurting me about the divorce, but my parents didn't want to hear my input. My parents always said that this divorce was about them being happy and they were doing what was best for them.

"What about the things that are best for my younger sister and me?" I'd question them.

Amid the divorce, my parents considered me to be disrespectful whenever I expressed how the divorce was impacting me. It was as if the divorce wasn't my business, even though it directly affected me.

While adjusting to New York, I found solutions to being financially drained due to my parent's divorce. At the age of fourteen, my mother helped me obtain a part-time job as a grocery bagger at the Fort Hamilton Commissary. The Commissary is a grocery store available on nearly every military base and it provides groceries to military members at lower prices than stores on the local economy. Sometimes the Commissary carried international food items for its military members.

While I was younger, I constantly found ways to be financially independent, so it didn't hurt to work part-time on the weekends. Grocery baggers working at the Commissary made their income by receiving tips from customers; there were no hourly wage involved. This meant that I'd have to work hard in order to earn money. I committed to working at the Fort Hamilton Commissary nearly every weekend from the grocery store's opening time, until their closing time.

I packed customers' groceries all day, loading it into shopping carts, and then walking the groceries to their cars. When I got to the customers' cars, I'd unload the groceries into either their trunk or back seat, depending on where they preferred their groceries. After loading all the groceries into their car, the customer would give me an optional tip of either $1, $2, $3, ... or sometimes $20. At the end of the day, when I counted my takings, I'd have on average about $70, depending on how busy the store was that day.

My mom, younger sister and I not only began to love the new apartment we were renting, but we also grew a bond with our landlord, who lived on the premises. My landlord owned a three-family home and occupied the first floor of the home, while we lived on the third floor of the home. Although we were only residents of my landlord's house, our relationship with each other started to feel like family.

On days my mom and landlord were both off work, we'd spend an entire day out in New York City together. When I first moved to New York, the city looked amazing to me because it was different from the suburban lifestyles I was previously accustomed to. I was fascinated with the architecture of the tall buildings, landmarks, and other detailed attributes of the city. The New York City sidewalks were extremely crowded and there were high levels of vehicle traffic. As I walked around Manhattan, I'd look up towards the buildings and sometimes get dizzy. Much of the city was shaded against the sun's rays because of the height of the buildings blocking the sunlight. Depending on the time of the day, the sunlight could beam down between the city buildings, resembling the way shadows darken around a sundial. I couldn't believe humans were brave enough to construct buildings at those soaring heights.

I immediately observed the diversity of New York City while walking around. It was common to hear people speak various languages other than English while strolling around the city. There were people from every ethnic and racial background enjoying their time in New York City. This impressive intermingling of people made New York even more awesome. I was exposed to so many cultures at one time that it was immediately apparent why New York is labeled the "melting pot". There's so much blend of culture. If you want, you can watch performances, eat food, and explore clothing from over ten different cultures all in one day.

While walking around the city, I never wanted to fall behind my mom or landlord because it could only take a few seconds before I'd get lost within the crowd. Much of the other pedestrians were taller than me and many people walked with urgency.

We visited many parts of New York City with our landlord, including 34th street Herald Square, Coney Island, Fifth Avenue, and the Prospect Park Zoo. It was customary for us to walk around New York City to view various beautiful sites. When we were done exploring the beautiful city of New York, we'd find a nearby restaurant, eat together, and when we were done eating, we'd return to our home in Brooklyn.

November 2008, Barack Obama was elected as the 44th President of the United States of America. Barack Obama made history by becoming the first African-American man to be the President. The students and staff at Middle School 61 celebrated the election of President Obama in nearly every classroom. It made people realize that no matter your identity, there is still a chance you could become successful.

I would hear some students declare, "When I grow up, I want to become the president of the United States of America." Obama's presidency developed confidence within many of the students attending Middle School 61, especially since the majority of the students were of color.

For, President Obama's election was captivating because as an African-American teenage girl, who is also a Muslim, I never thought I'd witness seeing an African-American man enter the highest office in the nation. The shocking thing was the conspiracies that quickly arose about Obama. Theories began spreading that President Barack Obama was possibly a Muslim and some people thought that he was not born a United States citizen. People began demanding proof of President Barack Obama's birth certificate, with suspicions that he was probably a Kenyan national.

President Obama continuously told the public that he wasn't a Muslim. Although he isn't a Muslim, these conspiracies demonstrated the reality of me never being accepted as a Muslim person in the United States. Honestly, the Obama conspiracy added to my insecurities of being a Muslim girl. This became the reason why I hid my Muslim identity from people. I normally waited until I grew a close bond with someone before saying, "I'm a Muslim." Watching the news and seeing the way Obama was being discriminated against, additionally made me realize the reduced chance I had of becoming a leader of the United States of America, because of my

Muslim faith. Watching the public attack President Obama because they simply *thought* he was a Muslim alarmed me and became the main reason I didn't want to wear the hijab. The hijab was a clear symbol that I'm a Muslim girl and I wasn't ready to be publicly identified as one.

During the Spring of 2009, the eighth-grade students at Middle School 61 assembled in the auditorium for our graduation rehearsals. On the last day of our graduation rehearsals, we were told we'd finally find out which high schools we were accepted to attend. The middle school seniors were called up one by one to receive their high school acceptance letters from the school staff standing on the auditorium stage. Nearly every student who went up to the stage and received their acceptance letters, left the stage delighted and cheery. Only a few students appeared to be disappointed after receiving their high school acceptance letter.

But then I was called up to receive my high school acceptance letter. I instantly felt a rush of anxiety before leaving my seat to walk up to the stage. I wanted to be pleased with the new high school I was attending; I didn't want to regret my choice. As I walked up to the stage, I began to feel even more uneasy. I received the envelope from a school staff member and walked back down the stairs to find a seat towards the back of the auditorium. When I got back to my seat, I opened the envelope.

I was selected to attend The Urban Assembly School of Business for Young Women. I wasn't exactly ecstatic about my high school choice, I only knew that the high school would provide me a comfortable learning environment. I made sure that I wouldn't attend a high school in New York City known for gangs, students possessing weapons, or drug use. The only thing I wasn't happy about was the fact this high school was an all girls' public school.

I told the other students in the auditorium about my high school choice whenever they asked me which school I was attending. "The Urban Assembly School of Business for Young Women recently relocated in lower Manhattan," I would tell the students. The other students attending Middle School 61 never heard of The Urban Assembly School of Business for Young Women. One of my friends approaches me to ask, "Hey, Julde, which high school are you attending?"

"I was accepted into The Urban Assembly School of Business for Young Women," I respond.

"*Soo...* is that an all girls' school?" she inquires.

"Yes, it is."

"Julde, did you know that most students who attend single-gendered schools either turn out becoming lesbian or gay?"

"Well I'm not going to become a lesbian."

"That's what they all say," my friend replies.

My friend's comment really stuck with me and I didn't respond to her. I did give it some thought, though. I knew that I'd be attending this high school for four years. For the next four years, all I would see for eight hours a day is females. I wouldn't have any contact with boys during the school day. I'd never had a boyfriend before. "How could I ever have a boyfriend if I attend an all girls' high school?" I contemplated to myself. Considering that I'm Muslim, it would be disappointing for me to let four years of high school turn me into a lesbian. I'm aware that there are other Muslims who turn out to be queer and they attend co-gendered schools. However, I knew that I'm attracted to guys, so it wouldn't make sense for me to become a lesbian suddenly because of an all girls' school. That's not how it works; you don't just get up one day and decide to become a lesbian because of the school you attend.

During the Summer of 2009, I was hanging out with the friends I made from Middle School 61. I gradually became an outcast to those friends because I wasn't bold enough to do all the bad things they were doing. My morals and values were especially conflicting with my closest friend from Middle School 61. My closest friend lost her virginity at the age of 14 years old and she was already sleeping around with men 4 to 6 years older than both of us around the neighborhood. I was frightened to engage in sexual activities at that age, so despite all the conversations my friend had with me, I avoided being in the mix of sexual activities.

The problem was, I could no longer relate to my friend, especially when she told me loads of stories of who she had sex with and where, but I couldn't share that same experience with her. Whether it was in a hotel, bathroom, or the school hallway, she always had a story. I sensed a disconnect in our relationship the more we hung out. At some point, my friend began acting strange around me, as if it bothered her to have me around.

Not only did my friend have sex with those men, but she also smoked weed with them.

My friend and I made plans to hang out with each other during the summer break and I wanted to get out of my house. All I did during the week was stay home, eat food, and watch television, which was becoming less entertaining. So, I committed to my friend's plans and we went out.

My friend mentioned that she met a boy who was a devoted Christian and helped out with the local church whenever they needed it. After all the sinful stuff my friend did, I was truly proud of her, especially for finding a Christian boy to date. I was hoping that this Christian boy could motivate her to do positive things in life. I knew that it would only influence her to be a better individual. She mentioned that this boy not only attended church every Sunday, but he also played for the church band. My friend's relationship with this boy could possibly be the reason she finally goes to church every Sunday and does good things for her community.

The group of boys played their instruments at the church while the choir rehearsed their vocals. My friend and I remained seated at the church until the church rehearsal ended. My friend mentioned that other teenagers were going to meet us at the church before we'd go to hang out at a nearby park. So, upon their arrival, we left the church as a group and headed towards the George W. Wingate High School field.

When we got to Wingate High School's field, all the boys from the church began rolling up weed. I was shocked. How could these children leave a church service to roll up weed in a football field? I know that people say weed is an herb and it's naturally grown in the earth, but there were people going to jail for possessing it. So, here I was, oblivious of my friend's plan to smoke weed in the park.

My friend knew that if I were aware of their plan, I wouldn't follow them to the park. In that moment, I realized that my friend only hung out with those boys because they were well-known within the church. My friend's parents wouldn't suspect those children of doing anything bad while hanging out with each other. These children were totally involved with the church and maintained their reputation within the community.

The boys start passing around the blunt to everyone and one by one everyone inhales the fumes of the blunt until the blunt gets to me. I nearly panic when I'm handed the blunt. I don't know what to do. I hold the blunt in my hand, feeling anxious, and my palms start to sweat.

"What am I going to do?" I think to myself.

Some people acquire serious conditions for smoking weed laced with other drugs and I have no idea whether this weed is laced with something else. I look down at the weed while the other teenagers chuckle at me. Then I bring the blunt to my lips and inhale some of the fumes. One inhalation makes me feel like something lit up in my body. I pass the blunt to the next person, then about five minutes later, two police officers approach my friends and me on the bleachers.

The two police officers flash their flashlights into our eyes to see our faces. We raise our arms over our face to block out the light coming from their flashlights.

"It smells like weed, are you kids out here smoking?" the police officers ask us.

Instantly, my heart begins to beat fast. I'm not ready to go to jail for smoking weed outside in a park. I hope that whoever took the blunt after me got rid of it. After some questioning, the police officers decide to let us go. Relieved, my friends and I start to head back home.

While leaving the park, one of the boys asks all the girls, "Are you a virgin?" Despite being fourteen and fifteen years old, each girl began saying they weren't virgins.

I try to avoid being asked the question, but he makes sure to get to me.

The boy then asks me, "Are you a virgin?" Honestly, I didn't want to answer the boy's question. I was the only girl in the group who was a virgin. And I wasn't planning on losing my virginity either because throughout my entire life, I was taught to marry first before having sex.

The boy chuckles before asking again, "So, you are a virgin?"

"Yes, I'm a virgin," I say, feeling embarrassed.

"Julde is still a virgin because she's pussy," my friend responds humorously.

"Julde's pussy!" all the girls laugh out. The girls continue to make fun of me for being afraid to have sex.

It was becoming hard for me to hang out with my friend because she was dragging me into situations I wasn't comfortable with. My friend became a professional at stealing from stores within our neighborhood. Sometimes some of the clothes and perfume she wore wasn't purchased. She took snacks from the local bodega and when she wanted me to steal, it was obvious to her that I was "pussy." I wasn't daring enough to engage in stealing. I was accustomed to making my own money, managing my money, and purchasing my own personal items. I was used to doing car washes, recycling cans, selling homemade popsicles, and doing yard sales. I already had my own bank account, and I enjoyed taking care of myself financially.

At various points in my life, I had adults tell me the consequences of peer pressure. I barely even started high school and I felt like the people I was hanging out with were pressuring me into doing things I disliked. Although I missed out on developing a bond with other children because of my military childhood, this was not the bond that I was looking to build. Not a bond that could potentially lead me to go to jail.

Several weeks later, I saw my friend walking around the neighborhood wearing a mini-skirt, high heels, and make up. I was still dressed up like a regular fourteen-year-old girl, so after greeting her, she looked at me in the most disgusting way. That day I realized that I was no longer on her level. I was too worried about the things I was already not doing right as a Muslim girl. Friendships with people like her were not healthy for my Akhirah[45].

Occasionally, I reflected on the disgrace I suffered from being a Muslim girl. I was more ashamed of being labelled a terrorist than being a Muslim, but people in the media often associated being a Muslim with being a terrorist. Calling all Muslims criminals because the action of one Muslim person is wrong, yet society was intensely heeding to those claims. This led me to feel trapped because I was confused with how I could still hold my Muslim values, but still hang out with people who could pull me away from those values. I was trying to find a balance between Islam and hanging out with my non-Muslim friends, who frequently did things against my religion. I knew that I was withering away from my oneness as a young Muslim girl. I really didn't belong around boys who smoked weed, people who shoplifted, and I especially shouldn't be associating myself around those who commit zina[46]. This wasn't what I intended for myself. This isn't what I was taught in Islamic school nor what my parents taught me to be. However, I have to admit that I was oblivious during my adolescent years.

I think back on the time when my classmates and I were out in the schoolyard searching for leaves to use for the Thanksgiving creative activity, and I finally understand what it was like to be that earthworm - having someone forcefully cut you in half and leaving you to live in two separate realities. I feel bad for that earthworm because I truly feel that this is what the American public is doing to Muslims. Are we testing out how faithful a Muslim can be to their religion if we repeatedly declare their religion a violent organization? And yet, we are still alive, just as that earthworm was still alive.

I ended my friendship with that girl because I knew that our friendship wasn't healthy for me. I continued working part-time at the Fort Hamilton Commissary on the weekends. During the week, I stayed home and on occasion, went to visit my landlord's apartment downstairs. I began saving

---

45 Akhirah: An Islamic term used to refer to the afterlife. The life that Muslims believe we live after the day of judgement.

46 Zina: an Islamic term which literally refers to an act of illegal sexual intercourse.

up money for my personal items, loving everything about working hard to purchase them. Working hard for myself made me independent.

Chapter Twenty: Knitting Family Ties Together

During the Summer of 2009, my dad arranged to get my younger sister and me from Brooklyn so that we can spend time with him for vacation. My parents had split custody over my younger sister and me, so my dad normally came to pick us up during the holidays. Due to the nature of my dad's job, my mom took care of us during the school year. My dad wanted us to go see his family in Virginia, so we travelled down to Virginia by car. The road trip took nearly two days because we made a couple of stops along the way, spending the night in hotels before continuing our road trip to Virginia.

Because my dad worked hard in the military, it was difficult for us to get to know our relatives on his side of the family. My dad was always stationed someplace far from his family, but now that I lived in New York, my dad wanted us to be more familiar with them. Since my mom, younger sister, and I lived on the east coast now, we could easily travel to Virginia and see my dad's side of the family. It was customary for my dad's side of the family to arrange family reunions or other family gatherings during the summertime. These gatherings always brought relatives together who hadn't seen each other for years, due to their careers or pursuing their education.

My dad's family is now scattered all over the east coast of the United States but originally, all my dad's family came directly from Hague, Virginia. Driving to Hague took roughly ten to eleven hours from New York.

Visiting Virginia brought back memories from the spring of 2003, when my aunt was sick.

I remembered some of the school activities I did while attending Cople Elementary School. Attending there was a unique experience for me because I got the opportunity to go to the same elementary school most of my relatives on my father's side also attended. It didn't matter that I only attended Cople Elementary School for a few months; what mattered was that I had the opportunity to do so - despite being an Army Brat.

My dad's family is from the Northern Neck of Virginia. Above the Northern Neck is the Potomac River and below it is the Rappahannock River.

Whenever we visited our family; my dad preferred staying over Nana's house. Nana is my Great Grandmother Mary Tolson. Nana's home was the main hub for my paternal grandmother's side of the family. Every time my family and I stayed at Nana's house, we'd run into other family members my dad hadn't seen for years. My dad would spend hours catching up with his family members if they came over Nana's house, which they did regularly to see how she was doing. Normally, Nana sat in her living room knitting various items with the different colors of yarn she had around her living room. Nana would knit hats, gloves, and blankets for our family members. Most of the time, the items she knitted were given away to her grandchildren or great grandchildren.

My Nana, Mary, was the mother to my grandmother, Daisey Ball. I called my grandmother Nany. Nany only lived a five-minutes' drive away from Nana's house. Nany's house was a small, three-bedroom home, and in front of her house was a screened porch.

Tall long stalks of corn stood in neat rows in front of Nany's house. The corn stalks nearly looked like they were trying to reach the sky and the driveway towards Nany's home was formed after cars had continually eroded the grass.

Although there were corn stalks growing in front of Nany's home, she didn't own the cornfield. The corn stalks were owned by a corporate farmer who Nany never met, but it added a pleasant southern landscaping for Nany's small home.

Sometimes I'd sit outside on Nany's porch to either speak with her, my aunt, or uncle. While talking to each other, we'd constantly find ourselves looking outside the screened porch towards the cornfield. Occasionally, one of my family members would go inside the house to grab a cigarette and smoke outside on the porch. While sitting on the porch, we'd hear the birds tweeting, crickets chirping and frogs croaking. Listening to the countless sounds of the countryside, we'd sit out front until the sun began setting, leaving the sky full of purple, pink, and orange streaks.

When evening approached, we'd all go inside Nany's house to eat dinner together. Before eating, Nany would ask someone around the table to say grace. We'd link our hands together, close our eyes and lower our heads as we listened to the person saying grace.

After eating dinner, my dad tried visiting other family members he hadn't seen for a while. Normally, our family didn't have problems with us coming over their homes late at night; we just had to notify them to see if they were home.

Many of our family members knew that we wouldn't stay in Virginia for long, so, generally, we'd visit them at different hours of the day.

Sometimes we'd visit my dad's other grandmother, Bertha Parker. My Great Grandmother Bertha had many visitors coming to her home throughout the day. Grandma Bertha's home was the point of connection for my paternal grandfather's family. Whenever visiting Grandma Bertha's home, you could easily run into other family members.

Grandma Bertha knew how to prepare many food recipes from scratch, especially the preservative jams which she made from scratch. Obviously, Grandma Bertha's jam tasted significantly better than the jam you can purchase from grocery stores. Not only did Grandma Bertha's jams taste good, but her baking was also delicious. One bite out of Grandma Bertha's cake and it instantly began dissolving in your mouth.

It didn't matter whether I was visiting my dad's maternal side of the family or paternal side of the family. Both sides of my dad's family knew how to throw down in the kitchen.

I spent my entire vacation in Virginia eating over various family members' houses. That summer, I gained a considerable amount of weight.

The couple of days that my dad took my younger sister and me down to see my family was a great way for me to reconnect with them and get to know who they were. I already knew much about my Grandmother Daisey because she came to stay with my family twice before in Texas.

Grandma Daisey was a crafty person because she could remodel an entire house by herself. She would sit in front of her Brother sewing machine and sew curtains, pillowcases, blankets and pretty much anything else. While Grandmother Daisey sewed, she'd gently press her foot down on the sewing machine's foot pedal. I never understood how Grandma Daisey maintained her patience while sewing all those items. She'd patiently sit under the sewing machine to place a single thread between the needle hole, then afterwards she'd place a thread in the bobbin. Once she got the thread in between the needle and bobbin, she'd begin sewing. Sometimes if it was taking Grandma Daisey a good amount of time, she'd ask me to help her.

I already knew Grandma Daisey was good at redecorating a house, but that trip, I noticed a new couch in my grandmother's living room.

"I love your new couch," I tell Nany.

"I made that couch," Nany responds in a nonchalant tone.

I was astonished, so I asked my grandmother again to clarify, "Nany, did you just say that you made that couch?"

"Yeah, I made that couch," Nany confirmed.

Like, honestly, I never thought I'd meet someone who could reconstruct or build a couch in the year of 2009. How many people do you personally know that could say, "Yeah, I made my couch?"

Well, exactly, that's my point. Most people purchase their couches from retail stores and get it delivered to their home.

Then, Nany went into her bedroom, searched through her photographs, and then she came out to the living room showing me the before and after pictures of her reconstructed couch. Nany reupholstered her original couch and made it look brand new.

On my trip to Virginia, I appreciated the originality of all my relatives. Nearly everyone was capable of making something from scratch, whether it was food, furniture, clothing, or home decorations. I didn't stay in Virginia long enough to learn the true nature of all my family member's talent, but it was then that I began to understand the foundation of my own creativity. I appreciated getting to know my family further because I believe that in getting to know the people I come from, it makes me understand myself better.

Chapter Twenty-One: Lady Liberty

September 2009, I began my first year of high school at The Urban Assembly School of Business for Young Women. Just before attending there, I purchased my school uniform from the Cookie's Department store in downtown Brooklyn. My high school required me to wear a white-collar shirt, a pink or grey skirt, grey slacks, black shoes and a burgundy vest or sweater.

After purchasing my uniform items, I prepared to get my hair done for my first day of school. I've always thought of it as necessary to get my hair done for my first day- I believe most people could also relate to that.

I went to a nearby beauty supply store in Downtown Brooklyn to purchase hair extensions. It typically cost me around $70 to purchase a bundle of human hair extensions, depending on how long I wanted them

Then I headed to the beauty salon and waited in turn to get my hair done. The air in the hair salon was humid and smelled like a blend of sweltering hair products. Some women were sitting under hair dryers with rollers in their hair, reading magazines or looking down at their cellphones.

While waiting to get my hair done, I watch the beauticians as they flat iron, curl, and relax some of the women's hair.

I spot one beautician blow dry her client's hair at such a high temperature that steam starts to escape from the other side of her client's hair. Every time the beautician passes the blow dryer, her client's hair becomes slightly straighter than before. Most clients came to that particular beauty salon with the intention of straightening their hair. The salon was owned by a group of African-American beauticians and most of their clients were also African-American.

Immediately after one of the beauticians gets done doing her client's hair, she calls me to sit at her booth, and then asks, "Which hairstyle do you want me to do for you today?"

"I want to get a relaxer and when you're finished, can you please add in these hair extensions?" I present the beautician with the packets of weave I bought from the beauty supply store.

The beautician takes the hair extensions and places them to the side before heading to a shelf, where she grabs the hair relaxer. Before applying the relaxer, the beautician places gloves on her hands. While carefully sectioning my hair, the beautician lays the relaxer at the roots of my hair. The roots are the main areas the beautician focused on. Most of the time, the ends of my hair were already straight, but the roots consist of new growth[47].

 The beautician continues placing relaxer at the root of my hair, instructing me afterwards, "Let me know when the perm begins burning so that I can begin massaging it into your hair."

"Okay, I'll let you know," I tell the beautician.

Fifteen minutes into adding the relaxer into my hair, "Ma'am, the perm is burning!"

The beautician rushes to massage the relaxer into my hair and then tells me, "Let me rub the perm into your hair a little longer so that we know for sure your roots will come out straight."

After rubbing the relaxer in my hair for five minutes, we rush to the sink to rinse out the relaxer.

Once she rinses my hair, the beautician washes my hair out with shampoo and conditioner to make sure any residual relaxer is completely rinsed out.

Rollers are added to my hair and I sit under the hair dryer until my hair is dry. After the beautician is done drying my hair, she adds the extensions.

"That will be $160," the beautician says upon finalizing my requested hairstyle.

"Okay! The extra money is for your tip," I tell the beautician.

It nearly cost me $250 to get a hairstyle which would only last me one to two months, depending on how well I took care of my hairstyle. This was

---

47 New growth: Newly grown hair at the roots, its curly texture is distinct from the chemically straightened ends of the hair.

the money I spent to fit the beauty standard of being an African-American woman. Even though I was fourteen years old, I understood that my natural kinky hair wouldn't be accepted as a "normal" standard of beauty.

I look in the mirror one last time before leaving the salon, admiring the work of the beautician, and I grab my shopping bags to go home.

It's late at night by the time I leave the beauty salon. My hair extensions and freshly relaxed hair bounce gently against my shoulders. As always, the city streets are full of traffic. Pedestrians walk and jostle their way through, on their way to who knows where. This is the first time I've lived in a state where people walk around outside during any hour of the day. New York City is literally the city that never sleeps.

While walking home, I look up towards the night sky and I can't help but notice an extension of navy-blue across the night sky. I try to view the stars, just as I did in other states. Then I realize, in New York City, you can't see the stars in the night sky. No matter how hard I try, I can't distinguish them.

Finally, I see a tiny yellow flicker in the night sky. "Could that be the only star in the sky?" I think to myself.

But then, how could it be the only star in the sky?

Then something odd began to happen; the yellow sparkle begins moving quickly across the night sky. Next to the yellow sparkle are flashing red and blue lights. I try to comprehend how a yellow star would have flashing red and blue lights near it, until I realize that I'm looking at an airplane. In New York City, you can't view stars like you can in the rural areas of the United States, but when you do see a sparkling light in the night sky, high chances are you're looking at an airplane.

The following morning, I log onto my computer, print out the Google maps directions to my high school, and get ready to drop my younger sister off at her elementary school with my mom. We take my younger sister all the way inside her classroom, meet with her teacher, and leave before continuing to my high school.

Despite having a printout of the Google Maps directions, my mom and I still happen to get lost within the New York City transit system. We follow every step in the directions; yet, because of transit service changes, we get lost on our way to my high school.

After finally reaching the subway station near my high school, it takes nearly twenty minutes to search for my high school's building. I was told that my high school was located at 26 Broadway, but oddly enough, my high school isn't located at that address. Instead, the entrance to my high school is located behind another building near Beaver Street and New Street. After turning onto New Street, my mom and I finally find The Urban Assembly School of Business for Young Women.

We take the elevator up to the cafeteria, where we're told to remain seated and wait until my principal comes out to introduce herself.

At first, there's utter silence within the cafeteria. Occasionally, there are moments of murmuring and whispering, but it never gets noisy. After several minutes of waiting, my principal walks in and grabs a microphone to introduce herself to everyone. My principal confirms that the high school recently relocated near Battery Park for the 2009 school year. Prior to that, my high school was located near 14th Street-Union Square. My high school was sharing a building with several other high schools at the 14th Street location. The 2009 Freshman class would be the first class to complete their entire four years at this school's new location. Since my high school is business-related, the school administration thought it would be important for our school to be near New York City's financial district; which is the reason why my high school is only a few blocks' walk away from Wall Street.

After the principal and other school staff finish introducing themselves, the students are given a tour around our new school building. Our high school is freshly renovated and incredibly clean. My freshman class sits in classrooms furnished with brand new equipment, textbooks, and supplies. The school's neighborhood is wonderful, and it appears that my high school has all the necessary equipment to teach the students. I don't have to worry about sitting in a classroom with broken equipment, shabby textbooks, or a filthy learning environment.

The start of my ninth-grade school year wasn't the first time I had to adjust to a new school environment. Upon beginning school at the Urban Assembly, I didn't know anyone, and this reminded me of all the other times I began school without knowing anyone. This school wouldn't be any different from other schools I attended, except that it's an all-girls' school. Throughout my entire life, I attended schools where boys and girls communally sat within one classroom. This would be the first time I'd sit in a classroom where my classmates are only girls.

It was the Holy Month of Ramadan when I began my ninth-grade school year at The Urban Assembly School of Business for Young Women. Ramadan would end one week after school began, but I wanted to make sure I'd finish fasting my remaining days. Sometimes I had urges to break my fast after watching multiple classmates eat their food, but I always tried to focus on the intentions of fasting and my inner spirituality. If I couldn't focus on the important concepts of Islam while fasting, it would be easy for me to break my fast. Fasting during Ramadan is great for any Muslim person's spirituality, especially since Ramadan is believed to be the month in which the first few chapters of the Quran were revealed to Prophet Muhammad (peace be upon him).

Given that it's my first day of school, all the teachers organized activities to help students get to know one another. During one of my class activities, the teacher mentions that the school created an acronym for our school.

The teacher says, "Instead of everyone repeatedly saying The Urban Assembly School of Business for Young Women, you can simply say, UASBYW. Can everyone say UASBYW?"

Then some of the students shout, "USA-BYW!" Even the shortened, acronym version of our school's name is too long for us to remember.

I join three new friends that I met for the lunch period at UASBYW. I must admit, lunchtime is a bit awkward for me, especially because it's Ramadan and I'm not eating in order to fulfill my religious obligation. So, I'm the only person among my friends sitting at the lunch table without a food tray in front of me. And to make it worse, we don't speak the entire lunch period. Instead, we just look around the school cafeteria in silence.

Lunchtime continues to be awkward until the school bell rings, signaling the end of our lunch period. At the sound of the bell, we part ways and head to our respective classes.

The common courses I took at UASBYW[48] was Math, English, Science and Social Studies. The extracurricular courses were Art and Dance classes. The staff at UASBYW replaced the standard physical education class with dance class because they believed that the dance classes would be more engaging for the students' physical fitness.

At the beginning of dance class, the dance teacher starts calling out attendance. Eventually the teacher calls out, "Juld Ball?"

"No, my name is pronounced Jul-DAY; the 'E' is not silent."

"Okay, I'll make a note of that, Julde."

There were countless times when I wished my name was common because I knew it would be easier for other people to pronounce. I cannot count how many times in my life I attended a school trip and couldn't find my name on a souvenir gift item. There were days I loved the individuality of my name; whereas, there were other days where I thought about how different my name was.

After calling the attendance, my dance teacher gives a brief introduction on her dancing career and tells us which dancing styles we'd learn that school year. The dance teacher informs us that we aren't in our permanent dance class. The principal is planning on renovating another classroom in our high school to become our official dance studio. Our new dance studio would have a mirror, barre, and hardwood floors, just like any other traditional dance studio. In the meantime, we'd continue coming to the untraditional dance class to begin some of the new choreography. By the time my dance teacher's introduction ends, it's time for all the students to leave for their next class period.

---

48 UASBYW: The acronym shortened version of the Urban Assembly School of Business for Young Women. My high school name was too long to say, so many of the staff and students referred to my school as the UASBYW.

I meet more friends on my second day of school at the UASBYW. Once again, I'm fasting, and I'm proud that I've remained committed towards fasting. I will be turning fifteen years old in December and I feel that I'm reaching the age where I can no longer make excuses of why I'm not fasting.

On the second day of school, all my teachers are prepared to teach us the material we need to learn for the school year. Each class begins with a "Do Now[49]," followed by an "Aim[50]," which I write in my notebook at the start of class.

The school bell rings to signal the beginning of our lunch period and while we walk towards the high school cafeteria, I can't help but inhale the cafeteria food, which instantly makes me feel hungry. Cafeteria food honestly cannot compare to home cooked or restaurant prepared meals, but when you're hungry, that food accomplishes its main purpose. Smelling the cafeteria food has me thinking about my failure in being the best Muslima that I could be.

"I will maintain my willpower," I fight to tell myself. "I want to receive the rewards for fasting this day, I'll be disappointed to allow my temptations in driving me to break my fast."

If I can keep my commitment to fasting this day, it could allow me to reflect on how sincere I am while practicing Islam. This would give me the chance to assess how true I want to be to Allah and his commandments to me. I was already having a difficult time of committing to my regular Islamic duties of praying five times a day. The disappointing part is that I'd contemplate about how much I desired praying, but I never took the initiative of getting up to do the prayers. I'd just sit there and think to myself, "If I do not get up to pray, I may lose my life and regret all the days I sat down wishing I could get up to pray."

---

49 Do Now: The opening class assignment which students are expected to work on once they enter the classroom.

50 Aim: the coursework objective or goal for the day. The Teacher would try to accomplish any learning material directed towards the aim for that day.

There were fifteen-year-olds my age losing their life, my life wasn't promised either.

So, Ramadan is important. It brought me back to where I needed to be in terms with my discipline in practicing Islam and it was truly a test of faith.

I meet another student from one of my classes named Aneesa and we decide to go to the cafeteria together. We both trail behind the cafeteria line to grab something to eat, but when it's our turn to grab food, neither of us grab a plate. Aneesa gives me a look of curiosity, before proceeding to ask me, "Umm, aren't you going to grab something to eat?"

"No, I'm fasting today," I respond.

"Really, do you want to know what's funny, Julde?" Aneesa asks me.

"What is it?" I ask, now curious myself.

"I'm also fasting," Aneesa replies. "What religion do you practice?"

"Well, I'm a Muslim."

"I'm a Muslim too!" Aneesa responds with delight. "Where's your family from?"

"I don't know exactly where I'm from," I tell Aneesa, but she gives me a blank gaze, so I go on to say, "My dad is from Virginia and my mom is from Sierra Leone."

"Which tribe is your mom from?"

"My mom is Fulani."

"Really because you don't look like a Fulani," Aneesa says with certainty.

I move on from the topic by asking Aneesa, "And where is your family from?"

"My family is from Mali," Aneesa replies.

My conversation with Aneesa becomes the foundation of a new friendship. Aneesa and I sit down in the school cafeteria without a food tray in front of us and continue chatting. One of the cafeteria staff approaches our table while looking concerned and asks, "Aren't you two going to grab something to eat?"

"No, we're fasting," we reply to her.

The cafeteria staff member thought deeply before saying, "Oh yeah! It's Ramadan. Are you two Muslims?"

"Yes, we're Muslims."

"So, why aren't you two wearing the hijab? If I may ask."

"We don't want to wear the hijab."

I can't speak for Aneesa, but I understood on my own that I wasn't ready to commit to wearing the hijab. And I was glad that my parents didn't force me to wear the hijab because I felt that I'd begin wearing the hijab whenever I was ready.

I always thought that wearing the hijab reaches beyond being simply identified as a Muslim woman, but the hijab also wasn't my modeled concept of beauty. I felt that by wearing the hijab, I'd be taking away from my youth, like I could no longer feel like I was a young girl. So, no, I wasn't ready to wear the hijab.

One week later, my family and I was celebrating Eid Al-Fitr[51], which marked the end of Ramadan. My family and I got up early on the day of Eid Al-Fitr to get ready for our obligatory prayers in observance of Eid.

We performed the ceremonial ghusl shower before getting dressed into our Eid outfits. Earlier in the week, I bought an Abaya which was Masjid appropriate for Eid because I understood that it's forbidden for women to wear revealing attire upon entering the mosque. I got the chance to finally wear my Abaya for Eid prayers. While wearing my Abaya, I realized that this is one of the rare moments which I could see myself walking outside as a Muslim girl. I rarely walked outside dressed up in full Muslim attire, except for religious occasions. My family and I rushed to the Mosque because we didn't want to be late for the Eid prayer.

Upon entering the mosque for Eid prayers, my family and I wish other Muslims, "*Eid Mubarak!*" Many of the other mosque attendees return the wishes. New York City has a huge Fulani community and many of the

---

51 Eid Al-Fitr: a holiday which marks the end of the holy month of Ramadan.

attendees were exclaiming their greetings to each other by saying, "*On Julee eh jan!*" Or "*Julama eh jan!*" which are two variations of saying happy Eid in Fulani. Then someone talking on their phone expresses excitedly, "*Hande Ko Julde!*" Today is Julde!

Then I ask my mom, "Why is that person saying today is me?" My mom didn't understand what I was trying to say, so I ask my mom, "What does *hande ko Julde* mean?"

My mom says, "It means 'today is Julde'."

My aunt, who was overhearing the conversation, tells me that my name, Julde, means Eid in Fulani. The person on the phone was saying today is Eid. For the first time *ever*, I finally find out that Julde means Eid in Fulani and it's alleviating to find out my name's meaning.

When my family and I finish praying our Eid prayers at the mosque, we get ready to spend the rest of our day out in midtown Manhattan. It's easy for us to take the New York City transit system toward midtown Manhattan, so we wait on the subway platform to board the next arriving train heading towards Manhattan. Immediately after arriving in midtown, we look around for a restaurant where we could eat Eid brunch together. Whenever my family and I recognize other Muslim families celebrating Eid out in the city, we exchange a warm smile and say, "Eid Mubarak!"

On that day, my family and I roam the countless parts of midtown Manhattan until the end of the evening.

After becoming more familiar with everyone in my high school, I began to realize how comfortable it was attending an all girls' school. With just girls being in my class, it was easier discussing certain topics because we knew boys couldn't listen in to our conversations. At any instance, teachers would stop teaching their lessons to begin a discussion about women's health or other topics in regard to being a woman. There were no boundaries as to how far our discussions could go. I shared significant moments with some of the girls attending my high school. Our relationships became more clustered and some of the girls attending my high school began breaking into cliques. After school, different group of girls left school together to hang out in the city. I'd join my friends so that we could explore lower Manhattan.

The girls who attended the Urban Assembly School of Business for Young Women came from every borough within New York City. Only a fraction of the girls attending my school lived in Manhattan, while all the other girls attending my school used public transportation to get to our school every morning. Manhattan is the center of the five boroughs of New York City, so it wasn't surprising that students living in other boroughs would travel a far length to attend our school. Manhattan is surrounded by four different bodies of water: the Harlem River, East River, Hudson River, and New York Harbor.

The Urban Assembly School of Business for Young Women was near Battery Park and the Staten Island ferry. Sometimes my friends and I would meet up after school and enjoy the scenery of Battery Park. Battery Park is full of tall trees, fresh green grass, and pigeons flying around the park. I appreciated the scenery because New York City lacked a natural environment due to its excessive amount of towering buildings. Battery Park not only provided me the feeling of nature, but looking at the New York Harbor was remarkable. The New York Harbor glistened under the sunlight while various boats sailed through the water. I took in the beautiful imagery of Battery Park while spending time with my friends.

While admiring the boats bouncing across the water, my friends decide that they wanted to ride the Staten Island Ferry and I decide to join them. The Staten Island Ferry is a free New York City transit ride towards Staten Island, but we want to take the ferry for our enjoyment.

The Staten Island Ferries are big bright-orange colored double deck boats. There is food sold at concession stands and an outdoor seating area for passengers who wish to look out towards the waves.

While sitting on the outer deck of the ferry, I stare at the Statue of Liberty from afar and admire Lady Liberty standing tall with her torch. Groups of pigeons circle around Lady Liberty's crown. The water looks greenish-black and while staring at the water, I notice that the waves look black and silver as they bounced off each other. The silver parts of the waves are just a reflection of the sunlight. The sky is a baby blue color and the clouds are spread out. I enjoy the ferry ride with my friends until we finally reach Staten Island's dock.

Everyone had to get off the ferry, including people who planned on returning to Manhattan. Some of the girls who lived on Staten Island say their goodbyes to us before parting ways. Afterwards me and all the other girls promptly board the next ferry returning to Battery Park.

After reaching Manhattan, all the girls heading towards Brooklyn enter the Bowling Green train station so that we could wait for the next downtown express train. All the other girls disperse into their own separate routes home. While riding the train back home, my friends and I get into great conversations.

Sometimes the conversations are so good that my friends and I are the loudest people on the train; however, at the time, we're carefree.

Yes, I must admit, my friends and I were those loud obnoxious teenagers who got on the train after school. It's quite funny because today as an adult, I get upset when loud teenagers get on the train. But then, I think back to the times when I was also that teenager, and I see myself in them, so then I attune to their noise.

The great discussions my friends and I had on our way back home gave me a chance to forget about everything that was happening at home. I was still being affected by the divorce and hanging outside with my friends helped me escape that reality. I didn't always want the divorce on my mind because it hurt to watch my family fall apart. I've always longed for my family's prompt reunion following my dad's continuous deployments to war. The same war that happened to be the reason why many children I knew as a young child could barely spend time with their parents. At home there were arguments, fighting, financial strain, and the apartment gave me a feeling of loneliness.

My friends began meeting up with each other every morning to ride the train together to school. After getting out the Wall Street train station, we would decide on which restaurant we wanted to grab breakfast from. It was expensive to get anything to eat from the Wall Street area; but, I felt that restaurant breakfast tasted better than our high school cafeteria's breakfast. While using the money that I made on the weekends as a grocery bagger at the Commissary, I'd purchase my breakfast and head off to school.

At the entrance of our high school lobby, we'd swipe our ID cards for attendance, head to the school cafeteria, eat our breakfast and wait for our first class to begin.

Everything I learned in class was beneficial for the New York State Regents Exams. In ninth grade, my teachers came prepared with PowerPoints, which allowed me to follow along the lessons with their slides. Being that the Urban Assembly School of Business for Young Women was in a new school building, we had the necessary equipment to facilitate our learning. On occasion, my teachers would use the whiteboard to emphasize a point they were trying to teach in their lesson. Most of the time, the teachers used the smartboard for presentations and if needed, our teachers showed us YouTube videos. By the time I made it home in the evening, I could figure out my homework on my own.

During my ninth grade school year, AIM and MySpace.com was my way of staying connected with the people I knew. It also happened to be the sites where I interacted with other teenage boys. Sometimes after school, my friends and I met up with teenage boys we met on social media to spend time with them in the city. We went out to Manhattan, taking countless strolls around the city. The problem was, no matter how much I liked a boy, my relationship with them never went far. I didn't believe in having sex before marriage and some boys thought that was humorous.

"Oh, so you one of those types of girls huh?"

"Yes, I'm one of those types of girls," I'd say.

I'm afraid of my judgement from God and I believed in getting married first. Some boys thought it was a joke, but I was sincerely concerned with my fate as a Muslim girl. Shortly after, the boy would stop talking to me because I was too boring to him. I quickly realized that certain boys wouldn't care about my personality; rather, they were seeking to benefit from our relationships. When boys thought that they can find another girl to meet their expectations, they'd leave me without any hesitation. I was afraid of being disgusted with myself for making the wrong decision.

This was challenging for me because some of the teenage girls attending my high school were already sexually active. Knowing my religion, I wanted to avoid falling into all the temptations surrounding me. Public schools educate teenagers about sex because there are consequences that follow - such as pregnancy or sexually transmitted diseases. There were clinics in New York which guaranteed teenagers their confidentiality for receiving birth control, condoms, and medical checkups without their parents knowledge. For most Muslim teenagers in the United States who don't have overly protect parents, they're less pressured to follow Islam's practices and their parents don't have extreme consequences for the slip ups. For those teenagers they either follow Islam's practices or slip up and get caught in the act of their peers. My parents advised me on Islamic practices and expected me to follow these practices for the sake of my personal deeds. However, it's unfortunate that there are a few instances of Muslim parents who have executed honor killings against their teenagers for being sexually involved, listening to music, or drinking alcohol. I had faith in Allah and I was afraid of his ultimate judgement in the Akhira. I was confused with what I really wanted and I knew that my freedoms wouldn't stop me from practicing Islam or joining peers in their activities.

I was afraid that I wouldn't make it into Al Jannah because I struggled with praying my five daily prayers and wearing proper hijab. I knew that if I didn't wear proper hijab, I couldn't pray the entire day. There was no way I'd stand up to pray in tight pants, short sleeve shirts, or a mini skirt. If I happened to be wearing hair extensions or fake nails, my prayer was automatically invalid. I knew that I didn't want to fall into any other encounters while being a young Muslim girl. Deep down, I was still in love with Islam, a love that I was having a hard time taking control of, but I honestly felt untrue to the religious practices. I felt constricted while practicing Islam because I was only being Muslim at heart. Externally, my practice of Islam wasn't evident.

I experienced countless heartbreaks by boys I met outside of my high school.

One day, I walk past my aunt's house with one of the boys I was talking to. At that moment, my aunt happens to yell out the window, "Julde, is that you?!"

Instantly, my heart begins pounding fast, but I answer my aunt because I knew that if I didn't answer her, she'd tell my mom I disrespected her, and my mom will believe it.

"Yes, auntie!" I respond.

"Julde! What are you doing with that boy?"

"Auntie, we're just hanging out."

"Julde, I HOPE SO! I hope that you two are just hanging out," my aunt responds from her window.

Then the boy asks me, "Who's that?"

"That's my aunt."

"Why does your aunt care if we're hanging out?"

In response to the boy, I simply shrug my shoulders and keep walking alongside him. I really didn't want to discuss anything with the boy, so I just ignore him. We hang out for the rest of the day and when evening approaches, I go home.

Later that evening, my aunt calls me and says that she wants me to come over to her house so that we can speak. I tell my aunt that we could plan a day during the week for me to come over.

The day I arrive at my aunt's house, she mentions that she wants to discuss the day she saw me walking outside with the boy. I'm not surprised by this because I figured that she had something important to tell me.

"Julde, I wanted you to come over to my house today, so that we can speak about the other day when I happened to see you walking with a boy. I hope that you're not doing anything with that boy," my aunt tells me.

"No auntie, I'm not doing anything with him."

"Are you sure?"

"Yes, I'm sure," I tell my aunt. "I'm not doing anything with that boy."

Then my aunt looks at me as if she's trying to examine every part of my face. But, all I do is stare back at her. Then my aunt says, "Julde, let me give you some advice that I hope you listen to. Make sure that whatever you do in life, you go to your husband's house a virgin. Julde, are you still a virgin?"

"Yes auntie, I'm still a virgin," I reply to my aunt awkwardly. I can't believe she's so comfortable in flat out asking me the question.

"Okay, I hope so, because today I'm going to tell you something that's very important. Sometimes if you marry a man who has knowledge that you weren't a virgin on the night of your wedding, he can hold that grudge against you for the rest of your marriage. Even if you claim that you only slept with one man prior to your marriage, he'll still ask you, 'how would I know you only slept with one man?'

"Sometimes there are men who call their wives hoes. If they know that they didn't marry their wife a virgin, they can use that against her for the rest of their marriage."

I'm shocked after hearing this. "There are men who call their wives hoes if the women didn't marry them as virgins?"

"Yes, there are women who are struggling with this today in their homes. You provide the space for your husband to disrespect you. You should be cautious in what you do with those boys," my aunt continues on to say.

Then I get quiet for a second, thinking about everything my aunt told me. I couldn't believe that any man could hold that type of grudge against his wife, but now I was aware of this obstacle, especially as young Muslim girl. This conversation made me reflect on what my expectations were. It's simple for a Muslim woman's virginity to be measured by the observance of a blood-stained white cloth on her wedding night, but there's no standard of measurement for a Muslim man's virginity on his wedding night. Muslim men are supposed to be married virgins, too; they're not better than Muslim women, but they don't share the same humiliation as Muslim women.

The white-cloth tradition is mainly rooted in cultures and not in Islamic rulings. Cultures existing prior to Islam, including my mom's Fulani culture, use this practice to determine a woman's virginity. If a cultural practice doesn't conflict with Islam, the culture can still be practiced, even after the introduction of Islam. I was interested in marrying any potential Fulani man and knew that the community would want to follow this cultural practice for my wedding. I was unsure of how I'd go about marrying a Fulani man if I didn't listen to my aunt's advice, especially in the alarming way she phrased it. Who would've thought a man would call his wife a hoe for a mistake he also probably made prior to getting married? Yet men are not penalized for losing their virginity before marriage.

"Julde, there are two things that I want you to know before leaving my house. First, I want you to know that you must always fear Allah. It's written in the Holy Quran that you should only fear the one Almighty Allah. Only Allah has the power to judge you for all your sins. I also want to remind you that sex committed outside of marriage is impermissible in Islam. Both men and women alike are instructed to guard their chastity until they're married. But, it's unfortunate that we cannot measure the virginity of men, so it's up to women to believe their husband married them a virgin. Even if your husband cheats on you while you're married, do not seek revenge on your husband because you're both going to your own graves and God will deal with you two justly. Allah watches over everything that happens and if your husband cheats on you, your husband will receive his own punishment on Al-Qiyamah[52].

Second, do not make room for your husband to disrespect you. Once you've granted your husband the opportunity to disrespect you, you'll surely have a hard time throughout your marriage. It shouldn't be this way, but this is the condition of women within our community who are proven to not be virgins on their wedding night."

I guarantee you that this discussion with my aunt remained with me from that point forward. I wouldn't let any temporary relationship become the reasons why I commit a major sin in Islam or invite my future husband to disrespect me. Honestly, a temporary relationship wasn't worth it. However, I began to question what that meant for me as a Muslim woman, especially since I wanted to marry a Fulani man. It could be that Allah set

---

52 Al-Qiyamah: the day of resurrection or the day of judgement.

the guidelines for both men and women to be married virgins, but how does a woman run from cultural practices which prove her virginity? These white cloth cultural practices are not mandatory in Islam, but many Muslim women have been humiliated in the process of this cultural practice.

Chapter Twenty-Two: American Muslim Teen

In 2010, I began my tenth grade school year at UASBYW- and by now, I was accustomed to the New York City lifestyle. During tenth grade, I had a different circle of friends; but, I still enjoyed my school.

My parent's divorce was still weighing down on me, and honestly, I didn't believe my opinion mattered.

I woke up early every morning to get ready for school. After brushing my teeth, I'd take a shower, and pick out my school uniform, I typically went on to doing my hair and makeup. When I felt that my hair and makeup was done, I'd dress up into my school uniform.

My school uniform was intended to look modest, but I found ways to make my school uniform revealing. I'd either wear tight pants or a skirt hemmed above knee length. After getting dressed, I'd check out my outfit to make sure that I was satisfied with my look. After feeling content with my look, I'd grab my school bag and cellphone and rush towards the train station.

The closest train station to my house was a thirty-minute walk, so during the walk there, I'd place headphones in my ears and listen to music. I listened to music at a low volume to remain aware of my surroundings. Sometimes listening to music helped me forget all the drama I was experiencing at home.

Unfortunately, now that some of the girls attending my high school were familiar with each other, there was drama at school. Some of the girls attending my high school went to parties together, drank with each other, and some of them even dated each other. Most of the drama at my school originated at social gatherings outside of the school grounds. Social media was gaining more popularity during this time and many of the students were using social media platforms to dispute their conflicts. No one really wanted a MySpace account anymore, so students began switching over to using Facebook. Students posted all their issues on Facebook, and then, the next day, students would fight out whatever problems they encountered on Facebook.

School administrators at my high school spoke with students several times to let them know that social media isn't the place to resolve personal drama. Teachers stressed going to the guidance counselors for help in disputing these situations.

"Girls, let the Guidance Counselors know the issues you're facing outside of school. The Guidance Counselors are prepared to resolve any conflicts you may be encountering with another girl here at school."

However, students never listened to the advice of school staff because they constantly found ways to handle disputes on their own - normally through fist fighting.

Countless times, girls made plans to meet up someplace after school and fight. If girls didn't want to wait until after school, they'd quarrel in the school hallway. I was rarely involved in drama stemming from social gatherings because I didn't want to be part of the life of drinking or smoking. My idea of fun was window shopping, eating at restaurants, or ice skating. I tried steering clear from friendships which involved a lot of partying because I didn't want to get caught up as a Muslim girl.

After school my friends and I would go out to Soho, Manhattan to hang out. At any given time of day, there are crowds of people shopping around at shops like Prada, Gucci, Ralph Lauren, Versace, Necessary Clothing, Victoria's Secret, The North Face, etc. Occasionally, my friends and I would purchase items from the stores, but for the most part, we'd window shop. More often, my friends and I were on a budget and given that most of the stores were expensive, we couldn't afford the products being sold at these stores. I normally spent the money I made from working at the Fort Hamilton Commissary on the weekends. Occasionally, my friends and I would purchase an item we couldn't leave behind.

My friends and I would take countless strolls around Soho. Many stores in Soho designed their storefronts to draw the customer's attention toward the store. The detailed designs of the store fronts often led me and my friends into entering the stores. If the store front looked interesting, but we didn't know the name of the store, we'd walk inside and learn more about the company. Frequently, my friends and I would learn that the store was a startup business which opened in Soho.

As the sun set and evening approached, my friends and I would go our separate ways home. I always reached home late into the evening, where I'd find my mom infuriated.

"Julde, didn't I tell you to come straight home after school!" my mom would yell.

"I wanted to hang out with my friends."

"Julde, I don't care what you want to do! Now you're on punishment."

My mom would turn off the television cable and take away my cell phone. I honestly didn't want to stay home every day; I wanted to go hang out in the city with my friends. I didn't want to be home, where all I felt was a tug-of-war between isolation and conflict. My older siblings had long moved out, my parents were divorced, and the house was a constant reminder that my life was changing.

The next day, I'd get up and get ready to go to school. Despite being on punishment, I would go out after school to hang out with my friends in Manhattan, not even caring about the consequences that I would face later.

My friends and I laughed together and made hilarious jokes. We spent the rest of our afternoons discussing our many dreams and aspirations. We knew that we wanted to become thriving members of our society. We spoke about the career paths we dreamt of pursuing, potential colleges we had in mind, or where we wished to travel as adults. With or without a phone, I was going to hang out.

On the weekends I continued commuting to the Fort Hamilton Commissary to make more money for myself. I made enough money to purchase meals during the school week and whichever excess money I made, I saved it in a box under my bed. Whenever I reached around $500 or $600 in savings, I'd go to the hair salon and get my hair done; then go to the nail salon to get my nails done and eyebrows waxed. I spent nearly $300 getting my hair and nails done. As for the $200 or so remaining, I'd purchase new outfits and shoes to wear on the weekends.

I made sure to look cute whenever I went outside. If that meant keeping up with my hair, nails, and eyebrows, I got it done. I especially enjoyed the new song that came out around the time by Drake called "Fancy" because I relived those lyrics.

I wore clothing, but the clothing revealed the shape of my body. I either wore extra tight pants with a blouse or a miniskirt which was above knee length. I had no regards or limits to how I exposed my body. Showing my body meant that I was liberated, and it celebrated my beauty, and I was content with how I dressed. I didn't feel uncomfortable before stepping outside. The moment I stepped outside, men from across the street would call out to me.

"Damn girl, you look good, you just need to get a lil' thicker!"

"Don't listen to him, you look good just the way you are!"

Every guy down the block had some sort of comment about my outward appearance.

The concept of self-image is ingrained within the American culture. In most cases, one man is telling me he liked my appearance, while the other man is evaluating how my body would have looked "better". Every man has their own say about my outward appearance. I knew that I was beautiful, but it made me more self-conscious that different men were commenting on my appearance.

Female celebrities invest money to enhance their outward appearance. Teenage girls are accustomed to watching these celebrities on television and they begin to admire the body image of celebrities.

As a teenager, I couldn't help but notice that in the beginning of the celebrities' careers, they look natural, but as their careers begin advancing, their body also begins changing. Later down the line, I begin to realize that the celebrity suddenly has bigger bosoms, fuller buttocks, and plumper lips. I watched celebrities in the mainstream media and I admired their success. I saw them as successful people and for that reason, I took them as my role model. As a result, I similarly concerned myself with my body image. I didn't want to wear modest clothing. I felt that modest clothing took away from my beauty. I thought that modest clothing was something someone's grandmother would wear.

I never considered modest clothing as a representation of self-respect; rather, I saw it as a constraint. So, I continued putting on my extra-tight jeans or miniskirts every day. Sometimes I'd put on a shirt which revealed my stomach or boobs. I didn't care.

"Damn beautiful, do you have a man?"

"Let me get your number, maybe we can hang out sometime."

"You're too beautiful to be frowning, put a smile on your face."

Was I fortunate of having multiple men always following me, trying to talk to me, or touching me without my granted permission? No, it was really aggravating; however, I never thought that dressing modestly was a resolution to being left alone by men. There was no way a guy was planning on respecting me, unless I dressed to be worthy of his respect. Women are taught that wearing revealing clothing grants them freedom, when instead, it makes them prone to cat calling and harassment as they walk down the street. Whenever a guy approached me, he was evaluating my looks, rather than my personality. This meant that the guy truly didn't care about the quality of my personality, instead he was lusting at my outward appearance.

Maybe if the boy was cute, I'd talk to him, but I knew that there was possibly no chance of him marrying me. I didn't want to be used or played with in the process of talking to a boy who didn't care about me.

Then, if the male was too old, I didn't want him talking to me, PERIOD!

I didn't want someone old enough to be my father or grandfather to think that we were going to date. The reality is, my clothing choices made me approachable to any man. Whether the man was young or old, cute or ugly; he was seeing me with the very same outfit everyone else was seeing me in. My outfit choices were the result of drawing that man's attention. How could I blame a grown man for talking to me, when my clothing choices drew that attention?

Academically, I was doing great at the Urban Assembly School of Business for Young Women, even though I went out nearly everyday day after school with my friends. I exceeded in my Science course, over all other courses. My Science Regents[53] Exam scores also happened to be better than my other Regents Exam scores.

By the time I reached tenth grade, I was familiar with the environment at UASBYW. The school building was not huge, our community was small, and everyone knew each other in the school.

A few incoming students who entered ninth grade were also Muslim, so I began hanging out with them. For the most part, we could only hang out during lunchtime or after school because they were in a lower grade level than me. But, we exchanged contact information, so we could hang out with each other on the weekends. Even though I wasn't current with my practice of Islam, the Muslim girls didn't judge me. The Muslim students were younger than me, but they were inspirational. They followed the religion properly, they were focused on studying for their classes and they didn't do drugs or drink alcohol. I knew that hanging out with them would be beneficial for me. All my Muslim friends were from some part of Africa and it was nice to hang out with them and see how similar their culture was to my mom's.

One of my Muslim friends had an overprotective dad and I believe my mom was nearly like her dad because she got in trouble for hanging out afterschool. What made my friend's dad different from my mom, her dad put a GPS tracker on her cellphone. If my friend's dad found out she was hanging out, she got into serious trouble at home.

After school, my friends and I were sad to see her go home, but she had no other choice. One day I suggested, "Why don't you leave your cell phone in the school locker so that you can hang out?"

"Trust me, my dad would find out," she replied.

"How is that even possible?" I asked her.

She went on to explain that one day her dad found out that she took her hijab off in school.

---

53 Regents Exam: a New York State exam which is used to assess a student's academic achievement within a particular course.

"Wait a second, how did your dad find out you took your hijab off in school?" I asked.

"I don't *know*, that's my whole *point*."

Then all my friends erupted in laughter.

As a solution to the problem, her parents didn't mind if we came over to her house to hang out. The problem was she lived all the way in the Bronx and I lived in Brooklyn, this meant that I'd have to travel two hours on the train to get back to Brooklyn in the evening. I decided that it would be better for me to go over to her house on Fridays or on weekends; whenever I decided to take off from working at the Commissary.

During the Summer of 2011, I hung out with some more friends I made in New York City. They weren't Muslims, but I enjoyed their company. They exhibited awesome personalities and whenever we spent time with each other, we would laugh for hours.

The issue is I didn't want to do the same things my non-Muslim friends were doing. Some of my non-Muslim friends could sit home with their parents to drink alcohol them, whereas this is something I'd *never* do with my parents.

Some of my friends were around sixteen and seventeen-years old, but their parents allowed them to drink alcohol. I wasn't willing to drink alcohol with my friends and their parents, for my *own* religious purposes. My unwillingness to drink alcohol set me apart from my friends. While they were drinking alcohol, I was off to the side drinking soda or juice.

My friends would always tease me and say, "At least we have someone who could drive us home after a party," I'd laugh along to their joke because I didn't mind taking that responsibility if I learned to drive. What mattered is that my friends would get home safe. If I could help my friends get home safe after a party, I'd gladly escort them home.

No matter how close we got, I didn't engage in most things my peers did. I enjoyed their choice to live however they wanted, but I didn't like for them to insist that I'd join them in those activities.

"No, I don't drink alcohol," I said one day. while I was at my friend's birthday party.

"Okay, we understand. You don't have to drink alcohol," everyone told me.

I began getting thirsty, so I asked the people at my friend's house, "Is there anything to drink?"

Everyone pointed towards the alcoholic beverages.

"No, do you have a non-alcoholic drink?" I asked.

"All we have is alcoholic beverages," they answered.

Then one of my friend's mother asked me, "Do you want me to make you a strawberry daiquiri?"

"Are you going to add alcohol?"

"No, I'm not going to add alcohol."

It was already past midnight and I was scared to drink alcohol, especially being that I would have to return home while using the New York City transit system. I lived nearly an hour away from my friend's house and I was around sixteen-years-old.

"Are you ready to go home?" I asked one of my friends.

"No, the party has just started. Why would we want to go home?"

The mother finished making my strawberry daiquiri and I took a small sip from the daiquiri before realizing she spiked my daiquiri with alcohol. I was disappointed. I wouldn't even do something like that to my friends. I sort of felt betrayed because if they needed help, I would've helped them. Now, I know that I cannot trust them because one of their mothers spiked my drink with alcohol.

I was stuck between going home alone or waiting for my friends, to ride the train home with them. I didn't want to be out alone in New York City in the hours past midnight. It wasn't safe for a sixteen-year-old girl to be out in New York by herself past midnight.

By the time my friends and I left the party, they could barely walk home, or even stand up straight. Their bodies swayed side to side as they leaned on each other for support. While walking to the train station, one of my friends grabbed onto me for support.

New York's city streets were normally busy, but in this case, everything was silent. Cars passed by occasionally, but not like they did during broad daylight.

My tongue began feeling dry because I barely drank anything that night. I made my way to a twenty-four-hour corner store to purchase a bottle of water.

It was a relief to finally get cool water to make its way down my system. It especially felt good to take my last gulp of water.

While walking to the train station with my friends, some guys passed by us and tried to flirt with us. We were all wearing revealing clothing, so it wasn't a surprise that they would try to talk to us. I was frightened with the idea of having my intoxicated friends being spoken to by older men who could easily grab and rape all of us. I knew that at that moment we were all vulnerable. Thank goodness we got home safe that night.

Later into Summer of 2011, my dad purchased airline tickets, so that my younger sister and I could go visit him in North Carolina, where he was stationed for work. We prepared all our belongings to get ready and take our flight heading towards North Carolina. My dad waited for my younger sister and I at the airport, so that he could pick us up and go to his new home. While driving to his home in North Carolina, my dad showed my younger sister and I the new military base that he was working at. My dad was now working on Fort Bragg, which he considered to be an enormous military base.

"There's Fort Bragg. You said that you work at the Commissary, right Julde?"

"Yes, I work at the Fort Hamilton Commissary as a grocery bagger."

"Well, yes, Fort Bragg has two Commissaries on their base, that's how big it is."

We ended up driving past Fort Bragg and heading directly to my dad's house. Immediately after entering my dad's house, he directed my younger sister and I to the room we'd be staying in. We placed our belongings in the room and enjoyed the rest of our evening at my dad's house.

For the next couple of days, my dad arranged to take my younger sister and I out to different parts of North Carolina. We went out to the movies, we visited a nearby water park, went shopping and he took us out to get our nails done. We did everything possible to spend time with my dad.

Chapter Twenty-Three: Finding Yourself is a Purposeful Journey

My dad takes my younger sister and me to the Fort Bragg Post Exchange. While shopping at their Post Exchange, I can't help but notice there's a jewelry box display near the cash registers containing religious chains and pendants. I decide to look through the chains and pendants to find a Muslim chain. I search repeatedly trying to make sure I didn't skip a Muslim chain by accident. I find chains with a cross or Star of David, but I can't find a chain with a crescent and star or lettering of Allah written in Arabic.

I notice that the chains and pendants sitting on display are only tailored towards people practicing Judaism and Christianity, but none catered to those practicing Islam. I feel a bit disheartened as I reflect on the countless times I've met Muslim men and women serving in the United States military who aren't offered a set of jewelry to accommodate their religious practice. I leave the Fort Bragg Post Exchange feeling like the Muslims living on base weren't of value; like we're less than our religious counterparts. Muslim families living on base lacked representation, but as members of the military community, our representation was as necessary as our Jewish and Christian counterparts.

In 2011, I began my eleventh-grade school year at the Urban Assembly School of Business for Young Women. At this point I was more confident about my future career path. I made sure to be hardworking and I took every necessary step to learn skills which would benefit me after graduating high school.

My high school staff was looking for girls to be part of the virtual entrepreneur class for the school year. The virtual entrepreneur class was going to teach the girls at my school how to work in an actual corporate office; however, there wasn't enough space for every eleventh-grade student to be part of the class. The staff at UASBYW took crucial steps to interview students whom would make ideal candidates for the virtual entrepreneur class.

"After lunch we'll hold interviews for students who appear suitable for the virtual entrepreneur class. Get ready for the interview and make sure to explain why we should pick you for the virtual entrepreneur class," the staff announces over the loudspeaker.

Before the selection process begins, I get ready for my interview. I prepare for what I'd say during the interview. I want to pursue a corporate career and the virtual entrepreneur class would prepare me for the corporate world. Just before lunch, I feel the butterflies in my stomach.

I wouldn't receive a second chance to be part of the virtual entrepreneur class if I messed this up. This interview is my one-time opportunity to prove why I should be in that class. When lunch ends, I go to my class and wait to be called in for my interview. After several minutes, the staff and some twelfth-grade students ask me to follow them in for an interview.

I feel anxious and my hands begin to sweat, but I have to make sure that I secure my spot for the virtual entrepreneur class. Despite being a nervous wreck, I walk into the interview room with confidence.

Without displaying any sign of nervousness, I say:

> *Ever since I was eight years old, I've had a strong passion for business. I mixed lemonade at home and sold it within my neighborhood. I went out in my neighborhood to neighbors who wanted me to wash their car. Currently, I'm part of the mentee program at the Urban Assembly School of Business for Young Women. I'm partnered with a mentor working at American Express. My mentor gives me insights about her daily working experience at American Express.*
> *I am the right choice for the virtual entrepreneur class because business is an ingrown passion. Business and corporation is what I was born to pursue.*

After some consideration, I'm selected among twenty-something other students to be accepted into the virtual entrepreneur class. This class was a passage for students seeking a career in the corporate world following their graduation from UASBYW.

My classmates and I sit in the virtual entrepreneur class for the first time learning information vital to the program. The virtual entrepreneur teacher informs us that we are going to compete with other high school students at the end of the school year. The competition would take place at a convention where judges would judge how each high school ran their business.

Every high school was provided a virtual money credit. Students are supposed to use this money credit to purchase products and services from other high schools. Considering that I loved business since I was a young girl, I feel ready for the class.

My classmates and I come together to design a business that we'd use for class. Following some debate, we agree to publish a magazine. So, my teacher asks, "If you're going to publish a magazine, what would be the main theme of your magazine?"

Immediately, students start speaking out of turn. The classroom grows noisy as we discuss which themes we prefer for our magazine. While discussing potential themes, we realize that the best theme for our magazine would be culture.

My classmates and I live in New York, which is enriched in multiple, thriving cultures. Most of the students in my classroom didn't even come from the same continents, countries, or cities, as each other. Being that we were already in a culturally diverse city, we had a special connection to the theme of our magazine publication. Our magazine was going to be about cultural diversity and this theme was associated with New York's unique identity. Each issue of our magazine would be about a different cultural practice that is done across the globe.

Together, we sit inside the classroom trying to determine what we'd title our publication.

"How about we title the magazine, COLORS?" someone shouts from the other side of the classroom.

Every student agrees that we should name our magazine COLORS, but we want to make the title an acronym as well. My classmates and I ponder hard about what COLORS could stand for. Finally, as a team, we come up with, "Cultural Opposites Learning Our Real Stories".

We divided the magazine into topics like: music, clothing, makeup, religion, history and lifestyle. Sometimes students can place their own writing pieces in each issue of the magazine.

We divide the work amongst ourselves. Some of the students in the class work as human resource managers, photographers, accountants, editors, website designers and publishers. I'm chosen to be an editor for the magazine. There are other editors on my team, with each of us assigned to cover our respective topics. The editor-in-chief chooses me to be editor of beauty. I'm to edit any articles in relation to beauty topics of any given culture.

The school guidance counselor created a club after school called Business Careers Etiquette Club. I was interested in joining this club because I wanted to learn the basics of business etiquette, considering I was planning on working in the corporate world. Right after school, I'd attend the Business Careers Etiquette Club.

The guidance counselor introduces both herself and the other instructor who assisted in forming the business careers etiquette club manual. After giving their introductions, we begin our first etiquette lesson.

The teacher hands every student a Business Careers Etiquette Club manual. Our guidance counselor allows us time to skim through the book. She wanted us to have an idea of the lessons we'll be learning in the club.

The teacher starts the club discussion by providing tips such as, "Everyone should always keep napkins and mints in their purse in case of emergencies. You do not want to push away business partners because your breath smells. Napkins are good just in case you need to clean anything unhygienic from your body. Make sure you do not drink from a cup while wearing lipstick, gently dab off the lipstick with a napkin."

She says that it's unpleasant to stain your glass or cup with lipstick. After the introductory class is done, we all leave to go home.

I felt good about my eleventh-grade school year. I was nearly finished with high school and it was crucial that I begin figuring out what career I was going to pursue. The virtual entrepreneur class and the Business Careers Etiquette Club motivated me to go for my future achievements.

The staff at the Urban Assembly School of Business for Young Women were actively preparing students for college. The staff planned numerous college field trips within New York State. Our school principal wanted to make sure that every girl graduating from the Urban Assembly School of Business for Young Women were all going straight to college.

Not only did we have numerous college trips; but, the school staff also prepared to have motivational speakers lecture us every week.

The school invited motivational speakers who'd push the students in achieving high career goals. The school staff invited businesswomen most of the time to discuss how they overcame the challenges of being women in the business world. This really motivated me and a lot of the other students, especially because we were an all girl's public school.

Other times the school invited male entrepreneurs who faced the challenges or battles of paving a way in the business world due to their race or ethnicity. Yet, despite all those struggles, they still found ways to become some of the most successful individuals in the world.

The whole purpose of the inspirational messages was for students to never give up on their goals or dreams. Despite the obstacles we may face in life, we should go out every day and try to pursue our dreams.

In the meantime, teachers handed out field trip forms for the students to go visit different college campuses in New York State. The college campuses that we'd visit would encourage us to go to their school.

"I'm going to apply for this college," some of the students would say.

The staff at the Urban Assembly School of Business for Young Women arranged to have tour guides walk us around the college campuses. While touring the different campuses, we couldn't help but admire the life of college students.

We visited a maximum of three colleges per day. Sometimes we viewed two colleges in a day if the colleges we were visiting had activities for the students to engage in. My classmates and I sat in numerous auditoriums listening to professors and students talking about what college was like.

In the evening, all of the students would go back to their hotel rooms and get ready so that we could go out and eat dinner with our teachers. Our teachers found reasonably priced restaurants in the area to take everyone out to eat.

Sometimes the college trips would take two to three days and then everyone would pack their belongings to head back to New York City.

My high school staff was concerned with every single student's attendance in college. We spent a few weekends on coach buses, which my high school rented, so that we could visit nearby colleges. The field trips rarely cost more than $25 and the staff always recommended that we bring pocket money in case we wanted to buy anything extra while on the trip.

Sometimes, we'd catch the New York City Transit together and tour colleges within our immediate neighborhoods. Of course, we could've viewed colleges within our neighborhoods on our own; however, our school staff took the initiative to take us there themselves. At this point, my parent's divorce slowly faded from my mind.

I began thinking to myself, "If I let my parent's divorce drain me, I'll never move forward with my life." I had to stop thinking about my parent's separation and worry about how I could better equip myself for the future.

I had no issue with being financially independent, but after the divorce I depended on my finances even more. My dad provided my mom with sufficient money to take care of me and my younger sister, but my mom's expenses were accumulating. This was hard for me because not only did I attend school, but I worked every weekend.

I continued bagging every weekend at the Fort Hamilton Commissary for income. Winter was fast approaching, and I wanted to save enough money to buy winter items.

While grocery bagging on the weekends, I developed relationships with some of the customers who regularly shopped at the Fort Hamilton Commissary. Some of these customers were active duty military, while others were retired military. The customers became so familiar with me that they often spoke to me like we were family.

They learned my name and requested I packed their groceries.

"Julde, I'd like for you to pack my groceries today."

"Okay, sure no problem, let me get a cart first."

I walk over to grab a cart and stand by the register waiting to pack the customer's groceries.

"Julde, what's your bagger number again?" the cashier asks me.

"My bagger number is 104."

"Okay, got it."

Then the cashier begins scanning all the groceries down the register for me to pack. I pack all the customer's perishables in one bag, cans and bottles in another, and fragile items packed and stowed separately.

"Ma'am, would you like to hold your bread and eggs?"

"Yes, thank you, that's the reason why I prefer you to pack my groceries. A few other people have broken my eggs or smashed my bread, but I know that you'll always hand them to me."

"Sorry to hear that, sometimes new baggers accidentally smash fragile items. When they get used to the job, they learn to hand the fragile items over to the customers."

"Oh, well, I don't want to take any risks and find my bread and eggs crushed when I get home, so I'd rather you just pack my groceries instead."

When I finish packing the order, the customer and I walk outside to the car and I begin placing the groceries into their trunk.

I did this all day: whether it was sunny, rainy, cloudy, or whatever the weather, I packed groceries and took the groceries out to the customer's car. At the end of my workday, I'd count all the tips I made for the day.

My workday ended at 7:00pm, at which point I'd head home, take a shower, and get ready for bed.

I put all the money I earned into a safe under my bed. Although I did have a bank account, my bank didn't have any branches in New York City to conduct my transactions, so I usually left the money I didn't want to save in my account under my bed.

I stare into the mirror on my dresser and while looking at my reflection, I realize that I have new growth.

It's that time of the month again, I have to go back to the salon to get another hair relaxer.

Maybe I'll go to the salon next week and get my hair done. Tomorrow is Sunday and I want to go back to the Fort Hamilton Commissary for work.

I get ready for bed and sleep into the next morning.

I wake up around 6:00 am to get ready for work. I go to the bathroom, brush my teeth, and take a shower. After my shower, I get out and prepare my flat iron to straighten my hair extensions. When I finish straightening my hair extensions, I try my best to lay down the new growth.

I don't like when the texture of my hair does not match the texture of my hair extensions. It doesn't look cute when your Afro-textured hair stands out from the Indian Remy extensions.

After fixing my hair the best I could, I dress up and head for work.

It takes roughly an hour using the New York City trains for me to reach the Fort Hamilton Commissary. Upon arriving at work, I put on my bagging uniform and wait until 10:00am for the store to open for customers.

My workday begins all over again.

I continue packing all the customer's groceries and taking the groceries to their cars. One of the customers who knows me very well requests me, but he doesn't know my name.

"I'd like to request bagger number 104 to pack my groceries!"

I get up from where I was seated, grab a cart, and prepare to pack his groceries.

"Hello, how are you today?" the customer asks.

"I'm doing good," I say while smiling. "And, how are you doing?"

"I'm doing the best I can. What's important, is that I woke up alive," the customer responds.

"That's true, unfortunately some people didn't live to see another day."

"Yes, that's unfortunate, and it's a blessing to be here today. How's school?"

"School's good," I say while actively packing the customer's groceries.

I learned that not only do I have to pack groceries, but I must be a multitasker as well. Some customers loved to talk while you packed their groceries.

When the cashier is finished ringing up the customer's groceries, the customer tells the cashier his payment method and pays for his groceries. As he heads for the exit, I follow behind him with a cart full of groceries, and we walk outside to his car.

While walking to his car, the customer says, "You're a very hardworking child. Every time I come here, you're out here working. Are you doing good in school?"

"Yes sir, I'm doing good in school. I come here on the weekends so that I can earn extra cash for myself."

"Well, you're a very hardworking child. Do you plan on attending college?

"Yes sir, I plan on going to college immediately after graduating high school."

"That's good, I like to see young African-American children bettering themselves. We didn't have a bright past here in the United States, but whenever I see a young African-American child like you, I hope that they're going to college. What do you plan on studying?"

"I'm going to be a business major."

"What part of business do you specifically plan on studying? Business is very broad."

"Well I'm interested in studying marketing."

"Marketing? Are you sure you want to study marketing? Do you even think you're going to get a good job in that field? You could always push for your dreams, but as an African-American, marketing is a tough field to enter. Initially, I thought you were going to say something like the medical or technology field."

"No, I want to pursue a career in marketing."

"Well, then pursue your career in marketing. You have surely paved a journey for yourself because you're an African-American woman. Your chances of entering the marketing field is difficult. Here, this money is for you, go buy your personal things and make sure you focus on school."

I was too naïve at that point to think that he was wrong about me getting into marketing. I never had uncertainty that my overall identity would make it harder for me to enter the marketing field. I was confident that by pushing myself, I'd certainly have that career later in life.

I walk back into the Commissary to continue my day's work.

Later that week, I go to the beauty salon to do my hair.

"Good Afternoon Jay! Is it okay if I call you Jay? I have a hard time pronouncing your name."

"My name is Julde [Jul-DAY], it's only two syllables! You can learn how to say that."

"Okay, just keep reminding me on how to pronounce your name. I'll eventually get it. Which hairstyle do you want today?"

"I want to relax my hair and add in some extensions."

"'I forgot the type of relaxer you usually use," my hairstylist says.

"I like the olive oil relaxers."

"Okay Jul... Julde? Did I say your name right?"

"Yes, you said my name right."

Two minutes later, the beautician comes over with the olive oil relaxer. She puts gloves on her hands, and begins sectioning my hair to place the relaxer on my roots.

While placing the relaxer on my roots, the beautician says, "Let me know when it burns."

"Okay, I'll let you know."

The beautician places the relaxer on my roots and slowly works it through my hair. Shortly after, my hair begins burning.

"It's burning!" I tell the beautician.

"Let me rub it in some more," the beautician tells me.

At this point, I'm in so much pain and my scalp feels like it's on fire. The beautician sprays oil sheen in my hair to ease the burning of the relaxer. Five minutes later, the beautician and I rush towards the sink so that she can rinse the relaxer out from my hair.

When the beautician feels that she's completely rinsed the relaxer out my hair, she places rollers in my hair and tells me to sit under the hair dryer. When I get out of the hair dryer, I sit back at the beautician's booth so she can add in my hair extensions. As she finishes putting all the extensions into my hair she says, "That will be $120."

I pull out my money and pay the beautician. After getting my hair done, I go to the nearest nail salon to get my nails done and eyebrows waxed. When I finish getting everything done, I go home.

Just as before, I spent approximately $250 trying to make sure that my hair fit the standard of beauty.

Why couldn't I just ignore the countless stereotypes revolving Afro-textured hair being "unprofessional" or "messy" and appreciate my hair's true texture? I wondered what my true hair texture looked like, but I wasn't ready to embrace it because I didn't know what to expect after going natural. I was used to other black people telling me, "Your naps are growing," Or "Your hair is nappy," when a short inch of new growth grew in.

Wearing hair extensions is not permitted in Islam and it makes my obligatory five daily prayers invalid. I couldn't help but think that everything I spent my money on would make it harder for me to carry out a valid prayer. I was divided between living up to the standard of beauty or being a loyal worshiper to the almighty Allah. Allah is the King, the Provider, the All-Knowing, All-Seeing, All-Hearing, Magnificent, and Nourisher, but I disobeyed him to live society's standard of beauty.

Chapter Twenty-Four: What's Your Vision?

In the winter of 2011, God had his own plans for me. One day, my friends and I were trying on makeup in a cosmetic store while I was wearing colored contact lenses.

The next day one of my eyes began turning pink. By the second day, my eyes turned from pink to red. On the third day, pus was leaking out the surface of my eye.

Nobody in my family had a clue what was going on with my eye. All we knew was pus slowly oozed out the surface of my eye. Whatever it was, it was becoming difficult for me to see.

I needed someone in my family to guide me to the hospital. It was my mom's workday, but she was the only person that could help me get there.

"Mom, look at my eye, there's pus flowing out."

"Julde, that's normal. Puss comes out of people's eyes while they are sleeping. Just wipe the corner of your eye and it will go away."

"No, Mom, this is different. I've wiped this pus from my eyes several times. It's coming from the surface of my eye."

"Okay Julde, let me look at your eye." My mom gets up from the couch and walks over to me. As she leans over to take a closer look, she suddenly jerks back and gasps.

Oh, my goodness, how did that happen?!"

"Mom, I don't know but I can barely see, and I need to go to the emergency room. Can you please take me?"

My mom is now a single parent and she typically doesn't like taking days off from work because she only works part-time, and it means she'd make less money for her bills.

But, who else was going to take me to the emergency room?

That morning, my mom calls her job to let them know she can't make it in for work. My mom tells her managers that this is an emergency and she'd have to take family medical leave. The managers at my mom's job approve her leave over the phone.

After getting approval for leave, my mom and I rush to the nearest emergency room, at Brookdale Hospital in Brooklyn.

When my mom and I arrive, the medical team isn't taking my condition seriously. The medical team try to convince me that my eye is just leaking regular pus.

"Ms. Ball, you know the pus that comes out from your eye when you wake up, *right*? That's what you have. Just wipe the corner of your eye and it will go away."

In that moment, I get frustrated with the nurse. The nurse clearly isn't listening to my concerns. Instead, she's brushing my condition off like I came there for no reason.

"Ma'am, can you just take another look at my eye? I understand what you're trying to say. This isn't the ordinary pus which forms after waking up. This is something different," I plead with the nurse, irritated.

The nurse takes a closer look at my eye and realizes that the pus was coming out directly from the surface of my eye. There's a second nurse in the room taking my vitals who opens a gauze pad and wipes the surface of my eye for me.

When the pus disappears, the first nurse thinks about sending me back home, but shortly afterwards the pus oozes out again. The medical staff immediately rush me into the emergency room unit and instruct me to lie down on the stretcher. Two physicians enter my room to ask me some questions.

The first physician asks me, "Ms. Ball, when did you initially realize that something was wrong with your eye?"

"About two days ago," I tell the physicians.

"Can I take a look at your eye?"

"Yes," I reply.

One of the physicians takes a gauze pad and wipes the surface of my eye. Both physicians watch wit dread as the pus slowly resurfaces.

At this point, both physicians look terrified; although, they never actually tell me that they're terrified. I also sense that neither physician has a clue what was going on, but they try to remain calm all the same.

The physicians leave me lying down on the stretcher and rush into another area of the emergency room before coming back with more medical staff. The additional physicians stand over me while I lie down on the stretcher.

Another one of the medical team members opens a gauze pad and wipes the surface of my eye, again.

"We have to send Ms. Ball upstairs to the ophthalmology unit."

"Okay, no problem. Ms. Ball, we're going to send you upstairs to the ophthalmology unit. They can better diagnose what is going on with your eye."

As I was lie down on the stretcher, the vision in one of my eyes begins to blur. I can no longer make out what I was seeing. The physicians send my mom and me upstairs to the Brookdale Hospital ophthalmology unit.

When my mom and I make it to the ophthalmology unit, the waiting room is packed. There are patients in the ophthalmologist's office for multiple reasons. Some patients have appointments, others are walk-ins, and there were other patients who had been referred by the emergency room, just like I had.

My mom and I sit in the ophthalmologist's clinic for hours. The doctors seem to be calling every patient in the clinic beside me. After waiting in the clinic for several hours, my mom and I begin asking the patient service representative at the front desk when I would be seen by a doctor. Every twenty to thirty minutes either my mom or I get up to ask when I would be seen by a doctor. Our impatience grows as the hours pass by.

Upset, I sit in the clinic waiting area, waiting for doctors to call me into the exam room. Although I'm an emergency room patient, there's no urgency for the doctors to see me.

The noise and foot traffic in Brookdale's ophthalmologist unit slowly fades as patients leaves the exam room. Finally, one of the physicians calls out, "Ball?"

When the physician comes out into the waiting area and sees that I'm a female, he says, "Ms. Ball, can you come and follow me?"

I'm the last patient seen by the physicians that day.

Three doctors come into the exam room to look at my eye. None of the doctors know what's going on. All three of the doctors look mind blown while they observe the condition of my eye, but they try to stay composed in front of me, as if they know what they are doing. This frustrates me even further because I'm the last patient seen by the doctors and they have yet to make a diagnosis for my eye condition. Unable to find a solution, the doctors tell me that they will provide me a referral to be seen at Kings County Hospital's ophthalmology unit.

The next day, my mom drops me off at my aunt's house. My aunt is supposed to take me to Kings County Hospital so that the doctors can check to see what is leaking out of my eye. When my aunt and I get to Kings County Hospital, we wait there for hours before being seen by an ophthalmologist.

Several doctors come into the hospital room to try to determine what was going on with my eye. None of the doctors have a clue what was going on. The doctors walk in and out of the ophthalmologist's office. They're trying to be attentive to my needs while keeping up with the other patients that were in their clinic. The doctors take note of what was going on with my eye, but still can't diagnose the problem, so they go off to help other patients.

The medical staff at Kings County Hospital speaks with medical staff at Brookdale Hospital. Both ophthalmology teams agree that they have no idea what's happening to my eye. The Kings County Hospital staff then tells me I would lose vision in that eye permanently.

They go on to say that they're going to send me to a hospital in New York which specializes in the treatment of eye diseases and conditions.

Specifically, I'm being sent to the New York Eye and Ear Infirmary of Mount Sinai.

My mom leaves work early that day to take me to the New York Eye and Ear Infirmary of Mount Sinai. I wait for my mom at my aunt's house, distraught. At this point my eye constantly stings and is extremely sensitive to light.

After thirty minutes, my mom arrives at my aunt's house and parks her car in the driveway. The New York Eye and Ear Infirmary of Mount Sinai is located near 14th street-Union Square in Manhattan. New York City's streets are full of heavy traffic daily and it's challenging to find free parking in Manhattan, so if we don't want to waste valuable time finding parking or paying to park in a garage, my mom and I know that it's best to travel toward Manhattan by using the New York City Subway system.

After stepping outside, I could barely open my eyes. My mom and I start walking to the nearest train station. It's very cold outside and all I can think of is putting my complete faith in Allah Almighty. The New York Eye and Ear Infirmary of Mount Sinai is about to be the third hospital to check the condition of my eye. None of the doctors at the prior hospitals could explain what was happening to my eye. Just by hearing the hospital's name, New York Eye and Ear Infirmary of Mount Sinai, I knew that if this hospital couldn't help me, I'd be going blind. I'm pretty sure that if they specialize in the treatment of eye conditions, but cannot help me, that I am doomed.

When my mom and I finally get to the subway station, my mom pays for both of our Metrocards. Then we patiently wait on the subway platform for the train that would take us to Manhattan.

I sit in silence. I don't want to talk about anything at this point.

I can only imagine how my life would be after becoming blind in one of my eyes - at the age of sixteen years old. After five minutes, the train arrives.

No one really knows what you are going through when you're boarding the New York City transit system. My vision was *so bad* that I can barely see where I'm going. One of my eyes is in good health, while the other one only sees shadows. It's getting hard for me to focus on where I'm walking.

The pus continuously oozes out of my eye. I accidentally bump into someone as I board the train and the guy starts behaving outlandish towards me.

"Watch where you're going, you just bumped into me!" the man scolds me.

"I'm sorry, I'm losing sight in one of my eyes," I reply to the guy.

Then I show the guy my eye. My vision might be going, but it's obvious I've left him speechless. I can sense sympathy from him before he manages a sheepish, "It's okay."

The New York City train is slow that day. I honestly don't think that the train could get any slower. Not to mention, there's train traffic and we're travelling during rush hour. The New York Eye and Ear Infirmary of Mount Sinai is about to close soon. The train rides past Wall Street and I instantly think about the days of high school I've missed. There's a good chance that next time I attend school, I'll be blind in one eye.

Finally, the train reaches 14th Street-Union Square. My mom and I search for the clinic that could help me with my condition. We run up and down 14th Street-Union Square asking people if they knew the location of the clinic. None of the people we ask know where the clinic is located.

With time running out, my mom and I finally find the clinic that we were looking for. It's still open, with the patient service representative sitting at the front desk. The patient service representative checks me in to see the doctor and then afterwards directs me to see the nurse. The nurse had already received information that I was supposed to see the physician for emergency circumstances, but the physician had left the clinic approximately ten minutes ago. Upon hearing this, I immediately break down in tears. At this point, nothing could keep me from losing my sight. The nurse feels bad, but there is nothing that anyone could do. The doctor didn't know if I was still coming because the clinic was closing, and the clinic never received a call from us.

My mom explains that she was rushing from work. She feels guilty for even going to work. My aunt, who was taking care of me the whole morning, also had three children of her own; so she was unable to take me to the clinic. She would have had to arrange for a babysitter to watch her children, which was near impossible on such short notice.

My mom and I start to head back to my aunt's house to get my mom's car. As we walk back to the train station, we call my aunt to update her about my visit at the New York Eye and Ear Infirmary of Mount Sinai.

My aunt feels bad that I couldn't meet with the physician that day. No one in my family knows what they can do to help me. I'm really not in the mood to talk to anyone after finding out we missed the physician by less than ten minutes.

When my mom and I arrive at my aunt's house in Brooklyn we thank her for her help. I didn't want to stay over her house, so my mom decides that we should get in our car and drive back home.

When my mom and I get home, I knew that my mom had empathy for me. My mom and I call my dad to update him on what happened with the third hospital. We tell him that we went to the New York Eye and Ear Infirmary of Mount Sinai, but the doctor left ten minutes prior to us arriving at the clinic.

I speak with my dad for nearly twenty minutes before deciding I wasn't in the mood to talk anymore.

My mom takes the phone from me and speaks to my dad further about the situation. She tells him that currently none of the hospitals had answers for my condition. When my mom gets off the phone, she looks at me, gives me a hug and tells me that she's sorry.

I knew why my family members were saying sorry. They were saying sorry because they felt bad and there was literally nothing that they could do to help me. Yes, I was helpless, but that didn't mean that they should apologize for this situation. My health condition wasn't their fault.

I didn't want my family members to tell me they were sorry because honestly, there was no reason for them to apologize about something that wasn't their fault. This situation only brought me closer to God.

I think to myself, "I'm only sixteen years old in the eleventh-grade and I'm about to go blind."

I go to the bathroom and decide to make wudhu for prayers. I take the necessary steps of making wudhu:

1. *I wash my hands three times.*
2. *Rinse my mouth three times.*
3. *Cleanse my nose three times.*
4. *Wash my face three times.*
5. *Wash my forearms three times.*
6. *Brush water on the top of my hair three times.*
7. *Wash each of my feet three times.*

When I was done with the necessary steps to cleanse myself, I dress for prayer. I get an abaya and a scarf carefully donning them. Then I get a prayer mat and begin praying.

I pray, but this prayer is different from any other prayer that I've prayed. I not only pray to God because I wanted my eyesight to be restored; rather, I pray to thank him for all the blessings I already had. Instead of focusing on what I'm losing, I want to express my gratefulness towards the blessings I already had available to me. My life would change after losing my eyesight; however, that isn't the thing that mattered. What matters to me is the stuff that I haven't lost in life.

Before every prayer, a Muslim opens the prayer with a surah from the Quran called Al-Fatihah, which literally means opening. The chapter is seven verses, which read:

1. *In the name of Allah, the Most Beneficent, the Most Merciful.*
2. *All the praises and thanks be to Allah, the Lord of the World.*
3. *The Most Beneficent, the Most Merciful.*
4. *The only Owner and the only ruling Judge of the Day of Resurrection.*
5. *You alone we worship, and You alone we ask for help.*
6. *Guide us to the straight way.*
7. *The way of those on whom You have bestowed your Grace, not the way of those who earned Your anger, nor of those who went astray.*

When I'm done praying, I make supplications. "Thank you for providing me with arms, legs, good health, a family," and I just go down the list. When

I'm done praying, my mom looks at me weird because prayer isn't the first thing she'd expect me to do in this situation.

"Everything is going to be alright, Julde," my mom tells me.

I give my mom a smile and respond, "Yes, everything is going to be alright."

My mom gives me a nervous smile back and in a curious tone asks, "How do you know everything is going to be alright?"

"Because at least I can see with my other eye, and that's better than being completely blind," I tell my mom.

My mom looks at me confused as she tries to hold back her tears. My mom and I both decide to end our conversation and prepare to go to sleep. We would have to get up early in the morning to see the doctor at the New York Eye and Ear Infirmary of Mount Sinai.

My mom and I get up early the next morning, got dressed and head directly to the New York Eye and Ear Infirmary of Mount Sinai. I'm the first patient to be seen by the physician. The physician mentions waiting for me yesterday, but after thinking we weren't coming, decided to leave. My mom and I tell the physician that we had no way of contacting them because we weren't given the direct extension number for the clinic.

At last, the physician diagnoses the condition of my eye. I have a corneal ulcer. The doctor at the New York Eye and Ear Infirmary of Mount Sinai grabs a sterilized medical swab to collect samples of the pus leaking from my eye for research. That same day, I'm instructed to head back to Brookdale hospital and follow up with the diagnosis. All three doctors pause on calling patients into their exam rooms. When there are no other patients in the back, they call me in so that they could follow up with the corneal ulcer diagnosis.

The doctors are now trying to figure out the nature of the bacteria developing on my cornea, so that they could medically treat my eye. I sit in the ophthalmology exam room as all three physicians take turns looking at my eye.

The doctors at Brookdale hospital explain that they needed to collect samples of the pus for lab research. They walk me into an adjacent exam room to collect samples of the bacteria. First, the physicians point to the bench for me to sit on. Then, the physicians recline the bench all the way back until I'm lying down. The three physicians get medical swabs and get ready for the specimen collection.

I'm informed that a proper specimen collection would require that the physicians clamp my eye open. The physicians show me the clamp and explain that the reason they're going to use a clamp was so I wouldn't blink the entire time they were collecting samples for research. I'm afraid of getting my eye clamped open, but I take a deep breath and let the physicians place the clamp on my eye. The specimen is sent to the lab for research and I'm instructed to wait in the waiting area until they receive the lab results.

After several hours of waiting, the physicians tell me that there is only one pharmacy which could make the eye drops for my eye. The pharmacist didn't know how he could treat my eye; but, he's a specialist.

One of the three physicians looks directly at me and says, "Due to the nature of the bacteria, this pharmacy is going to create experimental eye drops for your eye. The doctors mentioned that they were unsure how to treat this specific bacteria growing on my cornea his will be the first time that they make these eye drops for anyone."

After hearing the physician telling me this, I think to myself, "New York is packed with millions if not billions of people. There's hardly any space for buildings in New York City because of how overpopulated the city is. Nearly every building in New York City is a skyscraper with thousands of occupants residing inside and this is the first time any pharmacist in New York would make these eye drops?"

I was speechless.

I agree to take on this experiment because I have no other choice. What am I going to tell the doctors? No, I don't want to take part in an experiment which could possibly save my *eye*? The greatest choice I made was saying, "Okay, no problem, I'll take the experimental eye drops."

Corneal ulcers are a common infection, but the medical team weren't specifically familiar with the nature of the bacteria growing on my eye.

My mom and I head towards Kings Pharmacy on Flatbush Avenue. By the time we arrive, the pharmacist is nearly done creating the eye drops. He tells us that the treatment would require me purchasing two different bottles of eye drops.

Each bottle of eye drops costs $50, and that's after Tricare medical insurance pays their share of the medicine. My parents buy the two bottles of eye drops for a total of $100 so that I can begin my eye treatment.

The pharmacist instructs me to place eye drops in my eyes once every thirty minutes around the clock. He makes himself very clear about me needing to be diligent with his instructions.

"Ms. Ball, *make sure* you place the eye drops in your eye every thirty minutes around the clock. You need to follow these instructions if you want to save your eye. Alternate between the two eye drops."

For the next four days, I alternate the two drops in my eyes every thirty minutes around the clock. It's difficult placing eye drops in my eyes every thirty minutes, but considering how much I want to save my eye, I do it anyway. I lose a lot of sleep by constantly being up every thirty minutes. Each eye drop solution works differently. One eye drop burns my eye, while the other one soothes it.

I end up asking my mom, "Mom, can you please help me place these eye drops in my eye? It burns."

My mom walks over and helps me apply the eye drop.

"Open your eye, Julde. The drops aren't going to work if you close your eyelids."

My mom places her forefinger and thumb over my eyelids, holding them open to make sure she places the eye drops directly on my eye. The drops burn, but I take the pain and give the eye drops a chance.

Thirty-minutes later, I alternate to the eye drops which soothe my eye. I place those eye drops in my eye independently because it doesn't burn.

Constantly placing eyedrops in my eye is starting to get tiring, but I'm grateful that there's still hope for my eyesight to get better.

Later in the evening, I make wudhu for prayer. I mention in my prayer that even though the doctors figured out a way to treat my eye, I still want to give thanks for everything I have in my life. I may not be in perfect health, but there are other things in my life that are good. I need to be grateful for the things I have in life. One moment, everything could be going good in my life, and then suddenly everything can fall apart.

Throughout the night, I continuously reset my alarm to ring every thirty minutes to apply my eye drops. When morning arrives, I head back to Brookdale Hospital so that the ophthalmologists can re-examine me. The ophthalmologists stain my eye with a greenish-yellow eye drop.

After taking a close look, the doctors say that my eye is improving. However, when the three doctors move to the adjacent exam room, they start arguing about reasons why my eye wasn't improving. I had the right to know the progress of my eye; however, to spare my feelings the doctors avoided telling me the truth. It was painful to overhear the doctors arguing about whether my eye was improving.

"Are you *sure* my eye is getting better?" I ask the physician promptly after he arrives back in the exam room.

"Yes," he replies.

The doctor instructs me to keep placing the eye drops in my eye for treatment. After leaving the hospital, I only think about the positive things in my life. I don't want to focus on the negatives; that would bring me down.

The second night, I alternate the two drops in my eye again, every thirty minutes around the clock. It's now well over twenty-four hours since I started applying eye drops and I'm exhausted. I accidentally oversleep during one of the thirty-minute intervals and I wake up in anguish.

I begin to cry because I haven't slept well for the past two days, the doctors seem dishonest, and I'm learning how to adjust to this life-changing moment. I'm suffering from an eye condition that the doctors claimed they hadn't treated before.

By the third day, I don't have to show my identification or tell my name to the receptionist at the front desk; she already knew who I was. The patient service representative immediately asks me to sit down in the waiting area until I'm called to see the doctor.

"My name is Julde B...," I tried to tell the patient service representative.

She cuts me off, gives me a smile and says, "I know who you are, just go sit down in the waiting area until you're called by the doctor."

I sit down in the waiting area for nearly twenty minutes before I'm called by a doctor. After getting called into the exam room, I patiently wait for the doctor to check on the condition of my eye.

"Your eye is getting better, we'll send you to Kings County Hospital tomorrow," the doctor tells me.

"Isn't tomorrow Saturday? Will the clinic be open tomorrow?" I ask.

I'm confused because I never see medical clinics open on Saturdays; but, I have to put my trust in God and hope that the physicians working at Kings County Hospital could help me on a Saturday morning.

I go back home that evening joyful because my eye condition is getting better, and this time I can see the results myself. The pus is slowly disappearing and my eye looks like it's healing.

With the help of nearly twelve medical professionals, I was going to get my eyesight back. The most important thing was this situation brought me closer to God. For the rest of the night, I continue to alternate the drops in my eye every thirty minutes, encouraged by the Brookdale doctors' confirmation that my eye is getting better.

On the fourth day, my mom and I wake up, get dressed and head towards Kings County Hospital.

I walk into the ophthalmology clinic at Kings County Hospital and it's completely empty. From the lack of people in the clinic, I'm unsure of whether the clinic is actually open. There are no patients or receptionists in the clinic. And not to mention, we didn't have phone numbers to contact the physicians. Then, one of the physicians comes out into the waiting area to call me into the exam room.

The physician introduces himself by shaking my hand before walking us into the exam room. There are two physicians present at Kings County Hospital that Saturday. The two doctors use medical equipment to check on the progress of my eye.

Both physicians begin writing notes in their records as they examine my eye through the medical equipment. As I sit anxiously worrying about the results, I think to myself, "Maybe this will be my last night dropping eye drops in my eye."

Then one of the physicians looks up to give me a hard, stern look and says, "Ms. Ball?"

"Yes?" I nervously reply.

"You have saved your vision."

I nearly collapse with relief. I reconfirm with the physicians, asking, "If I saved my vision, do I still have to place eye drops in my eye?"

"No, you're no longer required to do that."

Then the doctor pauses for a long moment before proceeding to ask me, "How old are you again?"

"I'm sixteen years old," I told the doctor.

Both physicians stared at me in amazement, as if they almost didn't want to blink.

Then they said, "There are people much older than you who went blind because of a similar eye condition, just a different strain of bacteria growing. We instructed them to place their eye drops in their eyes every thirty minutes around the clock, but instead they'd sleep throughout the entire night."

The two physicians escort my mom and me out of the clinic and we immediately call my dad to update him on the progress of my eye.

After talking to my dad, I finally decide to contact my friends from high school and let them know why I had been absent for more than a week. After hearing the news, my friends were shocked. "Julde, where have you been?" my friends ask me before I proceed on, explaining the whole situation to them. My friends were glad I was doing okay. Now that my eye was treated, all I was worried about was sleeping in.

Promptly upon arriving home, I go straight to sleep.

The following Monday, I go back to school at the Urban Assembly School of Business for Young Women. My friends are thrilled to see me. The first thing my friends shout after seeing me is, "Julde!"

One of my friends jumps on top of me, knocking me over. My other friends joke by saying, "How could you just knock Julde over like that? Are you trying to make her blind again?" Then we all burst out laughing.

After returning to school, I still didn't wear the hijab; but I remained committed to praying. I prayed because despite doctors stating I'd go blind, I didn't go blind. I felt that the return of my eyesight wouldn't have been possible without the help of a higher power. At some point during my treatment, I believed in everything the doctors the doctors were saying. I accepted my fate of going partially blind and then committed to prayer.

Somehow during the quest to find a treatment for my eye, the physician at the New York Eye and Ear Infirmary of Mount Sinai was able to diagnose my condition, and the pharmacists at Kings Pharmacy made it possible for me to regain my eyesight. If it weren't for the guidance of Allah, I would've never came across these two skilled doctors who were the source of my eye treatment. They were two amongst the thousands of other doctors who worked in New York who could have been tasked with helping me. However, my treatment required teamwork. If it weren't for my trust in God, the medical staff, my health insurance, my family and me; there would have been no way I regained my vision.

I remained focus in school and after school activities. The experience of almost losing my eyesight allowed me to learn much about myself. I learned that I was disciplined, self-determined and whatever I wanted, I could get it done.

I had to catch up with my schoolwork, and it was especially difficult because I was roughly one week behind in my school work. With dedication, self-determination and time management, I was able to pass all my courses for the Fall 2011 term.

On the weekends, I continued working at the Fort Hamilton Commissary for tips. I wasn't going to give up on my goals. Yes, I was just a teenager, but I was trying to figure out the person I aspired to be in the future.

I was devoted to pursuing a career in marketing and despite what anyone said, I was going to pursue it.

I saved up to change my professional wardrobe. I felt that dressing up in professional attire would help me feel like a professional individual.

By 2012, much of the customers shopping at the Fort Hamilton Commissary really adored my personality. It didn't matter whether people tipped me or not, I treated everyone with the greatest respect. Many of the customers who shopped at the commissary regularly began wondering who my parents were. Most people working as baggers at the commissary were dependents of soldiers. People found out that my mom worked as a teller at the Commissary; however, since my dad didn't live in New York, they began asking about my dad. I told the customers that my dad is in the United States Army, but that he lived near Fort Bragg. If the customers asked me further questions, I told them that my parents were divorced.

That year, the store director and store administrator of the Fort Hamilton Commissary told me to apply for the sales store checker position. Both the store director and store administrator admired my work ethic. Since I was fourteen years old, they'd been watching me bag groceries at the commissary. They didn't want to let this opportunity pass me by, so they approached me about the job opening more than once. I completed every necessary step to apply for the position at the Defense Commissary Agency.

I went online at USAJOBS.gov to begin my online application. Within a couple of months, I received an over-the-phone interview and was immediately hired to be a sales store checker My first official paycheck job was for the Department of Defense.

The administrative staff at the Fort Hamilton Commissary told me every document I needed to provide them before beginning work. After submitting all my paperwork, I was told my hourly wage, and the date I was expected to report for my first day of work.

Before beginning work at the Fort Hamilton Commissary, I was to take an oath to the United States. The staff at the Fort Hamilton Commissary scheduled a day when I could state my oath in front of the American flag.

In April 2012, I began my first day of work at the Fort Hamilton Commissary. The store director, store administrator, administrative assistant and other store managers escorted me into a conference room. Collectively, the supervisory team at the Fort Hamilton Commissary congratulated me for getting the job. Then, I was told to face towards the American flag to take my oath.

I turned towards the American flag, raised my right hand and took my oath, repeating after my supervisor.

After saying my oath, I was provided with the address for the ID card office so that I could get my Department of Defense identification card. I completed all the mandatory training before beginning work.

I ran the cash register at the Fort Hamilton Commissary. I knew that being well-mannered would allow every customer to have a great shopping experience before leaving the Fort Hamilton Commissary.

Just as I did as a bagger, I politely greeted all the customers and asked them if they had a great day. Customers were thrilled to tell me everything about their day. Whether the customer had just finished watching their child's soccer game, seeing a newly released movie, or starting a new at-home business, they were delighted to communicate what made their day great. Afterwards, I'd share great details about my week. I spoke about my mentor program with American Express, the Business Careers Etiquette Club, or virtual entrepreneur program. When customers left the Commissary, they were happy with my customer service.

Not only was I concerned with providing customer service, I was also worried about paying close attention to the money in my register. I never lost money in my register, not even by one penny. If managers left me responsible with money, I tried my best to return the money without anything missing. Being off by one penny would have devastated me, even though the Commissary granted a grievance for money missing under $6.00.

I felt that my work at the Fort Hamilton Commissary reflected my values: integrity, loyalty, sincerity, truthfulness and trustworthiness.

I wasn't limited to working on the cash register. Sometimes I offered my help to managers overseeing other departments within the store. Sometimes I was instructed to look for expired items on the shelves, and when I did go looking for expired items, I made sure to take my time and check for every expiration date on the shelf.

"Julde, you found all those expired items?" my manager exclaims.

"Yes, I did," I reply while placing them in the warehouse.

"Really? Because I just sent two other people down that aisle last week to look for expired items and they told me there weren't any expired products on those shelves," the grocery manager says in amazement.

Nearly one month later, I began preparing for my high school's end of year business competition at the virtual entrepreneur convention. My high school selected a few students to represent COLORS magazine for the high school business competition and because of my school achievement, I along with a few other girls were chosen to represent our school.

The managers at my job gave me time off to meet with my classmates in preparation for the business competition. The business competition organizers scheduled a deadline for theme submissions, which was crucial to making sure that high schools wouldn't replicate each other's themes. Everyone in my class agreed that we'd use a Hollywood theme for the business competition.

The high school staff provided us with a budget for all expenses we planned on using for the business competition. The girls in my class purchased all the Hollywood-themed decorations and we pre-ordered shirts which read, "COLORS Magazine."

The afternoon before the business competition, my classmates and I went to the school gym where the business competition would be held to begin setting up our booth. We set up a replica red carpet, the Hollywood Walk of Fame, and decorated the booth with other Hollywood related items. Several girls in my class got their names on the Hollywood Walk of Fame, and I was one of the girls. My Hollywood star said, "Julde," which is obvious, but I was delighted to have my own star on the Walk of Fame.

The next morning, my classmates and I meet in the virtual entrepreneur class for the business competition. The teacher briefs all of us on instructions to follow for the business competition. Students from various high schools would begin the business competition with the same cash allowance and we were expected to use that allowance to purchase items from other high schools. High schools with the maximum number of sales would be the winners for the annual high school business competition. When the brief is complete, girls from my class go out to purchase products or services from other high schools. Other students are instructed by our teacher to remain at our booth and make sales for COLORS Magazine. The teacher tells us that we'd rotate shifts so that all of us would get a chance of purchasing products and services from other booths.

The other high schools thought of brilliant ideas to maximize their sales. High schools running food businesses had brought along actual food products for students to eat. One of the nicest booths at the business competition is an imitation ice cream shop, which looks like the genuine article. The ice cream shop is furnished with a menu including all the prices for the different flavors of ice cream, the queue is professionally roped for the customers, and there's a countertop where students can stand to purchase their ice cream. The realistic ice cream shop appears to be a good idea, until all their ice cream runs out. After hearing the ice cream shop ran out of ice cream, their dissatisfied customers go off to find other booths to purchase from. Other booths are selling unappealing items such as fake jewelry or cheap toys, but their marketing strategy would determine the high number of sales they could make at the business competition. Without a doubt, students with high confidence would sell the greatest number of items.

The gymnasium is flooded with high foot traffic. Music is playing throughout the gym and there is chitter chatter everywhere.

Then ultimately, there's my high school, the Urban Assembly School of Business for Young Women, selling COLORS magazine as our product.

COLORS magazine is a significant work because it not only displays the student's ability to conduct business, but it also shows that we're capable of research. It takes time and research for students in my class to publish our magazines monthly.

I speak about COLORS magazine with confidence at the business competition. I tell all my potential subscribers that the students in my class conducted research about specific cultures for each issue of the magazine we published. We investigate the lifestyles around those cultures including music, fashion, religion and we add our own unique writing pieces within the magazine.

I present an upbeat personality, promptly answering questions of potential subscribers. Overall, I'm well-informed about my high school's product. I instruct students from other high schools on how and where they could subscribe to our high school's magazine. When the business competition ends, everyone hands their receipt books over to our high school teacher and goes home.

The next day, I arrive in school and attend my regular school courses. The girls in the virtual entrepreneur class are told to wait on the results for the business competition —— until we met for our regular class period. The girls in my class are eager to find out the results. After entering class, we are told that our high school received an award at the competition. Our high school didn't receive first place, but receiving an award is enough to prove our hard work and dedication. Not only does the staff announce our class' accomplishment, but the staff also surprises me with an award I never thought I'd receive. To my surprise, I receive Employee of the Month for the virtual entrepreneur class.

The teacher mentions that the reason why I was receiving Employee of the Month was because I accomplished the highest number of sales in my class. At the end of the high school business competition, my teacher along with other high school staff, looked through the receipt books of all the students in the class. The staff couldn't help but notice that I made the most sales during the business competition. The teachers and students walk over to hand me the Employee of the Month plaque.

My weekly school schedule remained consistent as I continued working at the Fort Hamilton Commissary, and I remained committed to the Business Careers Etiquette Club and the American Express mentorship program. I finished my eleventh-grade school year by June 2012. That summer, I got engaged to Elhadj Ousmane Diallo.

Chapter Twenty-Five: Overlapping Identities

By the Summer of 2012, I had a longing desire to search for who I was as an African-American Muslim woman. First, I decided that I was over having boyfriends. I had had three boyfriends who aren't worth mentioning in this memoir, and I should probably refrain from saying horrible things about them.

In all three of the relationships, I had intended for them to eventually become my husband; however, I was not interested in marrying those boys. So, I began searching for someone who could be part of my life for the long term. My parents didn't have a problem with me having a boyfriend, but after continually reading verses of the Quran and reading hadiths, I decided that it was time for me to consider getting married. Not to mention, my aunt's speech from the year before haunted me.

I was scared that I'd be sinning in the eyes of Allah and falling astray due to the temptations of the hypersexual society surrounding me. I already took issue that I wasn't fulfilling my basic obligations as a Muslima teenager and I believed marriage could connect me with Islam. And just as my aunt asserted, I heard many stories of Muslim women getting mistreated for not being married chaste, and being that a Fulani boy would be my preference for marriage, I didn't want to have that dilemma. In the Fulani tradition, a female bride is expected to carry out the white sheet tradition and the man's family would verify the bride's virginity through observing a blood-stained cloth. The news of a woman's virginity would be told to the family and that wasn't a sin I'd want to share with an entire family for the rest of my life.

I was searching for a deeper understanding of my identity because not only am I black, but I belonged to two different black identities. What does it mean to belong to two different black identities? Well, being black is a racial group, but within being black, there are ethnicities like Jamaican, Guinean, Trinidadian, Malian, African-American, or Haitian. And each of our cultures are different.

My dad happens to be a Black American from Virginia. For generations, all my dad's family knew was American culture and practices. Yes, my dad's ancestors experienced a great deal of slavery, Jim Crow laws, segregation, and all the current issues of being black in America. Yet, despite those struggles, Black Americans established their own culture after being separated from Africa for centuries. My dad's family are practicing Southern Baptist Christians who enjoyed a culture established within the countryside of Northern Virginia.

My mom's family grew to know their homeland in Africa. My mom is an African whose family is heavily populated in both Guinea and Sierra Leone. My mom's family got the chance to understand their Fulani ethnicity and the ethnicities of other African groups. They experienced a great deal of colonization, corrupt leaders, civil wars, and a fragmented government. Despite all those struggles, at least my mom's family got to hang onto their Fulani heritage for generations.

My two black identities are equally important to me and I literally consider myself an African-American.

The problem was, I was rarely exposed to my mom's culture because I spent much of my youth on different military bases and my mom had assimilated into American culture. There were a few things that my mom was able to expose my siblings and me to; for instance, my mom cooked numerous African dishes, jollof rice being one of them.

So, when I was looking for a spouse, I was looking to find someone who came from my mom's Fulani culture. I didn't want to completely lose my mom's Fulani culture, which was especially important to me because I couldn't speak Fulani. I could still remember the times when I went to visit my family in Guinea; however, I had a difficult time communicating with my family. I loved everything about embracing my Fulani identity, yet language was a powerful factor to lose, especially because I wanted to remain connected with the people I knew in Africa.

I took my chances and began looking for someone I could possibly live the rest of my life with. I preferred to find someone who was Fulani because I knew that my Black American culture wasn't far out of reach. I finally found my wonderful fiancé, Elhadj Ousmane Diallo, who would later become my husband. My fiancé and I were teenagers attending high school at the time when we met. Elhadj, who I often call Ousmane, truly respected me. We went out to different parts of New York and hung out, he taught me some words in Fulani, and he taught me certain things about Islam that I didn't know.

It's interesting how I met Elhadj Ousmane Diallo. We met each other at his family's house for Ramadan Iftar in the years 2010 and 2011. My family and I went over his house several times to eat Ramadan dinner during those years. Ousmane said he always wanted to marry me since the first time he met me for Iftar dinner. We continued to get to know each other as young teenagers before getting married.

In the meantime, I undertook a transformation by slowly embracing my natural kinky hair. I stopped going to the hair salon to relax my hair and getting extensions added. I began watching YouTube videos of black women who were exploring their natural hair journey. Some of these women, just like myself, had never seen their natural hair before. I began to wonder how I would look with my natural kinky hair and I felt that this journey was beautiful. I began my natural hair journey in the beginning of 2013. I was passionate about buying natural hair products and searching for advice online on how to take care of my natural hair.

I also developed a disdain for relaxers because I observed science projects demonstrated by peers in my high school which demonstrated how relaxers could create scabs on the scalps of women using them. I had personally experienced getting scabs myself as a result of getting relaxers. Additionally, the process of getting a relaxer is painful and expensive. I know that people say "beauty" hurts, but why should I allow societies' rulings of beauty standards make me go through the pain every two to three months?

Some people made fun of me for wearing my hair out naturally. Sometimes I was hurt by being an object of ridicule; yet, I continued to wear my hair out. In the process, I made sure to keep reading the Quran and Bible.

Some Muslims began asking me, "Why are you reading the Bible?"

Well, I wanted to understand both scriptures. This was especially important because my dad converted from Christianity and I wanted to understand why he would convert to Islam. I also read the Quran because I wanted to assess the stereotypes revolving Muslims. My entire life, people have said Muslims are terrorists, or that they're violent. However, I grew to know Islam as a religion, a central guidance for my family, and a way of healing after turning to God.

I searched numerous videos on YouTube explaining Islam and Christianity. I was searching for something that I'd been confused about since I was a young girl: my overall identity.

YouTube was the best way for me to search for the authenticity of my identity because whenever I tried to find television shows I could relate to, it was nearly impossible. Most of the American Muslims depicted on television shows are either Arab or Indian (Desi). However, I am a Black Muslim and I needed a character on television that could relate to my story. I also found it uninteresting to watch television shows depicting Muslim women as oppressed, trying to find ways to take off the hijab, or they're role playing a terrorist.

I was especially saddened about the lack of black Muslims being represented in television series because we were brought to the Americas in 1619 during the slave trade. Yes, we most of our ancestors later converted to Christianity while they were under the hands of slavery, but recently there has been an influx of black American reverts to Islam. Television series seems to neglect that there is many black Muslims in the United States. Many black Muslims desire to see themselves in an authentic television show of what it's like for us to live in the United States. Not the storyline that the media has been trying to depict which is that Muslims are all violent, the women want to break free from hijab, and they're either Arab or South Asian.

I was eighteen-years old and searching for what it meant for me to be a Black American who was also a Fulani; who grew up as a U.S. Army Brat to a practicing Muslim family.

I remember going out one day, embracing my kinky hair. I feel the stares from people, but I no longer care. I flaunt my hair with confidence, even up to the point where another African-American girl tells me, "Julde, I cannot wear my natural hair, I think it's too difficult for me to deal with. Every time I try growing out my hair natural, I get fed up and relax my hair again."

I just listened to the girl express herself. It didn't change what I thought about *my* kinky natural hair. I just continued going out every day, just the way God made me. Some people chuckled when they saw my hair, other people reached out to grab it, and some people told me to get my hair done. But, I finally felt free.

I no longer felt limited to what society expected from me as an African-American woman.

I invested a lot of my money on purchasing multiple African garments. Sometimes altogether, my African garments totaled between $300 to $400. I wore my African garments whenever it was warm outside. I'd ask Ousmane to teach me new words in Fulani, so that I could expand my Fulani vocabulary.

Sometimes in the process of embracing my true self, I faced moments where I'd break down in tears, and Ousmane was there to listen to me. It took some moments of tumbling before I was able to discover who I was. Ousmane and I watched each other graduate high school. My husband attended my graduation ceremony in 2013 and I attended his graduation ceremony in 2014. My husband and I watched each other grow.

We went from playing video games on my husband's PlayStation 2 to growing past playing video games and planning for our future.

While I was getting deep into my research of self-identity, I found that the Fulani are also known as a nomadic group of people in Africa. The Fulani normally travelled between East and West African countries. Researchers believe that the Fulani brought Islam from the East Africa to the West Africa. While I came across this information about the Fulani ethnic group, I also found proof from the Quran and Bible that a Creator exists.

After completing the entire Quran, I was full of regret for always being afraid of practicing my Islamic faith. I realized that I wasn't really embarrassed of being a Muslim; rather I was embarrassed of being labeled a terrorist. It was my fear of people labeling me a violent person which made me avoid the hijab, and not the religion itself. I was unwilling to stand up against the stereotypes revolving Muslims. I was another statistic of a Muslim who was allowing the media and general public to successfully mislabel the entire Islamic faith.

I was interested in Black history in the United States and what it meant for Black people in America to finally accomplish integration in a system which they were previously divided from. It's especially important for me to understand the depths of my Black American heritage because they're the strong people who made it possible for me to live a better life today. They suffered countless beatings and torture in order to fight for the future improvements of Black children today. Black people are now finally able to sit in the same classrooms, movie theaters, and restaurants as their white counterparts. We're finally treated as humans here in the United States and I believe that there's no better way of thanking them for making our lives better as young Black Americans. There are still some challenges being faced today, but we cannot say that there weren't *any* improvements.

It's strange because although I'm black, my black identities do clash from time to time. Some of the Fulani people treat me differently because of my Black American identity, and similarly some of the Black Americans treat me differently because of my Fulani identity.

I love both of my black identities equally and if people from either side of my identity choose not to speak of me because of my mixed identity, I have no problem with that - they do not have to speak to me.

Sometimes there are stereotypes that trail behind my Black American identity and some people may be afraid that I inherited those stereotypical "traits." For instance, there's this impression amongst some people that Black Americans do not want to better themselves in life, that they're "lazier" than their black counterparts (African or Caribbean), or that they do not try to finish college. That's wrong! The United States is full of historically black colleges, including Howard University, Morehouse College, and Spelman College. Ruby Bridges is the young Black American girl that made desegregating schools in the United States possible in the historic *Brown v. Board of Education* case. Black people *have* invested in their communities inside the United States, but these communities continually get destroyed. One good example of an affluent black community which was destroyed in the United States was Oklahoma's Black Wall Street. Tulsa, Oklahoma had black millionaires residing within that community. Many of the occupants were working various prestigious professions. On June 1, 1921, the Ku Klux Klan and their supporters bombed the entire city, leaving 1.5 million dollars in damages.

Black people in America have always been trying, it's just a matter of them having been suppressed from moving forward. We always hear about reparations and how black people will be repaid for the slavery of their ancestors, but this problem is deeper than that. Their achievements are always being hindered.[54]

On the other hand, the stereotypes trailing my African identity is that Africans come from a place where they live in trees, ride animals for commute, and act uncivilized; when this isn't the case. There are some Africans which live in large, multi-floored houses, equipped with electricity. They drive cars to travel around their cities, they wear name brand clothing, and are educated in universities around Africa. The problem is, Africa is heavily colonized and nearly every country around the world is extracting resources from Africa. The people in Africa are still being captured today for present day slavery.

Some Africans fall short of enjoying the nicer things in life because they're being affected by numerous countries overwhelming them; therefore, making some Africans poor. Being poor is not unfamiliar to America either. A lot of the times, Americans like to point out the homelessness in Africa to explain poverty. When right here in the United States, we have homeless people sleeping in the train stations, under bridges, on sidewalks, stairs, in banks, or in front of cash checking places. There is homelessness in Africa

---

54 JOHNSON, SIMONE R. "A Holocaust: How Black Wall Street Was Destroyed." New York Amsterdam News, vol. 107, no.

26, 23 June 2016, p. 34. EBSCOhost, search.ebscohost.com/login.aspx?direct=true&db=a9h&AN=116503392&site=ehost-live.

like there is in the United States. But for the Africans who aren't poor, they go clothes shopping at their local malls, they enjoy fashion shows, music concerts, and some of them are millionaires; just as those type of individuals exist here.

By the Fall of 2013, my mom would leave me behind in New York City while I was attending my first year of college at Kingsborough Community College. My mom got a job transfer with the Defense Commissary Agency to work at the Fort Gordon Commissary. I was slightly terrified of the thought of living in New York City by myself. None of my immediate family would be in the city with me anymore. My mom and younger sister would be relocating near Fort Gordon, Georgia and my dad lived near Fort Bragg, North Carolina. I shared the experience of beginning my first year of college with Ousmane always there to check on me. At the time, Ousmane was still trying to finish up his last year of high school.

Fast forward to the early months of 2014. I was pleased with myself because I finally broke all the confrontations I faced as a young African-American Muslim woman. My natural kinky hair was growing longer, I was knowledgeable in my maternal Fulani roots, and I had grasped a deeper understanding of Islam.

It felt good to finally walk outside without wearing a $200 hairstyle because African-American hair was deemed as looking "unprofessional." Sometimes while walking outside, someone would tell me, "I absolutely love your hair, what products do you use for it?"

"I alternate between using Miss Jessie's hair products and Shea Moisture," I'd say.

"Wow, your hair is very beautiful, keep it up."

Then after thanking the person for their compliment, we'd go our separate ways. In other instances, a black person would approach me with praise by saying, "I love to see Black people embracing their natural hair."

There were many other Black people embracing their natural hair journey.

Gradually, my clothing preferences changed, and I preferred wearing lengthier clothing. On the days that I wasn't busy with school or work, I'd pack all my old clothing into a plastic bag and donate my revealing clothes to various organizations. If I had enough time, I'd go shopping to purchase clothes that were more modest.

While I was transitioning to modest clothing, it wasn't a direct root of my research in Islam. Instead, it was a response to always feeling naked. I don't know what it was, but I no longer felt comfortable walking outside with revealing clothing. It bothered me when men cat-called me, and I felt that changing my wardrobe was necessary.

When it was nearly reaching May of 2014, something came up in my religious research. I found that the hijab is older than Islam. In fact, I found that Islam didn't invent the hijab. Different lecturers referenced actual quotes from the Quran explaining the hijab. The lecturers explained that the head coverings that nuns wear are similar to reasons why Muslim women have to wear a head covering. The nuns are following the revelations of the Abrahamic prophecy. This became the reason why Jewish women - including Mary, the Mother of Jesus (peace be upon her), and many other women who previously followed the Abrahamic texts- covered their hair.

I began to truly consider my decision of wearing the hijab, but I thought it would be better if I gave myself more time before committing to it, so I researched the topic further. The more information I found in the holy scriptures, the more convinced I was of the existence of God. Islam is believed to be the last revelation sent down by the Archangel Gabriel. As Muslims we believe that the Archangel Gabriel assisted in sending the Torah, Gospel, Book of Psalms, and Quran. There's proof that the first three books were changed by man; even some college professors admit to that claim. The Quran is the only revelation which remains unaltered.

I wanted to postpone wearing the hijab, but every time I walked outside without one, something deep down didn't settle with me. There's a higher power which directed believing women to cover their hair; yet, I continued avoiding my obligation. After going home from a long day of work at the Fort Hamilton Commissary, I found some scarves in my closet that I could begin wearing. All my scarves were tacky colors, but I was going to wear them temporarily, until I could afford better looking scarves.

The next morning, I got up, and attempted to leave my house without a scarf over my head, but I was terrified. How could I test the Creator, the One who created the heavens and the earth, the One who developed the complexities of this life that no human can explain? How can I refuse his instructions after I've been provided all the proof that he does, in fact, exist? I stared directly into the mirror while looking at myself, taking deep breaths, because this has always been hard for me. I've always had a hard time with being noticeably Muslim. Committing to wearing the hijab might finally change this fear I always had.

Then I thought to myself, "What about my beautiful, natural, kinky hair? I've worked hard on embracing my natural hair and now I'll have to cover it with a *scarf*? I finally love the beautiful curls that I've never got the chance to see until now. How can I cover my beautiful kinky hair so soon? Astaghfirullah[55], isn't this the same hair that my Creator made? How could I choose my natural hair over wearing a scarf?"

I noticed that I couldn't choose my natural hair over a directive sent down by God, so I finally placed the scarf over my head. During May of 2014, I began wearing the hijab, and continued wearing the hijab from that day forward. I remember walking outside and feeling alive, reinvented, because now I was no longer dependent on the opinions of other people. I didn't wear the hijab because I was oppressed, I didn't wear the hijab because I was told to; now I was wearing the hijab to fulfill my religious obligations. I was always afraid of being mislabeled as a Muslim woman, being alone, or challenging the status quo. But no longer.

At nineteen years old, I finally felt like I had overcome every obstacle that I faced as a young girl. I finally accepted that people wouldn't care about me, but it was more important that I cared about myself. I no longer had to worry about what people said about me nor should I view myself as inferior to another person because of my overall identity. I was going to finally embrace every attribute of my identity and not care if someone liked me.

---

55 Astafirullah: an Arabic text which means, "I seek forgiveness of Allah."

Shortly after wearing the hijab, I began losing some of my friendships. Some of my friends waited to see if I was going through a phase, but when they realized that wasn't the case, they no longer spoke to me. Only a handful of people remained by my side when I began my hijab journey. My hijab journey was made to last a lifetime. I was hoping that nothing would stop me from wearing it. There are many women who unfortunately stop wearing the hijab, but I didn't want that to be me. I was lonelier than before because I lost friends, my mom had relocated to Fort Gordon, and my dad was living near Fort Bragg. The days I felt lonely, I thought to myself that at least Allah was by my side. I wasn't completely lonely because Allah's essence was always near.

Sometimes my remaining friends would invite me to hang out with them in the city. I always reminded them that I didn't enjoy going out places where there was partying, drinking, or smoking. My friends always said, "It's okay Julde, we understand that you don't like those things, just come and hang out with us."

So, I'd ask them, "Which places are you planning on going then?" because I wanted some insight on the type of place we were going to hang out. I wanted to know beforehand if tagging along with them would make me end up in a bar. But, my friends made sure that they told me, "Julde, don't worry, we won't go out to a place like that."

Surely enough, on the day we'd be hanging out, I would be wearing a hijab and somehow my friends would make their way to a club.

I felt disrespected and I also felt a rush of discomfort.

This wasn't right for me.

No matter how much I expressed I didn't want to drink, smoke, or go clubbing, my friends always found some way to pull me into that environment.

That night, I left my friends while feeling upset and I caught a cab home. I realized that my friends couldn't be my friends anymore. It's not like I didn't care about them, but if they cared about me, they'd have respected my wishes.

While I was still adjusting to my new life as a hijabi, I discovered how difficult it was to find outfits in retail stores that covered my entire body. I was still slowly cleaning out my wardrobe of all my revealing clothing, but in the meantime, I also wanted to purchase long Muslim gowns. I relied on a small portion of my money to purchase more modest clothing. Every month my mom sent me money in my account, so that I was able to take care of myself in New York. This money came from both of my parents and I'd use it to buy more modest outfits.

At the end of May 2014, I decided that I wanted to make a surprise visit to my mom in Georgia for her birthday. I wanted Ousmane to escort me on the Amtrak and I explained to him that I was scared to travel down south by myself, especially being that I was now a hijabi. Ousmane didn't mind escorting me, so we immediately booked our Amtrak tickets.

On an early morning, Ousmane and I prepared to catch our train at 34th Street Penn Station to visit my mom. I called my mom that day to wish her a happy birthday and make sure she wasn't busy, but I didn't tell her why I was always asking if she was busy for her birthday. Finally, after reaching Washington, DC, I called my mom and said, "Assalamu Alaikum mom, how are you?"

"I am doing good and how are you doing Julde?"

"I'm doing good."

"Julde, is everything alright with you?"

"Yes, why?"

"You keep calling me, what's going on?"

"Well, mom, right now I am in Washington, DC -," then my mom cuts me off.

"What are you doing in Washington, DC?!"

"Ousmane and I are coming down to Georgia to visit you."

"Really! I knew something was up. Is that why you kept calling me to ask if I was working on my birthday?"

I tell my mom the time she should expect me to arrive in Georgia and what train station she should pick Ousmane and I from. About five hours later, Ousmane and I reach our train stop in Georgia. We wait a little bit for my mom until morning. I'm sort of scared that something will happen to Ousmane and me as we wait outside of the train station, especially because I'm wearing hijab and we aren't familiar with that part of Georgia. Then about two hours later, my mom comes to pick us up from the train station. I can tell she's delighted to see us.

"I'm so happy that you two came to see me for my birthday! Wow, this is the best birthday gift."

Immediately after arriving in Georgia, we go to my mom's house, drop off our belongings, and go out to IHOP to eat breakfast. After ordering our breakfast, I start talking to my mom and asking her how she's been. My mom says that she's been doing well, but there's not much for her to do in Georgia. My mom lives in a suburban part of Georgia and it's very relaxed in comparison to New York's hasty lifestyle.

"Oh, so, you still haven't adjusted to Georgia's lifestyle?" I ask my mom.

"No, it's too quiet here for me. And you, how's everything in New York?"

"Well, everything is going well with school and work," I tell my mom.

"So, what made you decide that you were ready to wear the hijab?" my mom asks me.

"I did a lot of research and I found that wearing the hijab, is in fact, obligatory. I felt uncomfortable leaving the house without a head covering, so I began placing a hijab over my hair."

"I'm so proud of you," my mom says. "I think that I'm going to start wearing the hijab, too."

My mom used to wrap her hair in a head wrap or turban most of the time. My mom frequently wore the head turban and she was planning on transitioning into wearing the hijab before my visit to Georgia, but after seeing me wear the hijab, she decided it was finally time for her to wear the hijab the traditional Muslim way. It's highly advised that Muslim women draw their veils across their bosoms and my mom mainly wrapped her hijab up.

After some more discussion, the waitress brings our orders to the table. We eat our breakfast, and then my mom tells me she wants to take me to the Fort Gordon Commissary so that she can introduce me to her co-workers. When we get to the commissary, my mom parks her car and leads the way.

"Hello everybody, this is my daughter Julde. She came to surprise me for my birthday!"

"Oh, how sweet! That's the best birthday gift, to surprise your mother for her birthday. How are you doing?"

"I'm doing great and you, how's everything?"

"I'm also doing great."

"Are you in college right now?"

"Yes, I'm attending Kingsborough Community College."

"Which school?" my mom's coworker asks again.

"It's a community college in Brooklyn, NY," I tell her.

"Oh, that's nice. What are you studying?"

"I am studying Retail Merchandising-Marketing," I say.

It has always been my dream to pursue a career in Marketing. It's my passion and I have enjoyed business-related work ever since I was a little child selling items in my neighborhood, or the time I was the Editor of Beauty for my high school's magazine. My mom makes way to introduce me to everyone working there before we go to hang out at some other places on base.

I'm not going to lie, it was hard for me to wear hijab and be the unusual person on base. Sure, there are other Muslim families who live on U.S. military bases and yes, many of the Muslim women in those families wore hijabs on base, but this time was different for me. Some people stared at me like I didn't belong, some people gave me curious looks, and others greeted me.

I was still familiarizing myself to a new life of being a hijabi. This is something that I struggled with my entire youth and I was finally breaking this struggle at nineteen years old.

I just take a deep breath and continue walking to the game center. The weather is beautiful, the sun is shining, and the plants bloom in the beautiful May weather.

I enter the Fort Gordon game center and am immediately asked to provide my military identification card. I promptly provide my ID. The person sitting at the counter behaves like he wasn't expecting me to have a military ID. He looks at my card, shocked, and then grants me access to play at one of the pool tables. I collect the balls before heading to a pool table with Ousmane.

Playing pool was a sad joke for me, but Ousmane and I try our best to get all the balls into the pockets. When my mom calls to say that she's ready for us to leave Fort Gordon, Ousmane and I return to the Commissary to meet my mom.

Ousmane and I spend the rest of our week in Georgia with my mom. On the days that my mom has to work, we spend time on Fort Gordon doing various activities. While I'm there, I search on Fort Gordon for the mosque so that we can pray. Fort Gordon has a mosque, but it's closed during the scheduled prayer times. I meet other Muslim families looking to pray at Fort Gordon's mosque, but they too find that the doors to the mosque are locked. We try to see if we can get someone to open the door, but the chaplains say that the mosque is normally only open for Jummah, occasionally also opening for Laylatul Qadr[56] or Taraweeh[57] prayers. I decide to find another place where Ousmane and I could pray, and afterwards we continue spending time together.

---

56 Laylatul Qadr: means "the night of power" and occurs during the last ten days of Ramadan when Muslims try to fast the day that the Quran was revealed to the Prophet Muhammad. Most Muslims believe that Laylatul Qadr falls on the 27th night of Ramadan even though there isn't clear evidence of this.

57 Taraweeh: is a prayer Muslims perform during the holy month of Ramadan after the obligatory Isha'a prayer.

On the day of Jummah, my mom decides that she wants us to pray at a local mosque outside of Fort Gordon called Islamic Society of Augusta. There is a small Muslim community there and they have a lovely mosque, not so far from where my mom lives. The mosque has a large entrance, a kid's playroom, a gym, and a spacious prayer room.

I can remember the Khutbah from that Friday. Ramadan was soon approaching, so the Imam was discussing the Holy month of Ramadan. The Imam recently found a research article about the benefits of fasting and he explains that scientists discovered that fasting could lead to multiple health benefits. The Imam explains all the health benefits that fasting could provide, while also establishing why Ramadan is beneficial for Muslims. Not only are Muslims fasting Ramadan for a spiritual connection with Allah, but also because this commandment can provide Muslims with health benefits. Fasting can detox a person's system, change their bad habits, and draw you closer to Allah. When the Jummah Khutbah is done, the Imam ends the Friday services by praying Dhuhr. The next day, Ousmane and I pack our belongings and head back to New York City.

Part Three: The Hijabi Army Brat

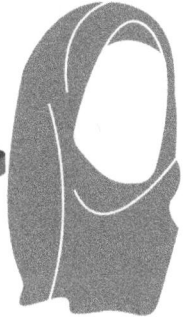

Chapter Twenty-Six: Get Out My Country!

I continued attending college classes at Kingsborough Community College, but I wasn't doing well academically. I was more focused on working at the Fort Hamilton Commissary than studying for school. I was also down because I was nineteen years old and trying to take care of myself in New York City. Every month, my parents provided me money so that I could get things done, but I felt like the money wasn't enough. I had to cover some of the costs of college, food, clothing, etc.

Ousmane was still trying to finish his last month of high school and sometimes I'd help him study for his exams. Ousmane was improving impressively when it came to his English. Ousmane mainly struggled with the English and reading portions of his exams because he came from a French speaking country. Ousmane and his family came as refugees from Guinea, West Africa. After enough studying, Ousmane was able to pass his exams and graduate in June 2014.

I attended Ousmane's graduation with his family. Ousmane and I watched each other graduate from high school, although I graduated a year before him. Ousmane began receiving college acceptance letters and we celebrated when he was finally admitted into Kingsborough Community College. I guided Ousmane on how to register for college and apply for his classes. When we were done, they told him that he would begin his college classes in August.

Because wearing the hijab was still new to me, I ran into many obstacles. There were countless times when I accidentally bumped into someone and said sorry, but the person would look at me in an unpleasant way. Sometimes I'd figure that maybe it was just a problem with that particular individual, until I received those looks repeatedly.

One day, while boarding the New York City transit to go to work, a black woman sitting across from me begins to rant, "You killed my daughter!"

At first, I don't pay her any mind because I know that she couldn't be addressing me. Then the black woman shouts again, "You killed my daughter! Why did you kill my daughter?"

That's when I look up at her to see who she's talking to. The woman looks me directly in my face and says, "I'm talking to you, you killed my daughter! Why did you kill my daughter? You took her from me, now I can't eat, I can't sleep."

Everyone on the train stops what they're doing to look at me and the woman. I'm confused, flustered, and can't believe I'm being accused of killing this woman's daughter.

"Ma'am, I didn't kill your daughter. I don't even know who your daughter is."

"Yes, you did! You killed my daughter, you *murderer!*"

Some of the people on the train observe the exchange with a smirk on their face while others just stay attentive to the situation without attempting to interfere. I, however, am very alarmed. I have no clue who this lady's daughter was, but I start to realize how easily someone can accuse me of anything. I know that this woman is blaming me for the death of her daughter because I'm wearing a hijab. But how could wearing a scarf connect someone to murder? It's obvious that because I wore a scarf, also known as a hijab, that I had this "terrorist" stereotype following behind me. Muslim women wear hijabs, so whoever murdered her daughter was probably Muslim.

I was being blamed for her daughter's death because I'm a Muslim woman. I was always Muslim, but being that I'm now recognizably Muslim, this would only be the beginning of numerous confrontations I would face in a day.

"Are you saying that because I'm wearing a scarf?" I ask the woman.

"No, I'm saying that because you murdered my daughter!"

"But I don't know you nor your daughter, so you must be accusing me of this horrible crime because I'm wearing a scarf."

So, I go into my handbag, pull out the bible, and read out 1 Corinthians, 11:4-6:

> *4. Every man praying or prophesying with his head covered disgraces his head.*
> *5. But every woman praying or prophesying with her head uncovered disgraces her head; for it is one and the same as she who is shaved.*
> *6. For if a woman is not covered, let her hair also be cut off; but if it is shameful for a woman to have her hair cut off or to be shaved, let her be covered.*

Then everyone on the train becomes silent.

"I wear a head scarf for religious reasons. Just because I'm wearing a scarf, it doesn't mean that I murdered your daughter. You're only accusing me of something like this because you're trying to make the claim that all Muslims are criminals."

Afterwards, the lady says, "No, I'm not saying that because you're a Muslim."

Finally, other Muslim men who were on the train jump to my defense. One of the Muslim men stands up and tells me, "Don't worry, I'm also a Muslim. Whatever this woman is doing isn't right."

Then the lady begins shouting at the Muslim man.

Another Muslim man tells her to shut up and leave me alone.

Other people who were observing our entire argument start to defend me, telling the woman, "Can you give it a break now and leave this girl alone? We're all just trying to go to work or school."

So, then the lady leaves me alone for the rest of the train ride. I realize that if I hadn't stood up for myself, this woman could've pranced on me and no one would have defended me. Without making the first step to defend myself, people would've continued finding our quarrel humorous, and the Muslim men sitting on the train probably wouldn't have got up to defend me. From this point forward, I quickly learn that I can no longer make any type of bomb jokes. Just like the jokes you make after leaving the restroom from taking a number two and saying, "Wow! I blew that toilet up!" or making references to the word bomb such as bomb bath fizzers. I had to entirely change the lingo that I used to protect myself from being accused of something I didn't mean to say.

I continue my ride to work thinking about the many conflicts I might face from this point forward, because taking off the hijab was no longer an option for me. I am going to finally face the struggle I avoided my entire youth: being an identifiably Muslim woman. I always had admiration for the women who could face the horror of wearing the hijab despite the numerous confrontations.

*   *   *   *   *

Working for the Department of Defense Commissary Agency was no longer the same after I decided to wear the hijab. Some of my coworkers and customers didn't understand my transition into wearing the hijab. There was a lot of curiosity and wonder revolving the hijab because people think that you're either oppressed, abused, or a terrorist if you wear the hijab. However, I chose to wear the hijab by myself and my situation isn't rare; there are other Muslim women who also choose to wear the hijab. Some of my customers would ask me, "What happened, why are you wearing that scarf?

"I'm wearing this scarf on my head because I'm a Muslim," I'd tell them.

"Is someone forcing you to wear that scarf?" they'd ask me.

"No, I decided to wear the scarf on my own." Then the customer would look at me with skepticism, without knowing that my entire youth I had struggled with how I could finally identify myself as a Muslim woman. I wasn't oppressed into wearing the hijab; rather, I was oppressed *from* wearing it. I was escaping being labeled as a terrorist for so long that when I finally wore the hijab, I felt like I had evolved. For the rest of the week, coworkers and customers would ask me about my hijab and I continued to let them know that I was wearing the hijab because it was my personal decision.

In the evening, I would get back on the New York City transit and make my way home. While sitting on the train, I'd get many stares from people who didn't understand me nor my religion. I'd try to avoid eye contact with some of the people on the train, but when I did avoid eye contact, I could still feel their eyes piercing down on me. Sometimes it helped to pull out my phone and play games or read my book. Eventually, I'd get home and lie down to rest. I had to attend school the next day.

Kingsborough Community College is a spacious campus, especially being that it's in Brooklyn, NY. Most of the college campuses in New York City are built sandwiched between other buildings in the city. Kingsborough Community College, on the other hand, is not located in an overcrowded area. The campus is in Manhattan Beach, which is ironically located in Brooklyn, New York. The campus has its own private beach where students and staff could swim during the summer.

Some of the friends I made at Kingsborough Community College when I initially started college nearly didn't recognize me after seeing me in the hallway.

"Julde, is that you?"

"Yes, it's me. I just wear the hijab now."

"What happened, why are you wearing a hijab? Did you convert to Islam?"

"No, I've always been a Muslim."

For some of my friends, they unexpectedly found out that I was a Muslim. For my other friends, they always knew that I was a Muslim, it just wasn't on a visible basis.

As time went by, I found myself feeling lonely again. It was either that my friends didn't like that I was pursuing my Muslim beliefs, or we simply couldn't hang out with each other. Whatever the case, I felt isolated, which was a horrible feeling. I rarely had someone around me who could understand my experience of being a new hijabi. Yes, I had Ousmane around, but he was a man. Ousmane wasn't obligated to wear the hijab nor would he ever know what it really felt like. Muslim men do wear hijab, but it's not the same type of hijab that Muslim women wear. Muslim women are required to wearing the Khimar[58].

Ousmane and I were still teenagers maturing together, understanding each other and sharing life experiences with each other. I communicated how challenging wearing the hijab was and Ousmane told me, "Julde, I'm proud of you for wearing the hijab, but if wearing the hijab is hard, you can just take it off." However, I wasn't wearing the hijab for Ousmane, I was wearing the hijab because of my belief in Allah.

Despite the challenges, every day I made sure to go outside wearing my hijab. I ran into a few other confrontations when people took it upon themselves to shove me or push me. People made rude comments aloud about Muslims directly in front of me. The rudest interactions that I had about my Islamic faith happened to be on the New York City transit.

One day, when a Latino preacher entered the train, he begins preaching, "You must turn to your lord Jesus Christ! You must repent! Do not make the mistake of dying before you turn to Jesus Christ." The man walks through the train car preaching to everyone he sees in sight until he reaches my area. When the man finally makes his way to my area, he shouts out to me, "You must repent to the Lord JESUS CHRIST!" I don't answer the man because I'm not in the mood to have a dispute with him. The man approaches closer to me and says, "Repent to your LORD JESUS CHRIST!"

Since he's in my face, I tell the man that Muslims already believe in Jesus, we just believe in him as a prophet.

Then I continue to say, "That Muslims do believe that Jesus (peace be upon him) would return to defeat the anti-Christ because he's the only person who can defeat him."

"Muslims are the anti-Christ!" the man yells in my face.

---

58 Khimar: a head scarf that is worn by Muslim women that normally covers their hair, neck, breast, and shoulders; only leaving the face uncovered.

Some of the passengers on the train are shocked to hear him yell that directly in my face. Then the man tells me, "Get out of this country, you do not belong here in the United States because you're a terrorist. Terrorista!" The man begins shouting in Spanish and occasionally, he goes back to calling me a terrorist.

"I don't know which country you want me to go to because this is my country," I retort.

"No, this isn't your country and you have to leave, you TERRORIST!"

"My dad is fighting in the United States Army and I grew up as an Army brat, so this is my country, too."

Some of the people on the train already feel bad for me, but this is when people start to intervene in the confrontation.

"Sir, you need to leave this young girl alone," one of the women standing on the train says. "Thank you for your dad's service," she goes on to say to me. Other people on the train join in, telling the man to leave me alone, until he finally departs.

Nearly every day, I got up and no longer cared. Even though some of the remarks I received from people were hurtful, I wasn't going to let those confrontations be the reason why I gave up on what I believed in.

One day while going into a local Subway, a black woman sitting in the sandwich shop begins talking to me.

"The man who makes the sandwiches will be right back," the woman tells me.

"Did he go to use the restroom?"

"I don't know, but he said he'll be back soon."

While waiting for the Subway shop employee, the woman engages me in conversation.

"Are you a Muslim?" the woman asks me.

"Yes, I'm a Muslim."

"Oh, okay, where are you from?"

"I'm from the United States."

"No, where are you *really* from?"

I pause for a second because I felt like I just answered that question.

"I just *said* that I'm from the United States," I tell the woman.

"Well, when did you become naturalized?" the woman asks me.

"I was born a United States citizen."

"Are you sure you weren't naturalized? You didn't have to take a test to become a United States citizen?"

"No, I was born a citizen."

"Okay, where were you born?"

"I was born in Germany."

"How could you be born in Germany but be a United States citizen? Do you have dual citizenship?"

"No, I was born in Germany because my dad works in the United States Army and he was stationed in Germany at the time I was born."

After going back and forth with the lady, I was relieved that the Subway employee finally got back to the counter to make my sandwich. After receiving my sandwich, I decided to leave the shop and eat while walking outside.

Chapter Twenty-Seven: Sweet Kenema

This question of where I'm from continually pops up whenever I am completing errands around my neighborhood. There's a lot of curiosity of where I'm from and this question is puzzling for me personally because although I'm an American, there are many layers to my overall identity and there are so many places that I've travelled to in the world. I've rarely lived in one location for a long period of time, except for New York City. First off, I was born in Germany while my dad was stationed to work on a United States military base near Kaiserslautern, Germany. People automatically assume that I have dual citizenship with Germany, but that isn't the case. I am entirely an American citizen. Although I was born in Germany, the United States grants citizenship to children of American citizens born abroad. Germany doesn't have birthright citizenship like the United States does.

In the United States, as long as you're born on U.S. soil, you're considered a United States citizen. On the other hand, the Germans do not care if you're born on their soil. You're still not considered their citizen. As far as travelling, I've also been to Mexico, Canada, France, England, Turkey, and other parts of the world. It would be gratuitous of me to recount my experiences in every country I've visited, so for the sake of brevity, I've only gone into detail about the places that played a significant role in who I've grown to become.

The one place that I do consider explaining my relationship with is Sierra Leone. Many people enjoy referring to me as a Sierra Leonean because it's my mom's original nationality, but I've only ever visited the country once, and that was for two weeks when I was eighteen years old.

I'm going to flashback in time to the Summer of 2013, a year before I committed to wearing the hijab. Way before I began encountering questions such as, "When were you naturalized?"

During the summer of 2013, before my mom decided to leave me behind in New York and make her move to Fort Gordon for work, my mom says that she misses her family and she's hoping to visit them before leaving for

Georgia. My mom asks me to accompany her to Sierra Leone because I've never visited the country and she'd like for me to see my family. Being that it was true, I was excited to attend this trip.

I'd only had the chance of visiting Guinea when I was younger and my mom promises that we'd make a stop in Guinea for one week so that I could revisit the country. I really miss Guinea, I just never want to go alone because of my language barrier and I'd have a hard time getting around the country if I couldn't communicate with the people. So, my mom and I agree that we'd make this trip four weeks: two weeks in Sierra Leone, one week in Guinea, and one week in Germany.

My mom asks me if I can afford to purchase my own airplane ticket, but I'm honest with my mom.

"Mom, you're about to leave me behind in New York to work in Fort Gordon. I don't want to spend too much money visiting Africa and Germany if I'll have to figure out how to live in New York alone afterwards."

"Okay, I'll purchase your ticket because I really want you to visit your family and I also want you to see my country. You've never been to Sierra Leone. I believe you're the only one out of your siblings who haven't had the chance to visit yet" my mom says.

"Yeah, and I'd really like to visit because last time you visited there, I didn't go with you."

"Okay, I'll buy your ticket."

When the time comes, we head off to John F. Kennedy International Airport for our trip. I haven't been on an airplane for a while. The last time that I flew on the airplane, I went to visit my Dad in North Carolina.

My mom, younger sister, and I fly on Brussels Airlines. The flight would make a stop in Belgium, then Senegal, before finally reaching our final stop in Sierra Leone. With all the connecting flights and stops, the flight to Sierra Leone nearly takes us an entire day.

I'm eighteen years old when I finally get the chance to see Sierra Leone's beautiful landscapes outside the airplane window. It was a couple of hours into the mid-afternoon and I observed the green surroundings at Lungi International Airport.

Before exiting the airplane, the crew members let down the stairs to the airplane, and then everyone walks down the stairs into the beautiful sunny weather. It's a short walk to the terminal, where we'd have to present our visas and go through international customs to gather our luggage. We wait for my Uncle Wurie and his friend to come pick us up from the airport.

After coming to get us from Lungi International Airport, we drive towards the ferry which would transport us to Freetown. Lungi International Airport is located on Lungi, a separate city from Freetown, which is divided by the Sierra Leone River.

Evening quickly approaches as we wait to board the ferry taking us to Freetown.

Inside the ferry, music plays and people sell items at concession stands. Some people dance, while others just stand at the rails, enjoying the waves. My family and I decide to remain indoors of the ferry, but there are windows looking out towards the water. The ferry rides slowly on the Sierra Leonean River Estuary, which is connected by the Bankasoka River and Rokel River.

While riding along the waves, I peak outside the window. This is a remarkable moment for me. I'm riding a ferry on the other side of the Atlantic Ocean, but this time off the coast of Sierra Leone. I remember the times when I'd ride the Staten Island Ferry in New York and now I finally got the chance to see the other end of that body of water.

The ferry finally reaches its dock in Freetown and we get off to load my Uncle Wurie's car with our luggage. The air smells of gasoline fumes. Most of the vehicles being driven are older models and this leaves the air in Freetown smelling like smoldering gasoline. There are many people hanging outside in Sierra Leone, preparing to go to clubs, braiding hair outside, or playing soccer. It's nighttime, but people still walk around the city, as if they didn't have any urgency to go home.

My Uncle Wurie says that we'd be temporarily staying with his friend's family, the Sesays, in Freetown for two days until we could drive to his home in Kenema, Sierra Leone.

For the short duration that my mom, younger sister, and I stay at the Sesay Family's house, my uncle promises to take us around to view Freetown. In Freetown, nearly everyone speaks English, although it's not like the American dialect.

My mom, uncle, younger sister, and I walk towards the nearest store so that we can purchase an ice cold soda before enjoying our walk around the city.

"Julde, which drink do you want?" my uncle asks me.

"Can I get a Vimto?" I tell the man seated at the store counter.

After making my request, everyone else in my family asks for the drink that they'd like to purchase. The man hands us four iced cold glass bottles of soda. Then the man assists us in opening our sodas with a bottle opener.

While walking alongside my family in Sierra Leone, I observe children playing soccer (*futbol*) outside. Before continuing our exploration around Freetown, my uncle advised me and my younger sister to limit our speaking around the city. The Sierra Leoneans who realize we speak the American dialect of English can begin price gouging items outside of their actual prices.

My Uncle Wurie wanted to show me and my younger sister some historic landmarks in Sierra Leone.

While slowly sipping our cold soda, my uncle suggests that we begin heading towards his car so that he could drive us to view West Africa's oldest university, Fourah Bay University. While driving towards Fourah Bay University, we drive past numerous people selling items alongside the road: oranges, bananas, fried donuts, cassava leaves, potato leaves, etc. There were houses built closely alongside each other. Some homes were strongly built, while other houses weren't built as strong, but were still livable.

Fourah Bay University is atop Mount Aureol and while driving in the direction of the university I observed the beautiful glistening water of Cline

Bay as ships rode across it. The closer you drive toward the university, the better the houses are built. After finally getting atop Mount Aureol, the view of Freetown was gorgeous.

As we slowly neared Fourah Bay University, I saw college students gathered outside the campus, listening to American rap music. Some of the students were dancing outside; others stood in a circle observing the dancers. Students were walking around the campus with textbooks in their hands and I felt that this was an honorable moment for me. I couldn't believe that I was on the grounds of West Africa's oldest university. My uncle said that this was the university that Nigerians, Liberians, and Ghanaians studied at before they could universities in their own countries.

After leaving Fourah Bay University, my uncle drove us to view the wealthiest neighborhood in Sierra Leone, Hill Station. Sierra Leone is still slowly recovering from their civil war, so although the neighborhood is wealthy, not all of the roads are well-built. After it gets late, my uncle decides that he'd drop us of at the Sesay family so that we could get some rest.

The next day, my uncle drives my family and I to go visit Lumley Beach. After setting up our items at the beach, me and my younger sister began running towards the beach. The ocean water was a clear greenish-blue color. While swimming in the water, I can remember the times when I was on the other side of the Atlantic Ocean swimming at Coney Island. The water was cleaner at Lumley Beach because it's not in a metropolitan area like New York City.

After swimming at the beach, my uncle drives us back to the Sesay family and he asks me, "Julde, do you know why we call this city Freetown?"

"No," I say. My Uncle Wurie says, "We call this city Freetown because many of the freed African slaves resettled here when they wanted to return to Africa."

"Really?" I ask.

The freed Africans coming from the Americas, West Indies, and Britain mainly resettled in Freetown, Sierra Leone; where they're commonly known as the Creoles.

So, I begin to draw the parallels in my identity that my maternal family is from Sierra Leone, the first West African country to build a university and a country where many former slaves were liberated. On the other hand, my paternal family is from Virginia, the first American colony and the state which produced the most United States presidents.

Unfortunately, Sierra Leone bore the burdens of a civil war beginning in 1991 often referred to as "Blood Diamonds". A group of rebels called the Revolutionary United Front (RUF) were trying to overthrow the corrupt political leaders in Sierra Leone. The Revolutionary United Front received aided support from Liberians to overthrow the Sierra Leonean president, Joseph Saidu Momah. Together, the rebels travelled from the border neighboring Liberia to Freetown. Revolutionary United Front and their Liberian partners didn't have enough money to keep up with their plan to overthrow the corrupt government in Sierra Leone, so they took control of all the diamond mines to fund their artillery. In the process, many Sierra Leoneans fled to Guinea to seek refuge, where most of my family currently resettled. In April 1992, President Joseph Saidu Momah was overthrown by the rebels and he sought asylum in Guinea where he later died.

Sierra Leone is still rebuilding its infrastructure from the civil war because many of their citizen's homes were broken down for diamond mining. Sierra Leone has high intolerance for a corrupt government, so political leaders don't commonly exceed their terms in office.

While driving around Sierra Leone, I personally took notice in their value for education. For the two weeks that I stayed in Sierra Leone, I noticed that the people hold graduation parades around the city. All the students belonging to one school would where their caps and gowns while marching around the city, celebrating their graduation. Parents and family members would trail behind the students while singing or drumming.

I feel bad for the condition of Sierra Leone. They've made progress since the civil war, but many of the people still face the traumas experienced during the war.

Aside from the traumas that Sierra Leoneans experienced from the war, it's a beautiful country and my uncle took us to go visit Bo and finally Kenema, where my uncle resides.

After reaching Kenema, my uncle took me to see the movie theatre he owns. My uncle says that he especially makes money in his theatre on the days customers want to view soccer games.

The air is much cooler in Kenema than it is in Freetown. Sometimes women would stroll by carrying heavy items over their head or they'll have a baby wrapped around their back. Together, the women in my family would stay at home cooking, cleaning, washing laundry, braiding each other's hair, and taking care of children. Family is highly valued in Sierra Leone. No one takes their children to daycare and elderly family members do not stay in nursing homes. The orphans in the neighborhood are fed by their neighbors after completing household chores.

I especially loved the way the neighborhood took care of a small two year old boy whose parents past away, leaving him an orphan. Every day, the neighborhood families played with him, provided him three daily meals, and helped shower him. There isn't a welfare system in Kenema, but the neighborhood seems to look after each other. I enjoyed the company of the people in Kenema for the short time that I stayed there.

The only time it could get difficult for families to take care of each other is if their health requires medical attention such as the disabled or people with chronic illness. The Sierra Leoneans commonly opt to local remedies by medicine men. These medicine men study herbs and the chemical reactions that these herbs have on the health of people.

Before leaving my short two week vacation in Sierra Leone, I especially reflected on how much the country could've accomplished if they didn't experience the civil war. My family left Sierra Leone to visit Guinea and Germany.

In 2014, one year following our trip in Sierra Leone, news hit that Kenema was one of the cities affected by the Ebola epidemic. A lot of the people living in Kenema began dying at rapid rates and my family had to escape from Kenema to avoid being hit by the outbreak. The Ebola Virus definitely affected Sierra Leone during a time they were slowly recovering from the civil war.

Chapter Twenty-Eight: Adversities of a
Black Muslima

In the Fall of 2014, I quit my job working for the Department of Defense. I made sure to write a letter of resignation to management at the Fort Hamilton Commissary letting them know I'd be leaving my position. I felt that this was the best decision for me because I was running into many confrontations with customers, particularly after wearing the hijab. I got into trouble for any minor issue and management rarely believed in what I had to say. I also believed that quitting my job at the Fort Hamilton Commissary would help me focus on college. I was running the risks of messing up my college education because I was trying to handle multiple responsibilities at one time.

I needed to concentrate because I was still working on my self-identity as a nineteen-year-old young woman. I was still getting everything figured out and it was hard managing the fact that I was in New York City with only Ousmane to look after me while my parents were far away. I was taking college classes and working. The worst thing that could happen is that I get fired from a Department of Defense Federal Job because I couldn't handle everything that I was doing, so resigning felt like the best option.

So, I continued focusing on school while my parents occasionally sent me money so that I could handle things on my own in New York.

While attending Kingsborough Community College, I found out that there was a Muslim Student's Association (MSA) located on campus. I began going to the MSA for three out of my five daily prayers. As time went by, I became familiar with some of the Muslim students who attended the MSA club. After getting to know each other, we exchanged phone numbers and began hanging out.

I was a solo act for nearly five months before making new friends, but this time, I made Muslim friends attending my college. In retrospect, being alone for those few months gave me a chance to learn more about myself. I could finally focus on myself and resolve confusions that I always had about my identity.

However, having Muslim friends helped me during my transformation because they sometimes shared their advice and experiences with me. It was approximately October of 2014 before I became well acquainted with some of the Muslim students attending Kingsborough Community College.

I told some of the students that I recently became a more traditional Muslim last year. I'd explain that I was a Muslim my entire life but now I was practicing more. Some of the Muslim students attending the MSA understood exactly what I was saying because they shared similar experiences as me.

It's unexplainable because I finally felt free, despite the news media constantly saying that Muslim women were oppressed. I now had control over who could see my body. As long as you're not married to me, I feel that you have no right to see the intimate parts of my body. My body is not for everyone to observe and assess. My intelligence or thoughts are more important for who I am as a person, not my body type. I feel free because I'm no longer objectified, and I prefer being known for my personality. I was glad that I grew from the young woman I was a few years back.

Before, I was trying to fit into society's definition of beauty. That a woman's beauty makes her successful, independent, and strong. However, a woman of any body type can be beautiful, and it's not up to the media to define what makes a woman beautiful. A woman can be chubby, skinny, tall, short, wide-hipped, narrow-hipped; it doesn't matter what body type the woman has, she should still know she's beautiful. Yes, women have every right to embrace those differences in their body types. A woman has the right to show off her different curves and I support it. She doesn't have to wear the hijab, especially if she doesn't practice Islam, but I want to reserve the right to wear the hijab because I do practice Islam.

I also require the right to cover up and conceal my body because I am trying to follow a commandment presented in my religion, Islam, just as the other women who don't follow my religion have the right to expose their bodies if they want to.

Even though I quit my job as a sales store checker at the Fort Hamilton Commissary, I went back to ask management if I could grocery bag on the weekends. The managers allowed me to come back and pack groceries for tips. I knew that it was better for me to grocery bag because I could work on my own schedule. If I had to study for school, I could let the managers know I wasn't coming in for work that day. Grocery bagging gave me the flexibility to work while also attending college classes at Kingsborough Community College.

The Fall 2014 semester was fast approaching, and I began preparing for my final examinations. The Fall 2014 semester also happened to be Ousmane's first semester at Kingsborough Community College, so I was also helping him get prepared for his final examinations. I gave Ousmane advice on how to pass his final examinations because I understood that college wasn't like high school.

Even though I had a rough time studying for my finals, I did pass all my college classes. My birthday approached immediately after finals examination week. This was the first time that I would be celebrating my birthday while properly practicing Islam. Muslims who wish to follow the sunnah of the Prophet Muhammad are advised to fast on their birthday. I wasn't sure if I was ready to fast for my birthday, but I knew that I wanted to do something special.

I couldn't figure out anything special to do on my 19th birthday so I decided to work. While at work some of my coworkers then ask me, "You're a winter baby?"

"Yes, I was born on December 20th."

"Oh, what's your zodiac sign?" one of my coworkers asks me.

"Well, they say that people with my birthday are Sagittarius."

"What are the personality traits of a Sagittarius?" my coworker asks.

"I'm not sure. Muslims aren't supposed to believe in zodiac signs."

"Oh, so, you don't believe in horoscopes?"

"No, reading into horoscopes is forbidden in Islam and I'm not sure if the description for my zodiac sign fits my personality traits. I'd be committing a sin for reading into my horoscope descriptions."

When I was younger, I was ignorant about the rules for astrology in Islam. My parents always made sure to stop me from looking at the messages inside fortune cookies, but I was unsure if zodiac signs were similar to fortune cookies. It's forbidden for Muslims to read fortune cookies, visit fortune tellers, or any sort of activities which may tell a person's future. We believe that by visiting a fortune teller, we'd be receiving readings by people associating themselves with the Jinn. So, after learning horoscopes have similarities to fortune tellers, I refrained from labeling myself a Sagittarius, even though I knew my birthday fell on that zodiac sign.

I attended various mosques within New York City because it didn't matter where I prayed. Non-Muslims commonly asked me, "Which is your regular mosque?" and I'd always tell them that any mosque could be my regular mosque. If I could make my five daily prayers on time, it didn't matter which mosque I attended. I was lucky if I could find a mosque which allowed women to pray at their mosques because certain mosques around New York City don't have a women's section for us to pray in, and if they do, it's normally a tiny space.

Immediately after entering the mosque, I take off my shoes and head towards the bathroom to perform my routine wudhu. When I finish making wudhu, I enter the Muslim women's prayer area and greet the women by saying, "Assalamu Alaikum."

Some of the women reply to my greeting by saying, "Walaikum As Salam." Some of the other women don't respond at all, they just give me a strange look. I stand in position for prayer. After praying, I put my shoes back on and leave the mosque. I feel bad that some of the women were rude enough to ignore my greeting; however, I brush this incident off.

On several occasions, I noticed that if I walk past my Muslima counterparts who weren't black, they'd rarely return my greeting. Many of them who were either Arab or South Asian would walk by me quickly, as if they didn't hear me greet them. On the other hand, I'd greet a Black

Muslima and the chances of her responding to my salam were much higher. I had to quickly learn that there was racism within the Muslim community, which is sad because the Prophet Muhammad was against racism in Islam.

Islam strictly prohibits racism against any individual. However, Muslims who are racists follow cultural practices which were introduced before Islam existed. Before Prophet Muhammad's (peace be upon him) existence, racism and slavery was strongly practiced with members of the Quraish tribe, who were mostly engaging in pagan practices such as worshipping statues. In fact, there were other problems faced by the Quraish tribe. Because they thought that birthing a female child was disgrace, they commonly buried their female babies alive.

Before the Prophet (peace be upon him) received his first revelation from the Archangel Gabriel, he was a merchant and he was commonly known as a trustworthy person (*Al-Amin* in Arabic) to his people. The Quraish were accustomed to worshipping to statues, burying female children alive, and treating Black people like animals, sometimes making their Black slaves sleep near farm animals.

Prophet Muhammad (peace be upon him) told the Quraish people that it was wrong for them to worship statues, bury female children alive, or treat Black people as their inferiors, but the Quraish felt insulted that Prophet Muhammad (peace be upon him) was correcting their traditional cultural practices. He was younger than many of them, including his Uncles who had raised him in the absence of his biological parents.

I never gave up on Islam because Prophet Muhammad clearly condemned racism within Islam. Racism in Muslim countries exists today because of cultural practices being passed down for generations, and it has nothing do with Islam or the teachings of Prophet Muhammad. Prophet Muhammad spoke out against racism during his time and he settled racial equality with the black Muslims who lived around him. An especially well known Black Muslim was named Bilal ibn Rabah, who's thought to be one of the first African slaves to accept Islam. Bilal was tortured by his pagan owner who starved him, dragged him around the streets of Mecca by his neck, and was forced to stand outside on the hottest days. After Bilal accepted Islam, Abu

Bakar, the Prophet Muhammad's wealthy friend, bought Bilal's freedom. Bilal was then restored to a healthy state under the care of Prophet Muhammad and his companions. Many Muslims are familiar with the hadith in which the Prophet Muhammad says in his final days of pilgrimage:

> *O people, your Lord is one and your father Adam is one. There is no favor of an Arab over a foreigner, nor a foreigner over an Arab, and neither white skin over black skin, nor black skin over white skin —— except by piety.*

It honestly didn't feel good to be experiencing rounds of anti-Muslim hate from non-Muslims and then to also experience rounds of racism from my very own Muslim counterparts. Especially given that Islam provides examples of why racism shouldn't be practiced by Muslims.

It's not fair to say that all Muslims are anti-black because that would be equal to saying all Muslims are terrorists, but it's good to acknowledge that racism does exist within the Muslim community so that we can resolve these issues.

We should also take notice that there are many Black Muslims who practice Islam, so this isn't a matter of religion Rather, it's a matter of racist culture forbidden in the Sunnah[59] still being practiced.

My Muslim counterparts sometimes fail to greet me, as if I don't exist.

While I was still starting my journey of a long-standing commitment to Islam, I didn't want to give up on wearing the hijab, but I considered possibly moving to a Muslim country. Maybe moving to a Muslim country could resolve all the issues that I faced here in the United States with the growing anti-Muslim speech. However, when I expressed this desire to other Black Muslims, some of them told me about the discrimination Black Muslims experience in Muslim countries being far worse than living here.

Unfortunately, the enslavement of black people is still legal in a good number of Muslim countries. If slavery isn't an issue within a Muslim

---

59 Sunnah: Islamic tradition and practices. Closely following the Prophet Muhammad and his companions as an example of moral behavior.

country, other issues may be present such as corruption. Some people argue that African countries are a sanctuary for black Muslims; however, that isn't the case. There's corrupt politicians in some of the African countries, and Libya is an African country with a 90%+ population of Muslims and they're still practicing slavery.

I don't understand where black racism originates from, but I knew that it affected parts of my life. I can still remember the first time that I was told I couldn't play with a group of children on New Argonner because I was black. However, that isn't the only experience of racism that I had in my life.

While attending the Urban Assembly School of Business for Young Women, the school staff provided each student with a New York City Metrocard. Each Metrocard allowed a student three subway rides on the New York City transit. One day, while entering the train station, two police officers quietly approach behind me and ask, "Did you just jump the turnstile?"

"No, I swiped my student Metrocard at the turnstile."

"Well, we saw you jump the turnstile. Do you have identification on you by any chance?"

It's truly my word against their word. I always paid for my fare, given that I had a student Metrocard from my high school. I reach into my school bag and give the police officers the only identification card that I had at the time, my U.S. military dependent card. Both police officers look at each other and then they look at my military ID. After searching for my dad's rank, they ask me, "Your dad's a Warrant Officer?"

As if that mattered; but I had to comply, so I say, "Yes."

"Okay, here's your ID card. Just stay out of trouble," the police officers tell me.

It's ridiculous to think that the only reason why the police officers let me go that day is because the identification card I provided them was my military dependent card. Prior to even knowing who I was, they saw a young black teenage girl and even though I didn't jump the turnstile, it was my word against theirs.

Years later, as a black Muslima who's wearing the hijab, I'm beginning to see the world through a lens I'd never seen it before. I'm beginning to notice the difficulties black people face globally because of our skin color.

I held resentment against the enslavements of black people in Muslim countries because it's legal, and no one wants to discuss those matters except for black Muslims. It appears that it doesn't concern our non-black Muslim counterparts that slavery is legal in Muslim countries because it isn't their problem.

Whenever topics of anti-black racism is brought up in Muslim gatherings, our non-black counterparts quickly lose interest in what we're talking about. The fact is, I genuinely love Islam, but I also love black people and it's embarrassing that black people are being treated badly in certain Muslim countries. I realized that being silent about the issue won't improve the conditions of black Muslims.

Topics of race have been brought up in Muslim settings, but it never really addresses solutions against the black racism. Instead, the topic starts off with, "It's really hard to be a brown Muslim."

I'm not discrediting the struggles of brown Muslims; however, they're more socially accepted than their black Muslim counterparts.

Sometimes I feel like asking, "What about the black Muslims who not only have to face the same amount of anti-Muslim discrimination as brown Muslims, but also experience racism due to white supremacy? The same black Muslims who fear police brutality, the KKK, and an institutional racist system. Black Muslims who might not feel safe living in Muslim countries due to their racist cultural practices, where black Muslims are being legally enslaved, victims of organ harvesting, and other countless wrongdoings because our darker skin appears 'inferior' than our non-black Muslim counterparts."

I really want to say, "It's really hard to be a black Muslim," but any black woman who speaks her truth is labeled the "angry black woman." No, I'm not an angry black woman, I'm just presenting the realities of black people, especially the plight of black Muslims.

Meanwhile, black people in the United States suffer a great amount of racism. If it weren't for the invention of cellphones or live videos, much of the public wouldn't see the dilemma of black people in America. Black people have recorded incidents of their counterparts calling the police on them simply because they're trying to enter their own apartment. Or sometimes black people are being killed in their apartments or homes for no reason at all because someone didn't think that was their residence. There are times when they're trying to enjoy the nice summer weather with a barbecue party and their counterparts are calling the police on them. There's evidence of police brutality which takes place against black people in the United States just because their skin color is darker. It's an abuse of power for a police officer to say, "Put your hands where I can see them," and then shoot 30+ rounds of bullets through a person even though they were complying, which was the case for Willie McCoy and Ryan Twyman.

Being that Islam condemns racism, it doesn't make sense to me that countries holding +90% population of Muslims such as Libya are not condoning the enslavement of black people.

I was torn between the Islamophobia present in the United States, the country in which I was raised in as a U.S. Army Brat, and the potential racism I could face in Muslim majority countries, which is prohibited in Islam.

I cannot give up on living in the United States simply because the way I'm being treated daily. I may be treated like I'm a foreigner, but I constantly think back to the times when educators took the time to teach me, doctors have treated me, and my neighbors have watched over me. I cannot give up easily because I've been discriminated against. I would be leaving the country I love for another country which I have no connection with other than my faith, and they too would discriminate against me. The United States is my home despite the mistreatment I may face daily.

Occasionally I find non-black Muslim sisters who greet me with "Assalamu Alaikum," and I reply "Walaikum As Salam," grateful that there are at least some non-black Muslims who're nice enough to greet me.

I would like to acknowledge the non-black Muslims who're active on calling out black racism. Linda Sarsour is an American Muslim who frequently speaks on the behalf of black racism. I truly respect Linda Sarsour for being at the Metropolitan Detention Center in Brooklyn to advocate for the inmates who were denied heat during the polar vortex of February 2019. Sarsour frequently organizes events for families who've lost family to police brutality and an institutional racist system. Imam Omar Suleiman is another American Muslim activist who isn't black but constantly brings awareness to the challenges black Muslims face. Suleiman often draws upon the examples of Bilal ibn Rabah and how he was made to feel a human after accepting Islam; something that wouldn't have been possible if Bilal was still a slave under his previous pagan owner. Amani Al-Khatahtbeh commonly provides a platform on MuslimGirl.com where black Muslims can post their true stories of what it means to be both black and Muslim. There are other non-black Muslims that I can highlight for their advocacy on the behalf of black Muslims and I want people to realize that they're challenging the status quo of their community so that people can understand the black Muslim's perspective.

Black people who aren't Muslim and hold anti-Muslim views also discriminate against me. If a black person doesn't share Muslim values, they may see themselves as superior to me because they don't share my faith.

I'm required to make visits to the hospital yearly to check on my physical health. While sitting in the doctor's office, I fill out all the application information regarding my family medical history. Some of the other information that's on the application includes race, ethnicity, and religion. I never understood why doctors needed to know my religion. I wouldn't want to be treated differently as a patient because I'm a Muslim. There's no possible way of me running away from being discriminated against, especially since I openly wear the hijab. I had no other choice but to put I'm a Muslim. I could only hope for the best and believe that the medical staff would treat me fairly despite knowing that I'm a Muslim woman.

There are countless stories in history of people facing discrimination in medical facilities because of their race, ethnicity, sexual orientation, disabilities or religious beliefs. Of course, morally, a medical staff member isn't supposed to discriminate against their patients, but that doesn't mean that discrimination doesn't occur. I would want to sincerely trust my medical staff, but I also understand the rise of Islamophobia could alter my medical treatment. There's no way of knowing whether your medical provider is anti-Muslim.

I sit in the patient waiting area, hoping that the doctor who sees me today will be kind, honest, and treat me like their other patients. What were the chances of me meeting an honest doctor? In an article called, "Critical Condition", published by The Crisis it states:

> *In the landmark 2002 Institute of Medicine (IOM) report, "Unequal Treatment: Confronting Racial and Ethnic Disparities in Health Care," researchers found that there was "inequality in quality" in health care. "Minorities tend to receive a lower quality of health care than non-minorities, even when access-related factors such as patients' insurance status and income are controlled," the report said. The study revealed that Blacks are less likely to receive medical procedures, such as proper cardiac care, kidney transplants and basic clinical services. It also found racial differences in appropriate cancer diagnosis and HIV care. Yet Blacks are more likely than Whites to receive the most intrusive procedures, such as amputations and castration. "What this study shows is that the color of your skin and the perceptions that go along with the color of your skin sometimes alter the care that you get. even if you had the same economic background, the same kind of insurance," says Celia J. Maxwell. M.D., assistant vice president for health sciences and director of the Women's Health Institute at Howard University. (Joiner, Page 23)[60]*

I took into consideration the discrimination I could face as an African-American Muslim woman, but I had to see a doctor. It's unfortunate that anyone should be afraid to trust the people they expect to receive medical treatment from.

---

60 Joiner, Lottie L. "Critical Condition. (Cover Story)." Crisis, vol. 111, no. 6, Nov. 2004, pp. 18–27.

Chapter Twenty-Nine: Surreal American Dream

One year later, in the Fall of 2015, I was completing my final semester at Kingsborough Community College. The department of Retail Merchandising at Kingsborough Community College required their final semester students to complete an internship to get credit for their RM9200 course. Marketing continued to be my passion, despite being told that I'd never make it in that career path because I'm an African-American woman, and now that I'm wearing hijab, it made it even more difficult for me to pursue this career path.

I was still working part-time as a grocery bagger at the Fort Hamilton Commissary, but my academic advisors told me that I couldn't be accredited for my RM9200 course while working as a grocery bagger. My advisors mentioned that the grocery bagging job was volunteering, and they wanted to make sure I had field experience in Marketing before graduating with my Associate Degree at Kingsborough Community College.

Searching for an internship was challenging, especially since my time for finding the internship was limited. I nearly had four months to find an internship so that I could get credited for my RM9200 course. I placed many applications for internships; yet, I barely received any responses. Whenever I did receive a response, they would contact me for the interviews. Nevertheless, I couldn't get past the interview process. I sensed that much of the reasons I had a hard time getting a Marketing internship is because I was an African-American Muslim woman. I refrained from thinking that my overall identity was making it difficult for me to gain an internship. Sometimes an interviewer would approach me hesitantly, with a sense of worry, as if they weren't sure about offering me the position to begin with. It completely showed in the interviewer's face and it was sometimes hard for them to control their facial gestures during the interview, even when they tried hard to do so.

I did the best that I could in hopes that I'd get a call back from the interviewer; however, in most instances I never received a call back.

I only had one more month for my Fall 2015 semester and I was one of the few students in my class who remained without an internship. Everyone else openly discussed the good news about their internships. My classmates and I received insights on what it was like for them to work a day at their internship job and I honestly felt left out. I spoke with my professor and let her know that I tried everything I could to get an internship, but I wasn't successful in acquiring one. My professor told me that I still had time before the semester ended. She also mentioned that she couldn't let me pass her class without the internship.

I spoke with another professor at Kingsborough Community College about my struggles of finding an internship for my last month of school. One of my professors at Kingsborough Community College had a friend who was a General Manager at a high-end retail store and the manager would be hosting a school trip for our college. My professor let us know that the store was hiring for the winter seasonal sales representative position and we could use that opportunity to get credit for our RM 9200 course.

In the meantime, I continued my volunteer job as a grocery bagger at the Fort Hamilton Commissary for tips. After work, I'd go spend time with Ousmane. I distanced myself from my social media platforms and the only social media app I maintained was WhatsApp Instant Messenger. Some of the girls who prayed at Kingsborough Community College's MSA added me to their WhatsApp group chats. On the group chats, the Muslim women discussed future Muslim club events occurring on other college campuses in New York City.

In my free time, I attended the other Muslim college events. There was beneficial knowledge that I acquired from these events. While socializing with other Muslim students, I was able to gain long-lasting friendships. I exchanged phone numbers with many of the Muslima women. Befriending the other Muslima women educated me in my religion. My family implemented Islam in my life as a young girl; but, there was only so much that my parents could teach me. Islam becomes more complex the deeper you get into certain subjects and I believe my parents wanted to teach me the simpler version of Islam.

On the day of my college trip to SoHo's Bloomingdales, my college professor, classmates, and I met at a location near the retail store. My professor took the attendance of all the students who attended the school trip. Some of the students had other obligations which limited them from attending this college trip; however, after everyone arrived, we entered Bloomingdales and waited for the General Manager to tell us about the company.

The General Manager introduces herself to us. She explains how she began her career working in fashion retail. Her career began when she was a college student, working seasonal positions at a specific retail store. She continued working at that retail store until she graduated college, then she was offered a permanent position. My classmates and I are given a tour of Bloomingdale's retail store. Since the store is in SoHo, the store workers say that most of their clients came to shop either at midday or late in the evening. SoHo is known for people partying and exploring the nightlife, so Bloomingdales' SoHo clientele preferred shopping in the evening. I love everything about Bloomingdales' customer service, company culture, and I'm interested in the brand names they sell. I'm wrapped up financially because I'm a college student, but I wouldn't mind purchasing the brand names they sold, if I had more money. The General Manager tells all my classmates to apply for the Winter Seasonal position and if we do good in the seasonal position, we could get a part time, permanent position.

When I get home that evening, I apply for Bloomingdales' seasonal position. Shortly after applying for the position, I email the Human Resources manager to let her know that I am one of the students who came for the college trip and I put in my application for the seasonal position. The Human Resources manager emails me back with information to come into the store for a group interview. I keep track of the date for my group interview. I knew that Bloomingdales would require me to wear an all-black outfit, so I search for all-black outfits that I could wear for my interview. This would be the last chance that I had to get an internship or job opportunity to receive credit for my RM 9200 course.

I go in for my interview and that same week, I receive a notice that I've been hired for Bloomingdales' seasonal position. I tell my professor that I finally got a job which could provide me credit for my course. After receiving approval from my professor, I start working at SoHo three times a week. The job offers flexible scheduling, so it's still easy for me to attend my college classes without the job interfering with my college classes.

I'm the only Muslim hijabi working at SoHo Bloomingdales at the time. At Bloomingdales, I often work in the costume jewelry or handbag section. I'm required to approach all Bloomingdales clientele to make sure they know I'm available for their assistance. Bloomingdales wants their clients to know that their associates are always ready to help them.

"Hello, welcome to Bloomingdales SoHo. May I help you with anything today?"

"Yes, I'm looking for a gift that I can purchase for my wife this Christmas. I know that my wife loves handbags, but I don't know which style I should get my wife. Can you help me?"

I would ask the client about which handbags his wife preferred wearing.

"We have a variety of handbags. Some of our handbags are crossbodies, totes, clutches, satchels, and bucket bags. We also carry a wide range of name brands. Some of the name brands we carry are MCM, Kate Spade, Rebecca Minkoff, Longchamp, and Dooney Bourke. Do you know which handbag your wife would prefer?"

"No, which is why I am asking you to help me find my wife a Christmas gift."

The client and I make our way around the handbag section speculating on which bag would be best for his wife. After hearing a little bit about his wife's preferences for a handbag, my client finally selects a handbag to purchase for his wife. I walk my client over to the register, complete his purchase, and wrapped his wife's gift. The Bloomingdales in SoHo doesn't have a gift wrap shop this year, so many of the associates wrap gifts for their clients.

Bloomindales' point of sales system can track how many sales you make in a day and the number of credit cards you open for customers. This information is important for management to evaluate whether you're keeping up with the store's daily sales goals.

However, I have a much difficult time keeping up with any of the sales goals and I believe most of it had to do with my visibly Muslim appearance.

"Hello, welcome to Bloomingdales SoHo. Would you like my assistance today?"

Sometimes I get brushed off and clients walk past me like I don't matter. Other associates who didn't look like me could easily help them. After several attempts to approach clients shopping at Bloomingdales, I'm deeply saddened. The other associates take advantage of me by taking clients I had been working with. Handbags are often stored in the basement of Bloomingdales, so while I make a run downstairs, another associate would prepare to ring up the client under their own name. All day I would work with a client, run downstairs, grab the handbag, and the other associates would ring up my sales. Some of the clients notice what's happening and make sure that I ring up their product.

"Um, this young lady was helping me the entire time," the client would say in my defense.

As I continue attending Kingsborough Community College, I start to think about the conversation I had with the customer who shopped at the Fort Hamilton Commissary. The man told me that a career in marketing was not for an African-American girl, but he also didn't know at the time that I was a Muslim. I begin thinking to myself that a career in Marketing wasn't for me. This is my final semester at Kingsborough Community College. It's too late to change my degree at this point, but it's a career that I was always passionate in.

I take the train home after a long day at school and work, thinking about the adversities I was facing. I ride the train home for nearly one hour and thirty minutes both ways every day and sometimes I contemplate about my identity. No one is truly going to accept me for who I am, except for me. I would have to accept who I was to be happy in life. I cannot continue to let people mistreat me because they feel that my overall identity makes me somewhat "inferior," but this is what stereotypes have created for me.

As usual, a preacher comes on the train car that I'm sitting on. Preachers, beggars, and dancers are a normal occurrence on New York City trains. I'm not enthusiastic about preachers though because of my previous experience.

The preacher who enters my train car is a black man with a Caribbean accent. The man starts preaching about Christianity and how he wants people to save themselves by accepting Jesus. The man makes his way through the train car and then immediately after seeing me, begins talking about Islamic terrorism. The man talks about Muslims who are committing violence around the world. The crimes that Muslims commit around the world may be true, but that doesn't make every single Muslim a criminal. I just sit down in silence, completely avoiding eye contact with the preacher. The preacher comes to my area and says, "ISIS is killing people all around the world. Muslims are terrorists and they're here to terrorize people!" I could feel people's eyes piercing down on me. I was the only noticeable Muslim hijabi on the train.

The man makes sure to approach me and continue his lecture about Muslim extremists. Everything the man says brushes past me because I'm already hurt about what I experienced earlier in the day. No one on the train knows me, nor do they have my back. Some people grin, smirk, and giggle as the man chants. Then, suddenly, the man says, "You ISIS Bitch!" while giving me direct eye contact.

"My dad fought for this country!" I say in distress. "I'm a US Army Brat and I have been for my entire life. My dad's a Muslim and he fights in the US Army."

The man stops his preaching at that moment. Some of the people stop smirking and giggling because now this was becoming a serious matter.

"Not every Muslim is a criminal. Not every Muslim is a terrorist!" I continue on.

"Yeah, but a lot of the terrorists are Muslim," the man tells me.

"Any person of any faith could be a terrorist!" I exclaim. "Terrorists aren't reserved for the Islamic faith."

Some of the people on the train finally jump to my defense, telling the man, "People of any religious group can be criminals. It's not right that you're targeting this young girl because of her religious beliefs."

One of the people defending me is a black woman. The woman is completely bald headed and when the man gets fed up with her sticking up for me, he tells her, "And you're bald headed? That is an abomination! Women should not be bald headed. Having no hair should be reserved for men!"

The woman looks sad and I feel bad for her. He doesn't even know the condition of this woman. She could possibly be suffering from cancer. The preacher gets off at the next train stop and the whole train falls silent.

I begin going over my recent Muslima friends' homes to eat dinner with them and their families, which is pleasant considering both my parents reside outside of New York City. While sitting in their house, the children would watch the countless Christmas specials as we sit in the living room talking amongst each other. During one of the commercials, "We Wish You a Merry Christmas" plays and my friend's brother begins singing along to the carol. All the adults who are sitting in the living room stop and look at each other before my friend's mom tells him to stop singing along to the carol. The child completely disregards my friend's mom and begins shouting out the lyrics while smiling, "We wish you a Merry Christmas, we wish you a Merry Christmas, and a Happy New Year!" When the Christmas commercial ends, my friend's brother then shouts out, "Thank You Jesus!" and we can't help but burst out laughing. Jesus (peace be upon him) is a prophet in Islam, and his Arabic name is Issa [Esa]. We just don't believe he was born Christmas Day or is the son or embodiment of God.

*   *   *   *   *

Bloomingdales selected the few associates that they wanted to keep from the seasonal jobs. The seasonal sales associates chosen to remain with the company had proved that they could fulfill the company needs of Bloomingdales. On the other hand, I struggled with fulfilling all the goals of Bloomingdales. It wasn't because I was a terrible worker, but because other associates took advantage of me and some clients wouldn't deal with me because I'm a Muslim. As an African-American Muslim woman, I wasn't profitable for the company. I would be a failed asset to hire if their clientele avoided my assistance simply because I'm a visibly Muslim woman.

The managers never told me why I lost the position. Management at Bloomingdales hired me knowing that I was Muslim, seeing as I wore the hijab for my interview. However, I wasn't successful in meeting the company's goals, and it was obvious that I couldn't meet those same goals for reasons surrounding the discrimination I faced. Some of my identity was a setback and there was nothing I could do. I was handed a notice that my position would end on January 2, 2016.

In June 2016, I finally graduated from Kingsborough Community College with my Associate's degree in Retail Merchandising-Marketing. My mom, Ousmane, Ousmane's dad and my younger sister all attended my graduation ceremony. My mom was excited about my graduation ceremony because I was the first of her children to obtain a college degree. I was unsure of what my future in marketing would look like, but that was still the only career path I was passionate about. I was already enrolled at Lehman College to acquire my Business Administration degree with a concentration in Marketing. I knew that I wanted to continue my college education; however, I didn't want to give up on Marketing. So, I didn't give up. I was going to push past all the barriers and try my best to defeat the stereotypes revolving around me. I wouldn't let my African-American Muslim woman identity put me down or make me believe that I wasn't suitable for a career in marketing.

During that same year, Ousmane and I finally applied to obtain our marriage certificate. We wanted to marry each other while we still in high school, but we were too young to take care of each other. The finances weren't there, considering that we were teenagers trying to finish high school and we didn't want to fall into that continual cycle of short-term committed relationships we saw our peers go through. We knew that we wanted to reserve our relationship for the bigger commitment, marriage. Our parents secured our engagement and implemented other practices so that our relationship could remain halal while we were trying to finish high school.

Now that I had completed my Associate degree and Ousmane had obtained his realtor license, we thought that we were established enough to obtain our marriage certificate. We still couldn't afford to have a more extravagant wedding, but we felt that if we had the basic gathering with a few witnesses, that'd be enough until Ousmane and I could head to the local courthouse in Downtown Manhattan to apply for our Marriage Certificate. Not only did Ousmane and I successfully get married in court that year, but we also got the exciting news that we'd be expecting our first child.

On November 8, 2016, Donald J. Trump was elected as the 45th president of the United States of America. Donald J. Trump's campaign stirred fear against Muslims because he discussed a potential "Muslim Ban" upon taking office. He always promoted using the term "Islamic Terrorism" when talking about Muslim individuals. President Donald J. Trump's election was an unexpected victory. I was terrified because not only was there anti-Muslim language coming from his campaign, but there was a rise of "freedom of speech" from the KKK and other white supremacy groups. If you could only imagine, this was a terrifying time for me as an African-American Muslim woman.

Chapter Thirty: The Lazy American

Leadership is very important, especially when you're leading a country with diverse citizens. America has developed a beautiful culture, far better than its segregated past. I love that I can experience different cultures from around the world because immigrants moved to America. Immigrants brought their food, music, languages, clothing, etc. Depending on the part of America you're in, you can learn something totally new about a certain group of people.

I didn't appreciate that the new administration incited fear against immigrants. When leaders can make comments such as, "Mexicans are bringing their drug dealers and rapists," it's implying that the only Mexicans who come to the United States are criminals. I have met many hard-working Mexicans in my lifetime. Many of those were so welcoming, and I can still remember living on New Argonner Kaserne as a child and having my good friend tell me, "Mi casa es tu casa".

I was especially disheartened by the rise of anti-immigrant rhetoric because my husband, Elhadj Ousmane Diallo, is a refugee from Guinea. I've had many talks with my husband about his childhood in Guinea. As a child, my husband never imagined living in the United States. Living in the United States was a dream my husband spoke of often as a child, but he never took it seriously. He never thought that his dream of living here would ever be possible. Now, my husband lives in the United States with better opportunities than he's ever had in Guinea. My husband's parents no longer pay for his school fees, like they had to in Guinea. Being a refugee provided my husband with education, healthcare, a home, and an overall safe environment. However, my husband grew terrified with the rise of anti-immigrant rhetoric. I also bore the burden of this rhetoric because I was pregnant at the time and being so worried for my husband wasn't healthy for my pregnancy.

I can understand when undocumented people are sent back to their countries for overstaying their visas or sneaking into the United States; however, Trump's administration was making it easier for Green Card holders to get deported. Green Card holders were especially considered for deportation if they were receiving public benefits, which made it harder for them to get their citizenship.

I was uneasy about the new immigration laws and policies because I didn't know how these new laws would affect my husband. My husband and I did some research and found that it was a great idea for us to photocopy all his legal documentation, and I also took the measures to photocopy all my legal documentation. People's family members were being deported out of the United States for not having their documentation readily available for the U.S. Immigration and Customs Enforcement (ICE), whenever they approached their residency.

I understand that many Americans fear that undocumented immigrants can negatively affect the United States economy; however, many of the undocumented immigrants are shared taxpayers to our economy without benefiting from programs like supplemental security income, subsidized housing, food stamps, and Medicaid. So, if undocumented immigrants can pay the same share of American taxes but not receive the same benefits, are they *truly* hurting the economy? I have a problem with the ways lower income *legal* immigrants are being restricted under the Trump Administration. Legal immigrants being sponsored by American family members will have a harder time obtaining their Green Card if they're proven reliable on public assistance. There are more American citizens reliant on public assistance than US permanent residents.

Immigration has been the main concern for many Americans because it has brought a surplus of bilingual speakers who are more preferred to companies than the average English speaker. Companies operating in a global economy would want bilingual employees to communicate with their foreign business partners. There's also an increase of consumers in America who don't speak English and bilingual speakers closes that communication gap.

I'd apply for a job where I fulfill all the educational and job duties, but then I'm not a bilingual speaker. Primarily, Spanish is the most requested language an employer is looking for. Americans are honestly not prepared for the results of globalization and its demand for multilingual workers.

Learning second languages wasn't thoroughly taught in our public schools, which has become a major problem for Americans in specific states where speaking a second language is more desirable; resulting in a challenging job search for Americans. Due to the Bona Fide Occupational Qualification, an entire firm's workforce can be exclusively reserved for bilingual speakers and it will be completely *legal*. President Trump did say that he'd want for every immigrant coming to the United States to know English fluently before assimilating into the workforce. However, this still doesn't solve America's lack of multilingual citizens in the long run, it only solves the language barrier in the short run. The federal government should make learning a second language *fluently* mandatory in all public schools so that our nation can remain relevant to the rapid growth of the global economy and Americans wouldn't struggle to find work.

I believe Trump did bring attention to some issues Americans are facing, but it's a matter of how he's implementing his strategies. How can we improve the language barrier in America for the long run? Does the border wall solve the issues of illegal immigration for the long run, given that a hole can be dug out in the wall? He won the electoral college, so it's important that politicians pay attention to the issues he may be addressing. I don't condone the racism that people claim is stemming from his base. Trump does have a diverse range of supporters, including some Muslim support. I'm not a Trump supporter, I was primarily a Bernie Sanders supporter, but I do respect the freedoms that fellow citizens expressed through voting and that could mean that they're seeking a change Trump promised.

*   *   *   *   *

I lost employment with a more recent clothing retailer because the managers could no longer accommodate to my pregnancy. I asked the employers if they could place me on unpaid sick leave; however, the managers told me unpaid sick leave wasn't an option for me. The managers at my job promised to rehire me after giving birth, so after frequently verifying that they would, in fact, rehire me, I took their advice and quit my job. I was around seven months pregnant when I stopped working. I wasn't physically capable of running around a clothing retail store at seven months pregnant, no matter how much I needed the job to pay my bills.

I truly relied on Ousmane to take care of me after I lost my job. We were saving up money for the baby, but it became nearly impossible to save with my husband being the only wage-earner in our relationship.

My due date was fast approaching, which meant that I had to attend my prenatal checkups more frequently. Ousmane and I were happy to know that our baby was healthy. We received sonograms of our new baby boy and patiently waited for his arrival. Medical visits weren't always a pleasant experience for me. Once, I was approximately three months pregnant when I went for one of my prenatal checkups and the doctor tells me, "Wow, you speak English so fluently!"

Like, am I not supposed to speak English fluently?

I only received comments like that after wearing the hijab, which is stereotypical. Apparently now that I wear the hijab, people assume that I'm a foreigner.

Six months later, I gave birth to a healthy baby boy. Ousmane and I were happy to finally become parents.

When I thought the time was right, I contacted the clothing retailer I was working for so that I could return to working with them. Unfortunately, I was blocked from reapplying for the position. Every time I tried applying, the application would state, "You already applied for this position." I notified human resources to let them know about this matter; however, they were no help. So, I decided to apply for another position, yet I wasn't given a call to be rehired. I was overwhelmed because I initially asked management to put me on unpaid sick leave. The managers insisted that if I quit the job, I could easily be rehired, but that wasn't the case. I felt like I lost my job due to my pregnancy.

Several weeks after becoming a new mother, I was unsure of how I could return to work. I had to begin applying for jobs and scheduling interviews so that I could secure a new job. The job search process is tough, especially when you have an infant who's about two months old. First, childcare must be arranged for your child so that you could meet with an interviewer. Then, you'll need longstanding childcare just in case you get hired for the position. At minimum, childcare centers charge a $1,000 tuition per month to watch infants. I was fortunate to receive subsidized childcare for my son.

Immediately after placing my son in daycare, I began going to numerous job interviews. I finally felt like I could accomplish other things while also being a mother. Every time I received an email or a phone call for a job interview, I got excited. I looked forward to meeting my potential employers.

On the morning of a job interview, I wake up extra early, get dressed, and then dress up my baby boy. When I'm done getting ready, I put my son in his stroller and take him to his daycare, which is a rough 20 minute walk away from my house.

After entering the childcare center, I always speak to the daycare teachers and maintain a constant flow of communication with them because I think it's important we keep up with the well-being of my child. Whether we're briefly speaking about my son's teething, required vaccinations, or changes in his behavior, we communicate these issues effectively. Sometimes, I go to a nearby store so that I can buy my son's diapers or baby wipes for the daycare. Altogether, it takes me nearly 40 minutes to drop my son off. I then catch the New York City transit to my job interview. I go to plenty of job interviews, but on this occasion, the job interview I have is with a bank.

I arrive for my bank interview early and wait in a nearby coffee shop. I start making minor fixes to my outfit like brushing off lint or straightening out creases. Lastly, I secure my hijab and make sure it looks neat before meeting with the hiring manager. I quickly glance over my resume and when it's less than 10 minutes to my interview, I enter the bank and tell one of the banking supervisors that I'm looking for the bank manager.

"Oh, yes, I can see that you're scheduled to have an interview with us," one of the banking supervisors says while shaking my hand. "How do you pronounce your name?"

"My name is pronounced Jul-DAY," I tell the banking supervisor.

"Okay, just wait right here and the bank manager will meet with you shortly."

I wait for the interviewer in an open area of the bank and after meeting in the waiting area, we both shake hands and introduce ourselves to each other. I'm ecstatic about this interview opportunity. I'm certain this interview will go well.

We walk into the interview room and immediately after entering the room, I hand my resume over to the interviewer. The interviewer takes a brief look at my resume and then asks me why I'd be suitable for the position.

Not skipping a beat, I tell the interviewer about my work history.

"My first paying job was with the Department of Defense. It was a food sector job, but I operated the cash register. I handled the money in my register carefully, I processed checks, credit card, and debit card transactions, and I was welcoming to the customers; making sure to greet all customers and hold conversations with them in a professional manner."

The interviewer nods at my words, and asks me several other questions before the interview ends. The interviewer provides me with her business card and says she'll keep me posted about the job.

In the meantime, I continue filling out more job applications while waiting to hear a response from the bank manager. More than a week passes without receiving a response, so I decide to email her. Someone from human resources emails me back on her behalf to tell me that they already hired a candidate for the position. But I'm not going to give up on my search for employment.

I go to several more interviews and I'm continually denied positions. Sometimes, before I can answer all the interview questions, the interviewer tells me, "This isn't the job you're looking for." Which is a painful statement to hear, considering the time it took for me to get me and the baby ready, just so I can make it for the interview.

If this isn't the job I was looking for, why would I wake up extra early, get dressed, dress up my baby, walk my baby to daycare, then travel to the interview location? I didn't tell the interviewer the process it took me to make it to the interview; however, I did think of the process.

In the meantime, I attended a few mosques regularly for their Halaqas. Attending Halaqas brought back memories of when I was a child. I used to follow my parents to Halaqas when we lived on Fort Bliss, New Argonner, and Schofield Barracks. Although my son was a baby, I felt like he was reliving my childhood of following my parents to the mosque. The mosque that I attended frequently with my son mainly consisted of West Africans, and they had a warm, friendly community.

The women at the mosque saw me nearly every week and as time went by my son began sitting up, crawling, then walking.

"Ma Sha Allah! Your son is growing up fast!" the Muslim sisters would exclaim.

However, the women at the mosque taught me something valuable. Every time the halaqas ended, I waited for my husband to pick my baby and me up. One of the women I knew from college would invite me to a sister's meeting held after the halaqas. The women commonly met in the mosque to discuss matters involving the community. Whenever there was a community member facing hardship, the women would discuss ways they could become more involved with those community members. The Muslim women discussed several things which displayed their compassion for humanity. These women took time out of their day to visit elderly people in nursing homes, patients admitted in hospitals, or families still facing the reality of losing a loved one. Through every conflict, these women made sure to be there for the community.

After staying home without work, I felt like I was losing my purpose in life. Yes, being a mother is wonderful, but I mainly stayed home to take care of my son. I began scheduling play dates with other mothers. My son and I routinely woke up around the same time every day to go outside for walks. We went out to various parks to enjoy the weather. Occasionally I'd go out with a family member or friend, but sometimes it was hard for us to make plans if they had busy schedules. Most of my family members or friends were either working or attending school at the time, which is why I frequently went out with my son alone.

I continued applying for job opportunities, yet many of the jobs rarely replied to my applications. Sometimes it would take me hours to complete a single online job application.

I never understood why online job applications would ask you to upload your resume, but still require you to fill out your job history into the application fields, one by one. After filling out an entire application, some jobs required you to submit an assessment. Some assessments were 50, 75, Or 100 questions in length.

"Wow, am I taking a college exam or am I just trying to apply for a job?" I'd think to myself.

Speaking of *no adult left behind.* But, I took the employment assessments anyway because I hoped it would get me a call for the in-person interview. I began using Indeed.com to apply for jobs because I felt that the process was much easier.

I created an Indeed account, uploaded my resume, filled out other necessary information, and I could simply apply for jobs on their site with a tap of a button. I attended job training programs, career fairs, workshops, and I continued going to job interviews; however, I unfortunately didn't find a job.

I attended a two-month job training with a nonprofit organization. The organization was training me on administrative and receptionist roles. Many people who took classes with the organization told me that they secured jobs promptly after completing the training. I was excited to take this opportunity and learn skills to work in an office setting. Despite going to the training every evening, I was still on the lookout for job opportunities. I quickly learned how to utilize Microsoft Word, PowerPoint and Excel for office work. I was trained to use multi-line telephones (AKA a private branch exchange system). The training wasn't only about phone etiquette, it was also about how to place clients on hold, transfer calls, take messages for management, and multitask phone duties while also paying attention to clients who enter the office. I learned many office skills and I was provided with an office internship opportunity.

While sitting in group interviews, I began to realize that my overall identity was still a factor leading to my continuing unemployment. I went to several group interviews and felt ignored by the interviewer. It's easier to realize you're being treated differently from other interviewees when you're part of a group interview.

I can still remember going to an interview for an administrative role. My training program sent me there with a few others from the training program. I was excited about this potential opportunity. The night before the interview, I looked through my closet and placed my interview outfit to the side. I researched the company, got my resume prepared, and googled the interview location.

The next day, I spend one hour and thirty-minutes getting my son and myself ready so I can drop him off to daycare. I get to the interview location on time. The others from my program make it to the location and we begin our group interview. There are four interviewees in the room, including me. When the interviewer is ready, she began asking the four of us questions. Whenever the three other interviewees answer the interviewer's questions, she attentively listens to their responses. However, whenever I speak to the interviewer, she constantly cuts me off, interrupts my sentences, or stops me from responding to her questions. At the end of the interview, the interviewer hands everyone a business card except for me. I ask the interviewer for a business card and in response she claims that she "forgot" to give me one.

I continued meeting with my Muslima sisters for potlucks, tea parties, community gatherings, marriages, baby showers, etc. I provided community service and volunteered regularly. Not long after, I had to resort to applying for public welfare programs. After my husband left for work in the morning, I would get my son ready for us to go to the public welfare office to collect benefits. My son and I sometimes sat in the public welfare office for up to five hours waiting to be called. There were plenty of other people also waiting in the welfare office to receive public assistance.

When people say things like, "People on welfare are lazy," it's not necessarily true. There are other factors which can lead a person to seek public assistance. It could be that the person is honestly looking for work, but discrimination is playing a part in their continuing unemployment. First off, it's better if your name sounds "American" if it's placed on a resume or application. If a person has a name such as Khadijah or Mohammed, it's easier for their resume to be overlooked. On the other hand, a person named Sarah or David is more likely to be considered for the position. African-Americans normally have a harder time with the employment process than their white counterparts. Not to mention, Muslims are unfortunately tied to a stereotype which insinuates that we're terrorists and people should be afraid of us. So there I was, seeking public assistance because I was rarely receiving a chance.

It's agonizing to discover that you've waited nearly five hours in a welfare office and the case worker cannot process your application because you're missing a single document. I began to think about my future, my son's future, and what it meant for me moving forward as a parent.

I spoke to other Muslim women about my struggles in finding employment. There were other Muslim women who didn't encounter problems while job hunting, although they do admit that they must work three times harder than their co-workers.

On the other hand, there were Muslim women who agreed with me, who said that they had difficulties finding employment. I spoke with Muslim women who were facing the same struggle as me and I especially felt bad for the Muslim women who wore the Niqab[61]. Some employers wouldn't hire them because they cover their entire face. Sometimes my Niqabi sisters had dreams to be teachers, medical workers, bankers, etc. Eventually, they took off their Niqab so that they could enter the workforce. Other sisters said that they'd get the job, but their coworkers were hostile toward them the entire shift. Sometimes they'd have to deal with this behavior for 40+ hours a week because they needed to earn an income to pay their bills.

I had to accept that my blessings had not arrived yet, so I patiently applied for more jobs.

---

61 Niqab: a veil worn by Muslim women that normally covers their entire body except for their eyes.

Whenever I looked at my son, I remembered different parts of my childhood. For whatever reason, I felt like I saw myself in him. I began to remember role playing during play time at Argonner Elementary School. When the children in my class would pull out their pretend work costumes. We pretended to be firefighters, police officers, medical staff, etc. Today, I can assume that most of my classmates from Argonner Elementary School aren't having trouble finding employment like I am. Although I applied for welfare benefits, I'm not lazy. As a child, I sold lemonade and frozen Kool-Aid. I went around my neighborhood asking people if they wanted car washes. I know that I'm not a lazy person; the opportunities for employment just didn't reach my way. I needed the help of my fellow Americans until I could get back on my feet and it has nothing to do with me doing nothing for myself. I was a holder of an Associate Degree from Kingsborough Community College and now seeking my Bachelor's Degree from Lehman College.

In the evening, after the sun sets, I look up to the night sky in search of the stars. It could be that I cannot see the stars from New York City because there are millions of buildings reflecting their own lights. This city is full of opportunities, yet I haven't been fortunate in obtaining employment. I worry about what life would be like for me as a parent and how I could continue to provide for my child if I'm not being treated fairly. I know that I'm not ready to give up on what I believe in. I wasn't taught to give up on my identity. I especially learned to not give up on who I was while attending the Urban Assembly School of Business for Young Women. Many of the motivational speakers invited to my high school didn't give up on their dreams despite their individual struggles, they kept on going. I'm going to make sure that despite whatever struggles I'm going through, that I keep pushing and believing in myself. That I turn to the mirror and let myself know that I'm valuable, like any other American who I walk alongside.

Chapter Thirty-One: Don't Let Your Obstacles Hinder Your Aspirations

The early morning sun rays pierce through the window curtain and my son wakes up at his usual time. I get up from my bed, walk over to my son's crib, pick him up and carry him to the living room, so that I can prepare his feeding bottle. After giving my son his bottle, I rush to the bathroom to get ready to go out with my son. I swiftly brush my teeth and take a shower because my son doesn't like staying alone in the living room. After getting out of the shower, I dress up quickly and pick out my son's clothes. I normally dress my son up last because I cannot count the times I've dressed him first and he needed a diaper change afterwards, or he spit up. After he's dressed, I put my son in his stroller, and we walk out of the house.

I love taking my son out for strolls so that we can enjoy the nice weather. Now that I've transitioned into my new life as a mother, I feel like it's easier for me to get stuck at home with the baby.

Sometimes the process of getting ready discourages me from going out to enjoy the beautiful weather. Before going out, I try to figure out if I'm packing enough essentials for my baby because I don't want to be short of any item while I'm out. During my preparations, my son will sometimes want me to pick him up, so he'll cry while I'm packing his belongings.

My son and I walk to the nearest train station so that I can take him to a park. I dislike taking my son to the parks around my neighborhood because I try to keep my son from seeing adults rolling dice, smoking weed, or selling drugs within our neighborhood.

Occasionally, people who do drugs in our neighborhood walk around the playgrounds while jittery, or collapse on the sidewalks. The parks exclusive of those undesirable activities are mainly in downtown Manhattan, which is a rough 35 minute ride away from where I live.

When I get to the subway station, I have to figure out how I'll carry all my belongings, including the stroller, down the train stairs, since there are no elevators. I'm grateful when people offer their assistance to help me down the stairs, but if they don't offer their assistance, I'm reluctant to ask. So, I carry the stroller and all my belongings down the steps on my own. While carrying all my items down the stairs, I risk tripping on my abaya; however, I'll do whatever it takes to get my son to the best neighborhood and enjoy the park. So, I pull up my abaya and continue carrying all my belongings down the stairs to the train station.

Thirty-five minutes later, my son and I get to Nelson A. Rockefeller Park, near Battery Park.

While my son and I are at Rockefeller Park; I push the stroller around so that we can enjoy the scenery. There are many children running around and playing in the sand boxes. My son is still seated in his stroller while watching the other children run around. The park is shaded by large trees which block out most of the sunlight. The sun still manages to shine through some of the leaves, allowing some rays to glimmer onto the play equipment. All the children in the park are happy, playing on the jungle gym, sliding down the slides, swinging on the swings, and building sandcastles.

While I'm pushing my son around the park he looks back and smiles at me. I smile back at my son, but his smile triggers memories of my childhood. I instantly remember the times that I lived on Fort Bliss and played around in my neighborhood. I was under the supervision of my family members whenever I played outside, but it was always within my immediate neighborhood.

I rarely take my son out to the parks in our immediate neighborhood because of the crackheads, meth heads and other drug addicts that sometimes come around. Don't get me wrong, they're nice people, but I don't want my son to grow up being exposed to their conduct. It may have an influence on my son's future. I want to protect my son from sabotaging his life.

It only takes my son's smile to feel hurt that I can't provide him the same childhood I had as a child. I didn't like constantly moving around as a child, but at least the neighborhoods weren't infested with drug addicts. It hurts because I'm not lazy, but my identity is constantly frowned upon by many potential employers.

My parents never had to go across the city to make sure that I played in a safe playground. In my situation, I have to go across the city to avoid playgrounds where adults are rolling up weed, rolling dice or selling drugs; just so that my son can play in a safer area.

I don't want my son to become a statistic, a black Muslim male in the United States who's engaged in illegal activities. I want my son to become a successful young man, who pursues a career, and takes care of himself.

I decide to purchase iced coffee from one of the breakfast carts around Battery Park. I especially love my iced coffees since giving birth, because throughout my pregnancy I refrained from drinking coffee. It's advised that pregnant women don't drink a large amount of caffeine and now I feel like I can finally enjoy coffee while strolling around the city with my son.

I get to the breakfast cart and ask for a medium vanilla iced coffee. While preparing my beverage the man asks me, "Where are you from?"

"I'm from the United States," I respond.

"No, where are you *really* from, like which country?"

"I just *said*, I'm from the United States."

The man stares at me in disbelief and proceeds to ask me, "Okay, which state are you from?"

"I don't know which state I'm because I grew up as a United States Army Brat and I moved around because of my dad's military career."

"When did you convert to Islam?" the man proceeds to ask me.

"I was born and raised as a Muslim Army Brat." At this point the man looks at me like he's just seen a ghost. He gives me a blank stare as if he is in disbelief that I could be a woman who grew up as a Muslim Army Brat, while also upholding the commitment of wearing a hijab.

"Okay where are your parents from?" the man asks.

"My dad is from Hague, Virginia; and, my mom is from Kono, Sierra Leone," I respond.

Oh! So, you're Sierra Leonean!" the man replies excitedly.

When the man finishes my order, I grab my iced coffee, place it in the cup holder of my son's stroller and walk off saddened. Lately, I haven't been feeling good. I've been doing a great job at finding out who I am as an individual, but people quickly label me however they want because they're uninformed that a black Muslim woman can also be an American.

I'm an African-American woman and even better, I'm a Fulani-American woman, but I'm not a Sierra Leonean. People may have a hard time associating me with being an African-American because of my maternal background and it's acceptable for me to be referred as a Fulani-American since that's, in fact, my ethnic background. However, my nationality is of the United States of America. My nationality is all that I grew up to know despite the troubles I faced. I stood for the American flag everyday singing the national anthem and feeling delighted while reciting every word of our Pledge of Allegiance, but the stereotypes that Muslims cannot be American has caused people to treat me like an immigrant. Cursing me, pushing me, giving me the side eye, treating me in the most despicable way as if I don't belong here.

If you're in my position, you'll begin to understand why the NFL players are "taking a knee." The NFL players are taking a knee in protest to the unjust treatment of Black Americans due to institutional racism, that we can get shot and killed in our own homes by a police officer and it can be justified. Some people who don't understand the concept of "taking a knee" make silly jokes like, "I'm taking a knee because my barista made me a caramel latte instead of a vanilla latte." I can name all the tasteless jokes made to ridicule NFL players simply protesting that we're also Americans, but we aren't given the same amount of respect and treatment as our counterparts because of our appearance. I began understanding why my middle school which was mainly serving students of color only played Whitney Houston's "Greatest Love of All" every morning before the start of class.

My husband was taking care of me during the months I couldn't get a job. Even if it was till his last money after paying all our bills, he'd try to get me all my essentials. One day I tell my husband, "You're lucky to be a Muslim man."

"Why?" my husband asks me.

"Because you're not required to wear a khimar," I tell my husband.

My husband chuckles and then says, "But I'm still a Muslim man, you don't think that matters?"

"I don't know, I'm just having a hard time, that's all. I'm more visibly Muslim than you are. People only know that you're Muslim after hearing your name. But, for me, people can immediately tell that I'm a Muslim because I wear the khimar."

"Everyone faces their own struggles, Julde. Sometimes things happen in life on purpose, to teach you a lesson. Just focus on school and everything will be okay."

My husband is right. Everything happens during its own time, for a purpose. My husband surely experienced discrimination as a Muslim man. I can remember my husband returning from work at his security job with a clean shave. Muslim men are supposed to keep their beard, but my husband said his employer would've let him go if he didn't shave his beard. For goodness sake! A security job? Not even a culinary job where he'd be working in a kitchen, but his security job threatened to fire him for having a beard.

A couple of months later, during the Summer of 2017, my husband receives a letter for his naturalization ceremony. After studying everyday, my husband passes his citizenship test. We make sure to tell everyone in the family about his ceremony and we didn't make any plans for that date.

I share the beautiful moment of watching my husband, Ousmane, a refugee from Guinea, West Africa become a United States citizen. He's seated while holding his American flag, waiting for the ceremony to begin. My mom, her new husband, my son and I watch the ceremony from behind and cheer when my husband is finally declared a United States citizen. My husband files for his United States passport within two weeks of getting his United States citizenship and he later receives his naturalization certificate.

Sometimes I turn the television on to the news networks and see coverage of family members being deported from the United States. The family members being deported from the United States are adopted children, biological children, husbands and wives. It doesn't even matter if a person is a military spouse, they were being deported. I feel for the families being separated for legal reasons because I'm afraid of facing those similar circumstances with my husband, Ousmane. Now that Ousmane is a United States citizen, I know that it would be more difficult for that to occur; however, I still have empathy for other spouses who may face this circumstance.

I continue to volunteer for various organizations during my free time. I can't help but help my community. I know that I can always be an excellent wife and mother while also being a positive person within my community. I love everything that I do for my community, but sometimes it's challenging to work and not receive income to pay for my bills. I still have to pay for college tuition not covered by federal aid, medical bills not covered by insurance, and basic living expenses for myself and my family. However, I enjoy volunteering for families who either face the same obstacles that I face or are affected by policies that similarly affect my family. I can relate to these families, which makes me passionate about what I'm doing.

I continued to struggle with who I am and yet, I stood my ground and thought to myself, "I will not give up on wearing the hijab, I will not give up on who I am, someone will accept me for who I am."

During the Spring of 2018, I began searching the internet to find other United States military brats who similarly faced the obstacles that I faced. I searched, yet I wasn't fortunate enough to find anyone online discussing their adulthood after being an American Muslim Army Brat. I would've loved to listen to another U.S. Muslim military brat's experience as an adult, especially a Muslima who wears hijab. I want to hear what it was like for them to transition into their adult lives as American Muslims.

I couldn't find anyone relatable, so I began talking to my family members and asking them about other Muslim families that we knew growing up, but my family said we lost contact with most of the Muslim military families after moving.

I decided to begin documenting my life and telling my experiences as a former American Muslim military brat. I faced challenges telling my story because I normally do not like discussing my private life, but I came across a few workshops in New York City which helped me break past my fear. I was definitely awkward in the beginning because I was shy, but I thought it was necessary considering the hardships that I was facing daily.

I wanted to tell my story.

Later into the year, I applied to be part of the Muslim Writer's Collective and the Moth storytelling workshop in Manhattan. Muslim Writer Collective and Moth were offering a handful of Muslims the opportunity to tell their individual stories, which would be recorded. I was slightly shy; however, after attending the workshop for two days, I began to feel comfortable telling my story. It felt great to express how I feel, today, as an African-American Muslim woman who is also a former United States Army Brat.

I was sitting in my living room one day and overheard news from the television that there was a Muslim woman running for congresswoman in the state of Minnesota. What caught my attention is that she also wore the hijab, just as I did. The potential Muslim congresswoman was Ilhan Omar, a refugee from Somalia, who had come to the United States when she was eight years old. While she was still campaigning to become a congresswoman, I hoped that she'd be elected in her state because her presence in the Capitol might help the Muslim families being impacted by the Muslim Ban. A few weeks later, I saw another Muslim woman named Rashida Tlaib, running for congresswoman in the state of Michigan. I hoped at least one of them would win a seat.

I felt that we needed them to win because electing President Trump as our president made me feel displaced as a United States citizen. People constantly treated me like I didn't belong in the United States and I felt that as Muslims suffered from a lack of representation.

In October 2018, I finally obtained part-time employment as a receptionist for a temping agency. I'd be working on-call with an agency to cover the receptionist and administrative shifts in offices around New York City. I wasn't always called to work every week, but whenever the agency received a job order, they'd call me and provide me the address to the work location. I was grateful that I could at least work sometimes because the income helped. The employment agent who hired me is friendly, easy going, and she makes sure to call me frequently about job openings; I truly love working with her and I'm glad she hired me to work for her.

I'm nearly done with my Bachelor's Degree program at Lehman College. I'll do whatever it takes to make sure that my child lives a decent childhood because he didn't ask to be brought into these circumstances. No matter how tired I am, I continue taking college classes with the intention of living a better life with my husband and son.

In November 2018, nearly two years after the election of President Donald J. Trump, Ilhan Omar and Rashida Tlaib were elected as congresswomen for their respective states. I was nearly on the edge, hoping that they could win their seats in congress, and they did. That was one of the sweetest moments for me as an American Muslim woman. Considering that I know their states aren't occupied with a Muslim majority population, it restored confidence in me that there are people who'd put the stereotypes aside and judge you on your character.

I was exhausted from the many confrontations that I faced daily: being pushed, shoved, cursed out, and not feeling safe walking around outside alone.

Despite getting home after a long day, I always reflect on how fortunate I am for never giving up on my overall identity. I remember being at work and meeting a man with a beautiful, radiant personality. He wasn't in the healthiest condition, but his smile gave a warm glow, and it was sincere. Unfortunately, the man relied on his wheelchair to get around, but that didn't stop him from enjoying the best of life. I greeted him and asked him how he was doing.

The man responded, "I'm doing awesome! I get the chance to live another day. I have nothing to complain about and today I get to hang with my best friend," and my heart nearly burst with admiration.

This man wasn't in his best condition, but he appreciated everything about life. The man then happily left from where I was standing after our short conversation. It's true, everyone faces their own struggles, and those

Growing Up an American Muslim Army Brat

struggles not only teach you a lesson, but it can also teach a lesson to the people around you.

After a rough seven months of documenting my life, I knew that I was certain about telling my story. I created a YouTube channel and other social media platforms to reach out to people within the community and let them know that I'm a former United States Army Brat who was born and raised as a practicing Muslim.

As the weeks went by, I began receiving messages from people who were either watching my videos or reading the blog articles I posted on my website. People were excited to hear my story and I was finally getting reconnected with other former American Muslim military brats. I didn't get a chance to speak with all the former Muslim military brats and I cannot even remember some of them; however, I look forward to catching up with them. My parents know some of the former Muslim military parents and I got the chance to speak with a few of them over the telephone.

I still have a lot to learn about myself and my overall identity, but I feel that I have accomplished learning much about my self-identity. I not only know what it feels like to be a black Muslim woman in America, but I also have concerns because I want a better future for the United States.

I really do not care if an American identifies as being a Republican, Democrat, or Independent; our differences shouldn't distract us from pursuing our main goal, a high achieving government. I believe every political view are equally important and our ability to debate issues and apply those to social change is what makes our government brilliant.

As a former Army Brat, I'm really concerned about improving public education within the United States. I understand that there are different state requirements for K-12 public education and I hope that somehow, the states can work together on creating grade-level requirements which are more uniform across the board. I personally struggled with transitioning my grade-level requirements to other public schools throughout my childhood while living on military bases. There are students in the United States who are given dissimilar opportunities due to their socioeconomic status. These different opportunities in public education became even more apparent while I was an Army brat of divorced parents.

There are Americans who rely on welfare benefits or public assistance and it doesn't necessarily mean that they're lazy Americans. Sure! There's a proportion of Americans who rely on these benefits and happen to be drug addicts or lazy, but most of the people are hardworking individuals who wish to get off these public benefits. Sometimes institutionalized racism, economic disparities and discrimination can play a part in the process of someone seeking to get off these benefits.

I experienced the benefits of being a recipient of Tricare Medical insurance, without worrying about being deprived of essential medical treatment. As an adult, I receive Medicaid and there's a limited amount of treatments which are covered under my health insurance. There's a medical treatment that I was supposed to get for more than two years that Medicaid continually rejects.

I understand what it means to live in the diverse socioeconomic statuses within the United States of America, while also facing the outcomes of stereotypes and prejudice revolving my overall identity.

I dream that there will be change from the discrimination and stereotypes which I or any United States citizen faces daily because of their identity. It's unfortunate that I suffer from the stigma of revolving stereotypes, but I'll never forget that while living in the United States or abroad, there was always someone who took the time to teach me to swim, dance, read, do math, solve science problems, play volleyball, give me life lessons, and support me during that process. During the times when I needed assistance, doctors medically treated me, caregivers babysat me, neighbors provided their support, and members within my community cheered me on.

I look at the mirror and reflect on who I am, and analyze myself while staring in the mirror.

I *know* that *I'm NOT* deserving of being pushed, kicked, shoved or followed.

Nor, am I an ISIS bitch, a terrorist, a lazy person trying to benefit off the government, or just that Muslim lady.

I am a hardworking individual, I care about my community, and I surely do not want to rely on the government.

I should feel comfortable praying at my local mosque without worrying about someone entering the mosque to harm me or other Muslim worshippers. I shouldn't feel that I'm an easy target to anti-Muslim rhetoric. I cannot go back to *my country* because the United States *is* my country. I share similar experiences to other American Muslims who face discrimination because of our religion. I worship the same God, Allah, as other Muslim worshippers in America. I'm no better than they are just because my dad served in the military. We all have different backgrounds or childhoods, but we still care about the advancement of the United States.

In the United States, people once said that they don't believe the enslavement of black people would end, that women would gain their right to vote, that women would one day join the workforce, that we would ever have an African-American president, that Montgomery would see its first black mayor, a woman as a primary candidate in the 2016 presidential campaign, a woman running a marathon against men, that two Muslim women would win their seats as congresswomen during Trump's presidency, nor have a man land on the moon. However, somehow, someway, the impossible became possible.

The United States has proven in history that there's room for improvement after continual advocacy. I believe in the phrase, "After every storm, there is a rainbow."

Yes, I've faced many adversities, but I don't believe in giving up. First Lady Michelle Obama used to say, "When they go low, we go high." And I'm beginning to understand more everyday what our former FLOTUS meant. Despite being mistreated, rejected, intimidated, and told that I wouldn't make it because of my identity, I'm going to keep going. I'm not going to give up because of the pressures of society. My dreams are just as important as any other person's dreams. I believe that even if I cannot reach for the stars, that one day I'll create my own sparkling star for the skies, and point to it to say, "Look! that's my star!" Granted that God paves a destiny for me that no one would've ever imagined.

Page Intentionally Left Blank

Glossary

Abaya: a large cloak or over-garment that is worn by Muslim women to cover the shape of their bodies or figure.

Adhan: an Islamic call for prayer. When Muslims hear this call, they know it's time for prayer.

Akhirah: an Islamic term used to refer to the afterlife. The life that Muslims believe we live after the day of judgement.

Al-Qiyamah: the day of resurrection or the day of judgement.

Astaghfirullah: an Arabic text which means, "I seek forgiveness of Allah."

Bismillah: a phrase that means "in the name of God" in Arabic. Regardless of an Arab person's faith they too say Bismillah, but this term is used a lot in Islam. This word starts every chapter in the Quran except for one chapter called Surah At-Tawba (aka Surah Baraat).

Bissap: a drink made from the sepals of a hibiscus flower, commonly known as sorrel. These sepals are boiled in hot water and then later cooled down to make a sweet beverage. This beverage is a tea, but is often referred to being a juice when it is sweetened and iced.

Bobo: a hair accessory that is used as a pony tail holder. Bobos [Plural] are wrapped around hair that is braided or twisted.

Creole: two or more languages mixed together. In my mom's case English, French and local languages from Sierra Leone are mixed together, to create a unique Sierra Leonean English dialect.

Deen: an Arabic term which means religion or faith.

Dhikr: a continuous praise of Allah, the God of Abraham. In Dhikr, a Muslim continuously says Allahu Akbar (God is Great), Subhan Allah (Glory to God), Alhamdullilah (Praises be to God), or Astaghfirullah (I seek forgiveness from Allah).

Dhuhr: the second daily prayer Muslims pray during the midday.

Dua: an informal act of worship in which a Muslim calls out or supplicates to our creator. This prayer form is like "saying grace".

Eid Al-Fitr: a holiday which marks the end of the holy month of Ramadan.

Fajr: the first daily prayer Muslims pray early in the morning before the crack of dawn.

Fulani: an African ethnic group which are nomads due to cattle herding in the Northern east and west regions of Africa. They normally travelled to countries they'd find food sources for their cattle so they can be found in many countries.

Halaqas: an Islamic gathering purposely for Muslims to study Islam and the Quran.

Hijab: a term used to mean cover or conceal. In most cases, hijab is used to describe a Muslim woman's head scarf or veil.

Iblees: the chief of Jinn which is believed to have rebelled against Allah. (He is also known as the Devil)

Imam: A Muslim leader who gives lectures and leads congregational prayers in a mosque.

Iqra: an Arabic word which means read.

Jannah: literally meaning heaven in the Quran. The highest level of heaven is Firdaus.

Jihad: an Arabic word which means struggle or effort. Muslims sometimes use this word to reference their personal spiritual struggle toward Islam. It is often erroneously translated as "holy war."

Jinn: a classification of spirit made from smokeless flames, different from an Angel because they can choose to be good or bad.

Jummah: a weekly Friday service which Muslims attend in a mosque around noontime, ending with a gathered prayer. (This religious service is an obligation for Muslim men; however, this religious service is optional for Muslim women.)

Kaserne: translates to meaning "barracks" in German.

Khimar: a head scarf that is worn by Muslim women that normally covers their hair, neck, breast, and shoulders; only leaving the face uncovered.

Khutbah: an Islamic preaching or sermons which presents the teachings of Islam.

Kumu: A Hawaiian Hula dance instructor.

Latrine: a pit dug into the ground with the purpose of people using it as a toilet for defecation and urination.

Laylatul Qadr: means "the night of power" and occurs during the last ten days of Ramadan when Muslims try to fast the day that the Quran was revealed to the Prophet Muhammad. Most Muslims believe that Laylatul Qadr falls on the 27th night of Ramadan even though there isn't clear evidence of this.

Lei: A lei is a necklace made from fresh Hawaiian flowers. The flowers are placed on a string or plastic wiring. There are different kinds of flowers that are placed on these leis.

Maghrib: the fourth daily prayer Muslims pray after sunset.

Mosque: a place of worship for Muslims.

Nikah: A Muslim wedding ceremony.

Niqab: a veil worn by Muslim women that normally covers their entire body except for their eyes.

PX: a short abbreviation for Post Exchange, a retail store that is found on military bases.

Regents Exam: a New York State exam which is used to assess a student's academic achievement within a particular course.

Salat: habitual prayer which is performed by Muslims, five times a day.

Shahadah: A Muslim's declaration that they only believe in one God, Allah, and Prophet Muhammad is the seal of the Abrahamic prophethood.

Sunnah: Islamic tradition and practices. Closely following the Prophet Muhammad and his companions as an example of moral behavior.

Surah: an Arabic word which means chapter. Any time this word is used it literally refers to the chapters in the Quran.

Tajweed: rulings which control the correct letter and vowel pronunciation within the Quran because mispronunciation of the Arabic words can misinterpret the meaning of the Quran.

Taraweeh: is a prayer Muslims perform during the holy month of Ramadan after the obligatory Isha'a prayer.

UASBYW: the acronym shortened version of the Urban Assembly School of Business for Young Women. My high school name was too long to say, so many of the staff and students referred to my school as the UASBYW.

USS: an abbreviation for United States ship(s).

Wudhu: a method which is used by Muslims to cleanse themselves before praying. This cleansing must be done, otherwise a Muslim's prayer is invalid.

Zina: an Islamic term which literally refers to an act of illegal sexual intercourse.

References

Alam, Mansoor. "The Quran: History of its Compilation." IslamiCity, 10 October 2019, https://www.islamicity.org/17075/the-quran-history-of-its-compilation/.

Cooper, Paul. "The Ancient Poems that Explain Today." BBC Culture, 21 August 2018, http://www.bbc.com/culture/story/20180820-the-6th-century-poems-making-a-comeback.

Cutolo, Morgan. "Can You Guess Which U.S. State Produced the Most Presidents?" Reader's Digest,

https://www.rd.com/culture/most-presidents-born. Accessed 8 October 2019.

Haretos, Chrisanti. "The No Child Left Behind Act of 2001: Is the Definition of 'Adequate Yearly Progress' Adequate?" Harvard Kennedy School Review, vol. 6, Jan. 2005, pp. 29–46. EBSCOhost, search.ebscohost.com/login.aspx?direct=true&db=a9h&AN=19737510 &site=ehost-live. Accessed 3 October 2019.

Joiner, Lottie L. "Critical Condition. (Cover Story)." Crisis, vol. 111, no. 6, Nov. 2004, pp. 18–27.

Lesch, Ann M. "Osama Bin Laden: Embedded in the Middle East Crises." Middle East Policy, vol. 9, no. 2, June 2002, p. 82. EBSCOhost, doi:10.1111/1475-4967.00058.

Levin, Gabriel. "On the Hanging Odes of Arabia." Parnassus Poetry, Vol. 30, Nos. 1 & 2, http://parnassusreview.com/archives/408.

McAuley, Denis. "The Ideology of Osama Bin Laden: Nation, Tribe and World Economy." Journal of Political Ideologies, vol. 10, no. 3, Oct. 2005, pp. 269–287. EBSCOhost, doi:10.1080/13569310500244305. Accessed 9 September 2019.

"No Child Left Behind [Documentary Film]." YouTube, uploaded by Boondoggle, 7 April 2011, https://www.youtube.com/watch?v=yiGN7kVyeaM.

Post, Jerrold M. "Killing in the Name of God: Osama Bin Laden and Al Qaeda." 2002. PDF file. Accessed 2 October 2019.

"Texas-Sized Nepotism." Utne Reader: The Best of the Alternative Press, no. 169, Jan. 2012, p. 21. EBSCOhost, search.ebscohost.com/login.aspx?direct=true&db=a9h&AN=69979040&site=ehost-live. Accessed 8 October 2019.

"The Origin of the Quran." Why Islam, https://www.whyislam.org/quran/originofquran/.

Ul Haq, Riyadh. "The Oral Tradition in Islam - Shaykh Riyadh ul Haq." YouTube, uploaded by Al Kawthar Academy, 28 April 2017, https://www.youtube.com/watch?v=xDIottFNnKw. Accessed 8 October 2019.

"US BUSH 2." AP Archive, uploaded by APTN, 17 Sept. 2001, http://www.aparchive.com/metadata/youtube/64b3224c6a68feebea1025c830c53242. Accessed 9 Sep. 2019.

About the Author

Photo By: Stanley Steril

Julde is an undergraduate Business Administration student at Lehman College CUNY where she serves as the secretary for the Muslim Women Leadership club. Enjoys volunteer and charitable work within her community. She frequently attends Muslim women tea parties, galas, interfaith conventions, Quranic studies classes, and Muslim Student Association events. As a Black Muslim woman who frequently faces obstacles, Julde grew an interest to begin writing about that challenges she faces with her overall identity. *Growing Up an American Muslim Army Brat* is Julde's first published literary work and she hopes to continue publishing work. Bringing authenticity of what it's like to be Muslim in America, challenges black people face within the Muslim community, and nonfiction stories of American Muslims. Julde hopes that her writing can bring future change to American Muslims like herself; while showing that being American and Muslim is not antithetical.

Let's Stay Connected!

Feel free to email me at: **author@juldehball.com**

Like and Follow me on Facebook, search my page: @OfficialJuldeHBall

Follow me on Instagram, search my page:

@juldehball

Visit my Author's website at: **www.juldehball.com**, where I'll post new blog articles and event information.

JULDE HALIMA BALL
AUTHOR

Thank You for your support! I hope that we stay connected. Please allow a couple of days for me to respond to messages.